THE UNIVERSITY OF CHICAGO

PRIVATE REDEVELOPMENT
OF THE CENTRAL CITY

Spatial Processes of Structural Change in the City of Toronto

DEPARTMENT OF GEOGRAPHY
RESEARCH PAPER NO. 112

By

Larry S. Bourne

The University of Toronto

CHICAGO • ILLINOIS
1967

Library of Congress Catalog Card Number: 66-30638

PREFACE

Existing theories of urban spatial structure provide only limited insight into the way in which cities are rebuilt and the nature of change in the standing stock of structures. Considerable research effort has been directed, on the other hand, to the spatial aspects of land use change, and to the movements of activities and social groups within the city. The current interest in improving the urban environment, and particularly of assuring more widespread and consistent change in the urban physical plant, demands a fuller understanding of the process of structural change.

This study treats one aspect of this process, the location and impact of private redevelopment within the central city of the Toronto Metropolitan area. Private redevelopment is defined as a continuous process of replacement in the structural or building inventory of the city. It represents the summation of all new construction and structural modifications generated in the private sector of the urban economy. In this sense, redevelopment acts as the complement of urban development or suburban expansions in the total process of urban growth and change. This is not a study of public renewal or redevelopment programs, or of the role of private investment in public-designated renewal and redevelopment areas, although the results will hold important implications for public policy formulation in the renewal field.

The largest proportion of investment in the urban physical plant derives not from public programs but rather from the aggregate of thousands of individual projects scattered throughout the city. New construction and modifications to existing buildings are the visible results of one phase of a complex mechanism of adjustment in the structural inventory of the city. Although most such adjustments take place without modification to existing structures, either through a change in location or the amount of space utilized at that location, new construction represents the strongest measure of long-run trends. The buildings of a city provide the physical space for urban activities and populations, and are influenced by and in turn influence, changes within these spheres. Clearly, the redevelopment process in this building inventory is an important facet of the complexity of changes affecting the modern city.

ACKNOWLEDGMENTS

The author would like to extend his deep appreciation to all persons who contributed to the formulation and completion of this study, and to the academic history from which it derives. Limitations of space preclude mentioning the appropriate scale of this assistance.

First, I would like to thank the Canadian Council on Urban and Regional Research (CCURR) for their generous support and encouragement of this project. Without this support the study could not have been undertaken. The opinions and conclusions expressed in the text, however, are entirely those of the author.

I feel particularly indebted to Professor Brian J.L. Berry, advisor, colleague and friend, not only for guidance of this research and the author's graduate training, but more important, for providing through association, the scholarly stimulation and perspective that are so rare.

Professors W.R. Derrick Sewell and Harold M. Mayer examined the final manuscript thoroughly and provided valuable insights and suggestions. Their willingness to take time from busy schedules despite inconveniences was most gratifying. Mr. Samuel Cullers, formerly of the Metropolitan Toronto Urban Renewal Study, Mr. A. Crerar, then of the City of Toronto Planning Board, and Professor Hans Blumenfeld of the University of Toronto, offered sound advice and assistance during the critical stages of problem formulation. Professor Eugene Smolensky, Miss. C. Nirmaladevi and Mr. P. Goheen read portions of the draft and extended helpful criticisms and comments. Most of the above, along with numerous others in Chicago and Toronto, will find their comments incorporated into the text. For this assistance the author is indeed grateful.

I am also indebted to the Metropolitan Toronto Planning Board for providing access to numerous statistical reference sources and for acting as co-ordinator and accountant for the author and the Canadian Council on Urban and Regional Research.

In addition, I would like to express my appreciation to the City of Toronto Planning Board, and particularly to Mrs. Eva Samery, whose efforts provided much of the wealth of information on which this study is based. The data were released by the Commissioner of Planning, and repeated enquiries by the author were answered in a most pleasant manner.

The cartographic materials are the result of the skill and perseverence of Mr. Gerald Pyle, who quietly responded to frequent deadlines. Mrs. Nancy Adelman, Mrs. Judith Taber, Miss Paula O'Neill, and Mrs. Clare McGough competently performed typing and editing duties.

The massive task of data processing was performed on the IBM 1401 of the City

Toronto and on the University of Chicago 7094-7040 computing system, with the able assistance of both staffs.

Finally, to the professors and graduate students in Geography at the University of Chicago, and to the staff and students of the Center for Urban Studies, who provided an atmosphere immensely stimulating for intellectual pursuits, I remain deeply indebted. The fruits of this experience may not yet be apparent, but for this failing, as well as for the limitations of the present study, the author assumes sole responsibility.

University of Toronto,
Toronto, Ontario,
October, 1966.

TABLE OF CONTENTS

    Problems and Processes of Structural Change in Cities
Study Purposes, Design, Objectives
Empirical Implications
Theoretical Contributions to the Study of Urban Growth
Synthesis and Organization

Urban Spatial Patterning
Space Organizing Concepts
Land Use Succession
Real Estate and Real Property
Differential Between Land and Building Values
Economics of Redevelopment and Replacement
Filtering and the Housing Market
Urban Renewal and Redevelopment Research
Synthesis: The Dynamics of Urban Structural Change

Land Use and Structural Change
Defining the Basic Concepts
    The Development-Redevelopment Continuum
    The Adaptation Process in the Structural Stock
    Concepts of Cyclical Change
    Cycles of Structural Change in Neighborhoods

Empirical Base
Toronto: Population
Evolution of the Existing Spatial Structure
Special Considerations: The Toronto Case
The Data
The Analysis
Measurement of Structural Change
Delimiting the Study Area: Rationale

LIST OF TABLES

LIST OF ILLUSTRATIONS

CHAPTER I

INTRODUCTION

Vast and complex changes are taking place in the spatial structure[1] of North

American cities. In recent years, rapid advances in technology combined with scale

shifts in the social and economic requirements for space and location have dictated new

patterns of metropolitan spatial organization. These, in turn, have created serious mal-

adjustments in the existing pattern of developed areas within the city. The trend toward

suburban sprawl, greater dispersion of activities and population, and lower densities in

central cities has been well documented.[2] Increasing rates of land consumption, decen-

tralization of employment and population, and widespread decay and deterioration at the

center attest to these trends.

Problems and Processes of Structural
Change in Cities

The factors producing these trends are varied and intimately interrelated. Here

we are concerned specifically with those factors which have acted to reduce the advan-

tages of central cities as places of work and residence and which have contributed to

decay and deterioration. The first consideration derives from the effects of growth

itself. Boulding's first principle of structural growth is that "Growth creates form, but

---

[1]The term "structure" is used in this text in two ways. The first is that of urban
"spatial structure," which refers to the framework, arrangement, and interrelationships
among urban phenomena as they are distributed in space. In the second case, "structures"
or "structural stock" are used interchangeably with buildings or building stock. This is a
more limited interpretation than that in common practice, in which physical facilities such
as roads and services are included as structures. The first usage is discussed more
fully in Donald L. Foley, "An Approach to Metropolitan Spatial Structure," in Explorations into Urban Structure, ed. Melvin M. Webber et al. (Philadelphia: University of
Pennsylvania Press, 1964), pp. 21-78; and is reviewed in Rosalyn B. Post, "Criteria for
Theories of Urban Spatial Structure: An Evaluation of Current Research" (Unpublished
Master's dissertation, Department of City and Regional Planning, University of North
Carolina, 1964), pp. 36-46.

[2]For an interesting cross-sectional discussion of these trends, see Lowdon Wingo
Jr., "Urban Structure as a Variable," in The Use of Urban Land (Washington: Resources
for the Future, inc., 1963), pp. 238-243; Benjamin Chinitz (ed.) City and Suburb: The
Economics of Metropolitan Growth (Englewood Cliffs, N.J.: Prentice-Hall, inc., 1964),
particularly the Introduction, pp. 3-42; Ronald R. Boyce, "Trends in Urban Land Con-
sumption," Professional Geographer, XV, No. 2 (March, 1963), 19-24; Melvin M.
Webber, "Order in Diversity: Community Without Propinquity," in Cities and Space:
The Future Use of Urban Land (Baltimore: Johns Hopkins Press, for Resources for the
Future, Inc., 1963), pp. 23-56; John Dyckman, "The Changing Uses of the City,"
Daedalus, Journal of the American Academy of Arts and Sciences, XC, No. 1 (Winter,
1961), 111-131.

1

form limits growth."[1] In cities, the existing spatial structure and building inventory act as a constraining framework for change. As there is an economic limit to vertical expansion, growth must continue to take place outward, and the expansion of activities within the city pushes others to the periphery. Equally obvious is that most central cities are now developed, vacant land is at a premium, and the intensification of existing uses, as an attempt to alter the existing form, is for most uses in large measure uneconomic. New growth has little alternative but to locate in suburban areas.

The principal dynamic elements in these trends result from an expanded range of locational and social choice for urban activities and populations. Rising real income, increased personal and functional mobility, and changing tastes have combined to provide both the means and the incentive for changing spatial relationships. Increasing the relative attractiveness of suburban locations has resulted in a "trickling down of the central city plant on the continuum of values."[2]

Technological developments, specifically those related to space and accessibility requirements, have also played a vital role. Combined with socio-economic pressures for change, such as the desire to escape undesirable neighborhoods, and the apparent preference for suburban living, the development of space-extensive technologies has reduced the demand for central city locations. At the same time, and in parallel with the increased demands for space, the automobile and the urban expressway have reduced the friction of distance, thus attracting new development to outlying locations and relocating existing activities from central areas.[3]

---

[1]K. E. Boulding, "Toward A General Theory of Growth," in J.J. Spengler and O.D. Duncan (eds.), Population Theory and Practice (Glencoe: The Free Press, 1956), p. 120.

[2]Scott Greer, Urban Renewal and American Cities (New York: Bobs-Merrill Co., Inc., 1965), p. 136.

[3]For example, statistical evidence of the suburbanization of urban activities and populations is given in Raymond Vernon, The Changing Functions of the Central City (New York: Committee for Economic Development, 1959); Raymond P. Cuzzort, Suburbanization of Service Industries Within Standard Metropolitan Areas (Studies in Population Distribution No. 10, Scripps Foundation; Miami, Ohio: Miami University, 1955); Amos H. Hawley, The Changing Shape of Metropolitan America (Glencoe: The Free Press, 1955); Donald L. Foley, The Suburbanization of Administrative Office in the San Francisco Bay Area (Research Report No. 10, Real Estate Research Program; Berkeley: Bureau of Business and Economic Research, University of California, 1957); and for industrial trends see, Mayor's Committee for Economic and Cultural Development, Mid-Chicago Economic Development Study, Vol. II, A Report Prepared by the Center for Urban Studies, University of Chicago (Chicago: Mayor's Committee for Economic and Cultural Development, 1966).

A third set of factors involves the aging and obsolescence of the physical plant, both physical deterioration and the economic obsolescence that aging implies. All other factors held constant, buildings, as an aging and declining asset, ultimately require replacement, which in itself will tend to encourage locational changes. Pressures for major structural expansion and improvement likewise encounter high land costs and the difficulties and costs of replacing what is already in existence. Thus while the demand for central area locations declines, buildings in these areas deteriorate and become less suited for the activities which use them, adding further stimulus to the decentralization process.

This has not always been the case. Central locations were formerly of such importance that replacement costs were justified and many areas of the city were rebuilt. In fact, rebuilding has been continuous since cities began, and much of the spatial struc-ture as it exists today in central areas is a result of this process.[1] Most downtown properties represent second, third, or even fourth stages of building. In this century, however, only relatively small areas in or near the central business district have been rebuilt. This spatial differential in the rate of change has left a legacy of deteriorating land and buildings in many areas for which there appears to be little potential re-use value.

In part the problem arises from the nature of urban investment.[2] Once a structure has been constructed on a parcel of land it is generally uneconomic to replace it with anything other than a more intensive use. In the case of rural land it is relatively simple to transfer productive capacities from one area or use to another. In urban areas, because of the durability of buildings, change is costly and slow. Where a reduction in intensity of use is demanded, change is largely impossible. Thus, the rate of replace-ment in the physical stock of the city is considerably slower than that of the activities that use these structures. Moreover, the physical and economic life spans of buildings are not the same. This difference tends to inhibit change and allows buildings to con-

---

[1] For example, the widespread demolition of buildings for road and railway improvements in London and Paris in the nineteenth century. See Steen E. Rasmussen, London: The Unique City (London: Penguin, 1961), p. 128.

[2] Some of the more interesting general treatments of this subject are: Ralph Turvey, The Economics of Real Property: An Analysis of Property Values and Patterns of Use (London: George Allen and Unwin Ltd., 1957); R. L. Nelson and F. T. Aschman, Real Estate and City Planning (Englewood Cliffs, N. J.: Prentice-Hall, Inc., 1957); Ernest M. Fisher and Robert M. Fisher, Urban Real Estate (New York: Henry Holt and Co., 1954), especially chapters xiii and xiv; Leo Grebler, Housing Market Behavior in a Declining Area (New York: Columbia University Press, 1952); and A. M. Weimer and Homer Hoyt, Principles of Real Estate (3rd ed.; New York: Ronald Press, 1954).

tinue in existence long after their apparent economic usefulness has been realized. The result is that with the passing of time the character and distribution of the building stock of a city become increasingly out-of-phase with the demands for physical space. It is this conflict between fixed real estate resources and highly mobile social and economic demands which underlies many of the basic maladjustments in the spatial structure of modern cities. From a geographical viewpoint, the problem of central concern is that of differential rates of change in the physical plant among areas of the city.

This problem has been described by Lowdon Wingo in economic terms as one of net disinvestment.[1] Wingo accounts for this phenomenon with two sets of factors. One set embraces those changes which reduce the productive capacity of the facility--obsolescence, aging, and capital consumption. The other consists of elements which affect the demand for urban real estate through their impact on "income earning expectations." In the latter case, there is a decline in demand, or what he calls a reduction in the flow of capital-replacing investment, because of structural effects and externalities. Structural changes are largely secular trends in technology, and in social and economic organization. Externalities derive from the interdependence of investment in urban real estate, in that the condition of one property influences the value of its neighbors. The uncertainty of investment in any property usually results in lower investment in all properties.

These trends should be set within a broader theoretical framework of urban structural change. Change in the basic urban pattern and the standing stock of buildings takes the form of an adaptation process. In economic theory there is an implicit assumption of equilibrium between present and optimum use of urban land and physical space.[2] At any point in time, the city is considered to be in balance with all activities in their optimal location given existing conditions. In reality, of course, no such state exists, although there may be a discernible trend in that direction.[3] The reasoning continues

---

[1] Lowdon Wingo, Jr., "Urban Renewal: A Strategy for Information and Analysis," Journal of the American Institute of Planners, XXXII, No. 3 (May, 1966), 147.

[2] The terms building space and structural space refer to the total building floor area inventory in the city. The use of the term space, in the sense of physical space, in preference to area, is deliberate. Space as a concept implies at least three dimensions, whereas area is explicitly two-dimensional. This distinction is critical in this study because of the parallel treatment of redevelopment as a process involving both land area and building space. For an interesting discussion of the varying interpretations of the term "space" in geography, see National Academy of Sciences, National Research Council, The Science of Geography, Report of the Ad Hoc Committee on Geography (Washington: National Research Council, 1965); and F. Lukermann, "Geography: de facto or de jure," Journal of the Minnesota Academy of Sciences, XXXII, No. 3 (1965), 189-196.

[3] For example, J.V. Giffor, Jr., "The Nature of the City as a System" (Paper presented before the Bay Area Systems Group of the Society for General Systems Research, San Francisco, November 15, 1962), p. 16.

that the addition of one element to this "system" changes all locational advantages, and the process of adaptation begins. Over time, activities and populations in the city essentially adjust themselves to these conditions in an attempt to re-establish equilibrium.

These adjustments tend to follow distinct patterns. Most demands are accommodated within the existing stock of buildings by a change in the location of a given use or in the amount of space consumed by that use. Without modification of existing structures, these adaptations lead to considerable spatial rearrangement of land uses and locational shifts in particular activities and populations. Only when the demand for change is sufficiently strong, however, is there modification or replacement of the physical plant. The actual replacement of buildings is the most drastic and least widespread phase of this continuous process, but it is part of the process.

Buildings themselves go through a continuous cycle of change with increasing age and external pressures for re-use. The cycle begins with new construction and a period of increasing or sustained value, followed by a long period of maintenance and depreciation, with possible modification of the building to accommodate new activities. Finally the cycle is repeated by replacement of the building. Replacement as a form of adaptation in the spatial structure of the city is therefore directly related to replacement in the life cycle of individual buildings.

Thus, not only is there a need to modify or adapt the nature, distribution and allocation of building space among different areas and activities, but this space, unlike the land on which it rests, must be maintained and eventually replaced.[1] These are continuous processes which operate simultaneously and in an interrelated fashion as the physical expression of urban growth and change. Given the existence of these forms of spatial adaptation and the life cycle of buildings, it is not surprising that large areas of our cities appear deteriorated. The problem is not that such conditions exist, because this is inevitable in a changing society, but rather that they persist.

Study Purposes, Design, and Objectives

This study attempts to analyze one aspect of this complex process of adaptation and renewal in cities, the nature and spatial pattern of private redevelopment. The principal focus is the standing stock of structures or buildings in the city and the process of change within this stock. The emphasis on structures is deliberate. The main concern is with changes resulting in new building construction, and major structural modi-

---

[1] This does not mean, of course, that all buildings or areas need be subjected to redevelopment. Many structures remain sound over long periods of time, and demands for their continued existence are strong. Public buildings, as well as those of historic, or monumental appeal, are examples.

fications. Limiting the analysis to structural change represents an attempt to isolate factors which derive from and affect the building stock, and which are influential in accelerating, retarding or prohibiting change in the geography of the city.

In the context of this study, redevelopment implies two different concepts. Most generally, redevelopment means simply to "develop again," and refers to any change in land use or rebuilding following the initial conversion of land from rural to urban use.[1] It thus complements urban development as a geographical process of urban growth in the form of a spatial continuum. This continuum ranges from new construction on vacant land in the suburban fringe to redevelopment in the city center where all new construction involves the replacement of an existing structure. More specifically, redevelopment refers to the actual demolition and replacement of existing buildings.[2] In this sense, redevelopment then becomes an integral part of a process of spatial and structural adaptation to changing socio-economic demands and increasing age.

To most readers, the terms "urban redevelopment"[3] and "renewal"[4] imply purposeful public action directed at the removal of slums and blighted areas and the

---

[1] For example, the Ontario Department of Municipal Affairs, Urban Renewal in Ontario (Toronto: Department of Municipal Affairs, Community Planning Branch, 1964), p. 10; and Miles Colean, Renewing Our Cities (New York: Twentieth Century Fund, 1953).

[2] For example, Donald H. Webster, Urban Planning and Municipal Public Policy (New York: Harper and Brothers, 1958), p. 490.

[3] The Central Mortgage and Housing Corporation, the Canadian Federal housing agency, defines redevelopment as " . . . a programme of acquisition and clearance of slums and blighted areas and the rebuilding of those areas for appropriate uses. . . ." Central Mortgage and Housing Corporation, "Urban Renewal," National Housing Act Brochure (Ottawa: The Central Mortgage and Housing Corporation, 1964). In the United States, redevelopment has been defined as " . . . the assembly of land in blighted areas, the clearing of titles, and the sale or lease of the assembled tracts to a private or public developer." For example, Harold M. Mayer, "Urban Geography," chapter vi in American Geography Inventory and Prospect, ed. P.E. James and C.F. Jones (Syracuse: Syracuse University Press, 1954), p. 156. For a discussion of recent additions and modifications of definitions in the Housing Acts of 1949 and 1954, see Greer, op. cit., chapter ii, pp. 13-43.

[4] Urban renewal is a more recent and inclusive term than redevelopment. Borrowed originally from the writings of Patrick Geddes and clarified by Miles Colean, renewal has generally been taken to represent the summation of all processes both private and public directed at maintaining urban vitality. Within this context, however, it is used to represent two distinct concepts. One refers to a range of activities, such as slum clearance and public works, and the second refers to what Weaver calls an "institutional form" and is restricted primarily to renewal programs at the federal, provincial, or state level. See, Patrick Geddes, Cities in Evolution (London, 1915); revised Williams and Northgate Ltd., 1949; Colean, op. cit., p. 28; Robert C. Weaver, "Current Trends in Urban Renewal," Land Economics, XXXIX, No. 4 (November, 1963), 328; and "The Rise and Development of Urban Renewal," chapter ii, in The Urban Complex (Garden City, N.Y.: Doubleday and Co., 1964), pp. 39-93.

maintenance of urban "vitality." This is not a study of public programs related to slum
clearance, public housing or plan implementation. Nor does it deal with the policy
experience of private investment in public renewal areas. The results may hold implications for such policy, but no qualitative judgments will be made concerning the presence
or absence of slum conditions in any area of the city, or in the establishment of priorities
for the removal of such conditions. Buildings are not synonymous with slums, although
some buildings because of their age, condition, or location, are more conducive to slum
formation than are others.[1]

Because of the complexity of information necessary to examine changes in individual buildings through time, the detailed empirical analysis is limited to one city,
Toronto[2] (Fig. 1), for which suitable statistics are available, and covers the years 1952
to 1962 inclusive. In an attempt to control the obvious problems that result from a
single case study and a single time perspective, priority is given to the theoretical basis
of urban spatial patterning and the replacement process in structures, rather than the
empirical analysis of new construction in Toronto. The unifying these is "process,"
with the city of Toronto as one example.

The analytical approach and study organization mirror this rationale. Initially,
the approach is to examine the visible results of a complex process of urban change.
This analysis is set within a conceptual framework designed so that generalizations
concerning the location of urban redevelopment are first drawn from the literature on
urban spatial structure. These generalizations offer a series of conceptual expectations
which may then be related to the empirical results.

Three aspects of redevelopment activity could be considered, the total amount,
its allocation among land use types, and relative location within the city. The total
amount of private redevelopment that occurs in any city is largely determined exogenously
to the economy of that city. Although the industry mix and economic health of an urban

---

[1] Miles Colean draws an interesting distinction between the "renewal" problem
and the "slum" problem in his study for the Twentieth Century Fund. The renewal
problem is essentially economic and structural, focussing on how to construct, maintain,
and rebuild the various parts of the urban structure ignored by the renewal process in the
private market. The slum problem, on the other hand, is related to social pathologies
and is basically a problem of attitudes and behavior. Confusion results from the close
coincidence of the two in the modern American city. See Colean, op. cit., p. 40; and
David L. Hunter, The Slums Challenge and Response (Glencoe: The Free Press, 1964),
particularly pp. 12-24.

[2] The City of Toronto throughout this text refers only to the area within the
municipal boundaries of the city. Metropolitan Toronto, or "Metro," refers to the
officially incorporated municipality consisting of the City of Toronto and the twelve
adjacent suburban communities (see Fig. 1). Reference will also be made to the
standard census metropolitan area and the Metropolitan Planning Area, which includes
"Metro" Toronto and additional fringe municipalities and townships.

8

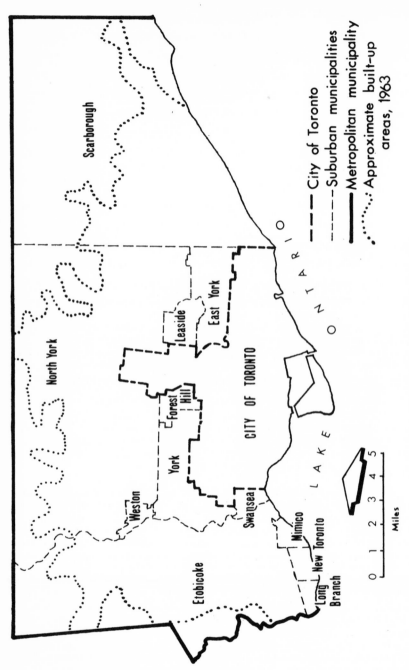

Fig. 1--The City of Toronto and its Metropolitan Context

area influences its competitive position within a national system of metropolitan economies, the absolute investment potential available depends on current national conditions. Likewise, investment in different types of redevelopment, that is, among subdivisions of the construction industry, depends on national growth conditions and preferences in financing, as well as on the composition of the local economy. In the formulation of this study no attempt will be made to analyze national factors or the relative position of Toronto in the Canadian metropolitan economy, although constant reference is made to such conditions.[1] The amount of investment in redevelopment in Toronto is basically taken as given, and the problem then becomes one of accounting for the spatial variation of this investment within the city, and the differential allocation among areas (see Appendix C for Zones of Analysis).

As the concern here is with redevelopment as a process within the context of the "normal" real estate market mechanism, the analysis excludes all government, public, and institutional land uses, as defined in the basic data source (see Chapter IV and Appendix B).[2] This also excludes all public renewal efforts, and private redevelopment in publicly-designated renewal areas.[3] By limiting the analysis in this way,[4] it is possible to make certain basic economic assumptions about investment decisions in new

---

[1]It is likewise obvious that the magnitude of redevelopment activity in a given period, as for all construction activity, depends on the capacity of the building industry. This is by no means a minor factor, particularly in an upswing in the business cycle during times of prosperity.

[2]The preferable method of defining public and private action would be based on the location of decision-making power. As this definition is operationally difficult to control, it has largely been ignored in urban research. For one interesting attempt in this direction see W. L. C. Wheaton, "Public and Private Agents of Change in Urban Expansion," in Explorations into Urban Structure, pp. 154-196.

[3]Excluded for the moment are the effects of code enforcement and rehabilitation on the condition of the building stock of the city. The short-run effects of these measures are likely to be substantial, and there is little doubt of their value in improving the urban "condition." The primary effect will be one of lengthening the economic and physical life of individual buildings, and thus of diverting investment from new construction to the existing structural stock. In this regard, rehabilitation measures are likely to alter the magnitude but not the relative operation of the processes of change. For example, the effects of various types of public policy including code enforcement are assessed in A. H. Schaaf, Economic Aspects of Urban Renewal: Theory, Policy, and Area Analysis (Research Report No. 14, Real Estate Research Program; Berkeley: Institute of Business and Economic Research, University of California, 1960).

[4]It is also not possible to treat in this context the external effects of public renewal and redevelopment action as a catalyst in stimulating private investment in areas adjacent to such projects. Evidence suggests, however, that this impact particularly in Canada, has not been substantial.

construction. No single set of generalizations appropriately spans location decisions in both the public and private sectors.

Empirical Implications

The problem of encouraging more widespread and consistent structural change and redevelopment in cities is receiving increasing attention.[1] The obvious breakdown in the private renewal process in the removal of deteriorated structures and the maintenance of urban vitality, as well as the social, economic, and visual pathologies that result has led to increasing public response. Large urban renewal projects in Canada and the United States, combined with expanding investment in schools, roads, and other municipal services testify to this increased role. In part, the increasing awareness of the magnitude of the problem is due to the very enormity of the building and rebuilding taking place. The Royal Commission on Canada's Economic Prospects,[2] for example, estimated in 1956 that within the following twenty-five years investment in Canadian cities and towns would equal and likely exceed all that has been inherited from the past.

It is agreed that private market processes will not be sufficient to improve urban environments in their entirety and that public participation is necessary, both as a substitute where private initiative is lacking, and as a form of guidance where it is

---

[1] For example, among the more recent reviews of the problem: Jane Jacobs, The Death and Life of Great American Cities (New York: Random House, 1961); C. Vereker and J.B. Mays, Urban Redevelopment and Social Change (Liverpool: University of Liverpool Press, 1961); E.A. Gutkind, The Twilight of Cities (Glencoe: The Free Press, 1962); T.F. Johnson, J.R. Morris, and J.G. Butts, Renewing America's Cities (Washington: Institute for Social Science Research, 1962); Leonard J. Duhl, The Urban Condition: People and Policy in the Metropolis (New York: Basic Books, 1963); Mitchell Gordon, Sick Cities (New York: MacMillan and Co., 1963); American Institute of Real Estate Appraisers, Urban Renewal and Redevelopment, Articles from the Appraisal Journal (Chicago: The Institute, 1964); York Wilburn, The Withering Away of the City (Birmingham: University of Alabama Press, 1964); American Academy of Political and Social Science, "Urban Revival: Goals and Standards," The Annals, Special Issue, Vol. CCCLII (March, 1964); Bernard Frieden, The Future of Old Neighborhoods: Rebuilding for a Changing Population (Cambridge: M.I.T. Press, 1964); F.J. Tietze and J.E. McKeown (eds.), The Changing Metropolis (Boston: Houghton Mifflin Co., 1964); Duke University, School of Law, "Urban Problems and Prospects," Law and Contemporary Problems, Special Issue, Vol. XXX, No. 1 (Winter, 1965); Charles Abrams, The City is the Frontier (New York: Harper and Row, 1965); John C. Bollens and J.J. Schmandt, The Metropolis: Its People, Politics and Economic Life (New York: Harper and Row, 1965); Scientific American, Cities, Special Issue, Vol. CCXIII, No. 3 (September, 1965); Greer, op. cit.; and James Q. Wilson (ed.), Urban Renewal, The Record and the Controversy (Cambridge: M.I.T. Press, 1966).

[2] Central Mortgage and Housing Corporation, Housing and Urban Growth in Canada, A Brief to the Royal Commission on Canada's Economic Prospects (Ottawa: The Central Mortgage and Housing Corporation, 1956), p. 5.

operative.[1] In both cases, therefore, public and private decisions must rest on a thorough understanding of the private market if their incentives and directives are to achieve maximum success.[2] Currently, if market processes are not entirely ignored, assumptions about their operation seem to be based more on speculation than on fact. As William Grigsby points out, the fundamental criticism of present public efforts in the renewal field is the inadequate consideration given to the realities of the real estate market. His criticism is pointed:

> The widespread recognition of the need to renew our cities
> has not been accompanied by an equal appreciation of the
> complexity of economic forces that surround the apparently
> simple task of tearing down the old and replacing it with
> something new and beautiful.[3]

Theoretical Contributions to the Study of Urban Growth Processes

Existing theories of the spatial patterning of urban land uses do not take into account the variable character of the structural stock and the process of change within this stock. Renewal and redevelopment as part of this process have been largely ignored by theorists in urban research. Descriptions of the internal structure of cities have been static, without reference to process, and primarily concerned with land use

---

[1] There have been some dissenting voices in the widespread criticism of private market processes. One of the most stimulating and controversial is a study of the Federal urban renewal program in the United States by Martin Anderson. His argument is simply that evidence to date indicates that the private market is capable of improving urban environments and housing without the aid of Federal assistance, as it has done in the past, and that this assistance is wasteful and in fact unconstitutional. See Martin Anderson, The Federal Bulldozer, A Critical Analysis of Urban Renewal 1949-1962 (Cambridge: M.I.T. Press, 1964); as well as his two following articles on the same theme, "Fiasco of Urban Renewal," Harvard Business Review, XLIII, No. 1 (Jan.-Feb., 1965), 6-21; and "The Sophistry That Made Urban Renewal Possible," Law and Contemporary Problems, XXX, No. 1 (Winter, 1965) 199-211. Anderson's conclusions have since come under severe criticism. For some interesting counter-arguments, see the reviews of Anderson's book by: M. Berger, "Checkmate Professor Anderson," Appraisal Journal, XXXIII, No. 2 (April, 1965), 199-202; Herbert J. Gans, "The Failure of Urban Renewal: A Critique and Some Proposals," Commentary, XXXIX, No. 4 (April, 1965), 29-37; Robert P. Groberg, "Urban Renewal Realistically Reappraised," Law and Contemporary Problems, XXX, No. 1 (Winter, 1965), 212-229; and the book review by Wallace F. Smith, in Journal of the American Institute of Planners, XXXI, No. 2 (May, 1965), 179-180.

[2] Kristoff describes the problem as one of maximizing private investment and minimizing the competitive effect between public and private efforts. Frank S. Kristoff, "Housing Policy Goals and the Turnover of Housing," Journal of the American Institute of Planners, XXXI, No. 3 (August, 1965), 241.

[3] William C. Grigsby, Housing Markets and Public Policy (Philadelphia: University of Pennsylvania Press, 1963), p. 332.

and population distributions.[1] Where a time perspective is provided, the empirical base is highly generalized, dealing with land use in the aggregate,[2] or has provided great detail for small areas in the central business district[3] or suburban fringe. Traditionally, geographers concerned with redevelopment have concentrated on public project planning and not on the continuous process operative in the private land market.

Thus, in addition to a lack of empirical documentation concerning recent modifications to the urban physical plant, the existing literature does not provide a logical basis to account for such changes. One purpose of this study is to address these imbalances. Careful study of scattered redevelopment in the City of Toronto provides the opportunity.

Research on urban renewal and redevelopment has, in the past, been directed at preliminary analysis for public renewal programs, and is therefore of minor direct interest to this study. Most such studies have been concerned with economic feasibility,[4] the planning and execution of public programs,[5] and include lengthy dialogues on the reasons why the private market mechanism has failed to maintain a more continuous

---

[1]The literature on urban land use in general is voluminous, and numerous detailed bibliographies are available. As examples, see C. Shillaber, "A Review of Planning Bibliographies," Journal of the American Institute of Planners, XXXI, No. 4 (November, 1965), 352-360; the Urban Land Institute publications on Urban Real Estate Research; and for Canadian references, The Canadian Council on Urban and Regional Research, References, 1945-1962 (Ottawa: The Council, 1964). For a general review see, Raymond E. Murphy, The American City, An Urban Geography (New York: McGraw-Hill, 1966), pp. 205-206; and for one suggestion of needed research see, J.W. Simmons, "Descriptive Models of Urban Land Use," Canadian Geographer, IX, No. 3 (1965), 170-174.

[2]For example, H. Bartholomew, Land Uses in American Cities (Cambridge: Harvard University Press, 1955); J.H. Niedercorn and E.F.R. Hearle, Recent Land Use Trends in Forty-Eight Large American Cities, Memorandum RM-3662-1-FF (Santa Monica: The Rand Corporation, 1963); and Louis K. Loewenstein, "Location of Urban Land Uses," Land Economics, XXXLX, No. 4 (November, 1963), 407-420.

[3]John Rannells, The Core of the City: A Pilot Study of Changing Land Uses in Central Business Districts (New York: Columbia University Press, 1956).

[4]For example, Max R. Bloom, "Fiscal Productivity and the Pure Theory of Urban Renewal," Land Economics, XXXVIII, No. 2 (May, 1962), 135-144; Otto Davis and A.B. Whinston, "Economics of Urban Renewal," Law and Contemporary Problems, XXVI, No. 1, (Winter, 1961), 105-117; and Hugh O. Nourse, "The Economics of Urban Renewal," Land Economics, XLII, No. 1 (February, 1966), 65-74.

[5]Probably the classic statement is the two-volume summary of the Chicago Redevelopment Study (1948-1951) edited by Coleman Woodbury, Urban Redevelopment Problems and Practices (Chicago: University of Chicago Press, 1953); and The Future of Cities and Urban Redevelopment (Chicago: University of Chicago Press, 1953).

process of rebuilding.[1] There is no theory of urban renewal as such; rather a "philosophy" of renewal has evolved to justify the intervention of government in the operation of a private market.[2] Few studies have sought to establish the nature and process of structural change in the standing stock of buildings in a city, and to describe the characteristics of the sites and areas undergoing change. This study may assist in bridging the gap between these research orientations.

There are several benefits to be gained by approaching the dynamics of urban change through the changing condition of its standing stock. These changes represent a summation of an enormously complex array of factors which are acting to alter the spatial structure of the city. An analysis based on the isolation of individual factors and their interrelationships would be tedious and costly, if at all possible. The nature and location of new construction represents an expression of these factors, and one that is directly susceptible to measurement and evaluation. Moreover, since the standing stock of structures in a city responds slowly to the interaction of supply and demand forces in the market, replacements in this stock represent adjustments to locational trends over the long-run.[3]

The use of structural criteria as the definitional basis for an analysis of change is not entirely new. Donald Bogue, for example, in his report on Needed Urban and Metropolitan Research,[4] suggests the use of changes in the structural stock of a city as one approach in urban structural analysis, and outlines a methodology which approximates that employed in this study. He regards one decade as a suitable time period for detailed analyses because of rapid fluctuations in the array of factors producing change, but extends the analysis to several decades, each acting as a "layer" of building activity superimposed on previous layers and in turn conditioning the future pattern. This is not

---

[1] For example, R. Heindahl, Urban Renewal (New York: Scarecrow Press, 1959).

[2] The philosophy of urban renewal is essentially a concept of social responsibility. See William L. Slayton, "Urban Renewal Philosophy," Planning 1963, Selected papers from the ASPO National Planning Conference, Seattle, May 5-9, 1963 (Chicago: American Society of Planning Officials, 1963), pp. 154-159.

[3] The designation of long-run trends is arbitrary and has no direct relation to the length of the time period under discussion, except to permit the assumption that new building will take place only once on a given site during this time. Buildings are usually designed and financed with an ultimate capitalization period of from 30 to 50 years, but often much longer. In this case, the term long-run is used in the sense of stability in contrast to the rapid changes and instability that characterize the locational patterns of individual urban activities and populations.

[4] Donald J. Bogue (ed.), Needed Urban and Metropolitan Research (Scripps Foundation Studies in Population Distribution, No. 7; Oxford, Ohio: Miami University, 1953), p. 23.

meant to imply that the spatial structure of the city at any one point in time is the result of a single definable set of forces, but rather as Bogue suggests, it is "a composite of several successive sets of forces acting at various times." In this study, a decade is taken merely as an operational and arbitrary division of this sequential process which has meaning in terms of the relative uniformity of economic conditions.[1]

Likewise, Rowlands cites the need for research into the dynamics of urban land use and argues for a systematic analysis of change based on studies of individual properties. He concludes:

> Studies of the decisions to build or to alter buildings can be expected to reveal trends in the financing of buildings and in the changes that have taken place in the space requirements of various types of businesses. . . . More importantly, it could evaluate the factors that retard or encourage investment in buildings in different locations.[2]

Obviously, changes in the physical plant of a city cannot be studied meaningfully apart from the processes of change in the socio-economic and political functions which use it. Conversely, neither can one understand the full complexity of urban change without an understanding in depth of the determinants of change in investment and replacement in the structural stock. This stock provides the permissive space for urban activities and populations, conditioned by and in turn conditioning broader social changes. Furthermore, the size of capital investment in the urban physical plant renders it of central concern for both theory and policy. As Wingo comments, the physical plant ". . . represents a large proportion of the total wealth of a nation, and the flows of investment induced by its growth and change are a significant fraction of our gross national product."[3]

Synthesis and Organization

To summarize, the principal objectives of this study are: (1) to examine and evaluate existing theories of urban growth and spatial patterning for insight into the process and patterns of urban redevelopment; (2) to outline a theoretical framework for redevelopment within the context of processes of structural change and renewal in cities;

---

[1]Note that the period under study is from 1952 to 1962 inclusive, a total of eleven years.

[2]David T. Rowlands, Urban Real Estate Research (Urban Land Institute, Research Monograph No. 1; Washington: Urban Land Institute, 1959), p. 25.

[3]Wingo, "Urban Renewal: A Strategy for Information and Analysis," loc. cit., p. 151.

and hypothesized location factors; (6) and to develop

(3) to describe and analyze the nature and spatial pattern of redevelopment in Toronto;

(4) to assess its impact on the physical plant of the city and suggest possible implications;

(5) to determine the spatial relationships between these changes and models to assist in evaluating the relative importance of these factors in producing spatial variations in redevelopment activity among areas of the city, and for the succession of land uses that results.

The initial three chapters review the relevant theories in urban research, evaluate these theories for insight into the nature and location of urban redevelopment, and introduce the concepts of redevelopment as a spatial process of urban structural growth. Chapter IV outlines the Toronto study and describes the data, analysis, and measurement procedures. The fifth chapter attempts to pull together from the literature, the specific location factors and constraints in redevelopment and to establish hypotheses to be tested in the Toronto context. Chapter VI summarizes the descriptive statistics on change, and suggests major trends and implications. The following chapter (Chapter VII) leads back into the theoretical discussion of the first section, relating the change summaries to the hypothesized location factors. The second section of this chapter examines in detail the nature of land use succession resulting from redevelopment.

CHAPTER II

CONCEPTUAL BACKGROUND AND FORMULATION

The conceptual framework for this study consists of a strikingly diffuse body of theory pertaining to urban spatial structure and the dynamics of urban change and renewal. This chapter reviews the traditional theories of urban spatial patterning in an attempt to extract insights into the patterns and processes of urban redevelopment. To provide a broad explanatory base for understanding the forces and mechanisms of change, relevant concepts from renewal, housing, real estate and planning research, and property economics are included. Finally, in this and the following chapter we will attempt to merge the approach of redevelopment research and the postulates of land use theory, to provide a conceptual framework for urban redevelopment as a spatial process of urban change.

Urban Spatial Patterning

Urban land economists have generalized the pattern and process of locational change in terms of the competition among land uses for urban space. Urban ecologists have described the process as one of competitive bidding among alternative users for individual sites, and have postulated spatial models based on the concepts of invasion and succession in neighborhoods and a filtering-down process in the housing market.

In economic theory, space and location are commodities subject to the forces of supply and demand in the "urban land market." Assuming perfect competition, each parcel of land is occupied by the activity which can utilize it most "efficiently," paying in rent an amount up to the savings in transportation costs that result from the accessibility of that site to the urban market. Ratcliff comments that "the structure of the city may be thought of as determined by the dollar evaluation of the importance of convenience."[1] In theory all activities compete for the same sites, but in effect only a

---

[1]Richard U. Ratcliff, Urban Land Economics (New York: McGraw-Hill Book Co., 1949), p. 375.

17

certain range of sites are attractive to individual types of land uses. This produces distinct submarkets for urban space, depending on the value placed on different locational attributes by individual users of space.

This interpretation of the competition for space and location derives from the classic statements of Hurd[1] and Haig.[2] In the Regional Study of New York in the 1920's, Haig postulated the assignment of activities to subareas of the metropolis in accordance with the principal of minimizing the "costs of friction." Locational decisions are viewed as based on a trade-off between accessibility and land costs, or between transportation costs and site rentals, which form the costs of overcoming the friction of space. Accessibility then acts as a substitute for transportation, but both must be paid for, the former in land rent and the latter in time, inconvenience, and the costs of transportation.[3] According to this theory, each user of space determines its unique and optimal location by obtaining the desired level of accessibility with a minimum of site costs based on the marginal rates of return for both. In the aggregate, the pattern tends toward the most efficient, in other words, that which minimizes the total cost of "friction."[4]

In this framework, land use and land value are simultaneously determined.[5] The spatial pattern that emerges both for land use and land values shows a strong focus on one point, the city center, with gradients sloping off in all directions. The center is occupied by those activities most valuing accessibility to the entire urban area and capable of operating at relatively high densities. Activities that cannot or desire not to compete are forced increasingly to the periphery where land costs are less, and where lower densities are economically feasible. Complicating these interactions of location,

---

[1] Richard M. Hurd, Principles of City Land Values (New York: The Record and Guide, 1903). Hurd argued that value depends on economic rent, rent on location, location on convenience, convenience on nearness, thus value depends on nearness.

[2] Robert M. Haig, "Toward an Understanding of the Metropolis," Quarterly Journal of Economics, XL (May, 1926), 179-208.

[3] R. T. Ely and G. S. Wehrwein, Land Economics (New York: McMillan and Co., 1940), p. 444. They attempt to include in the costs of friction some measures of the "disutilities" of travel, as does Ratcliff (Urban Land Economics, p. 372). In a more recent publication, Lowdon Wingo includes the value of travel time in assessing the interrelation between transportation and land use patterns. Lowdon Wingo, Jr., Transportation and Urban Land (Washington: Resources for the Future, Inc., 1961).

[4] Richard U. Ratcliff, "The Dynamics of Efficiency in the Locational Distribution of Urban Activities," reprinted in Readings in Urban Geography, ed. H. M. Mayer and C. F. Kohn (Chicago: University of Chicago Press, 1959), p. 302.

[5] The argument over whether values determine use or vice versa has been a continuing one in urban research. See Haig, op. cit., p. 405; Alonso, op. cit., p. 9; and for example, James A. Quinn, Human Ecology (New York: Prentice-Hall, Inc., 1950), p. 449.

use, and value, however, is the size of site, or amount of space consumed. To compensate or substitute for costs of access, activities alter not only their location but also the amount of space consumed at any location. Thus, while unit costs for land will decline steadily away from the city center the actual total costs of land may remain much more constant.[1]

A slightly different approach is taken in two recent studies which focus on communication or "linkage" requirements between activities.[2] By tracing the linkages or "movement systems" for and between establishments, some additional insight is provided into the locational pattern of urban land uses and variations in the degree of spatial association between individual uses.[3] Changes within an establishment generate different demands for movement and alter location requirements. For example, the cycle of family formation and growth is clearly related to the locational choices of individual households. Although it is difficult to extract theory from these discussions, the emphasis on the dynamic interaction between location and activity rather than on accessibility alone, represents an important addition to existing generalizations. In much the same line, the abstractions of Webber[4] and Meier[5] view urban spatial structure as the result of human interaction systems, including both spatial and behavioral dimensions.

Space Organizing Concepts

Attempts have been made to describe the spatial patterns that result from the operation of the processes just discussed. The traditional views of concentric rings, sectors, and multiple nuclei are sufficiently well known that only general reference need be made here.[6]

In large part these descriptive models of urban structure have been suggested

---

[1]William Alonso discusses this point and attempts to incorporate lot size into his theoretical model of the urban land market. See "Theory of the Urban Land Market," Papers and Proceedings of the Regional Science Association, VI (1960), 149-156.

[2]Robert B. Mitchell and Chester Rapkin, Urban Traffic: A Function of Land Use (New York: Columbia University Press, 1954).

[3]Rannells, op. cit.

[4]Melvin W. Webber, "The Urban Place and the Nonplace Urban Realm," in Explorations into Urban Structure, pp. 79-153.

[5]Richard L. Meier, A Communications Theory of Urban Growth (Cambridge: M.I.T. Press, 1962).

[6]See C.D. Harris and E.L. Ullman, "The Nature of Cities," The Annals of the American Academy of Political and Social Science, CCXLII (November, 1945), 7-17.

and tested by ecologists and thus are primarily concerned with residential space.
Burgess, and the ecological school in Sociology at the University of Chicago, described
the arrangement of land uses and the pattern of growth as forming general concentric
zones around the center of the city.[1] Five zones were recognized and defined, from the
central business district and the surrounding zone of transition to the higher income
commuting suburbs. Growth takes place by the simple expansion of these zones outward,
each zone invading the adjacent outer zone, replacing less by more intensive uses in a
process of succession.

Homer Hoyt disagreed with the concentric zonation theory as it applied to residential structure and growth. Instead, he postulated that residential areas showed marked
sectoral variation, and tended to grow outward along distinct radii.[2] If a certain sector
of the city develops as a high rent area, it will retain that character and migrate outward
with city growth. The high income area, which usually starts near the retail and office
district in the city center, acts as a magnet in pulling the growth of other residential
areas.

Despite their simplistic nature, and probably as a result of it, these generalized
models have withstood the pressures of criticism,[3] but with some modification. Harris
and Ullman recognized that cities have not one but several nuclei which act to orient land
use patterns.[4] Moreover, cities are characterized by both concentric and axial patterns,
as suggested by Hurd much earlier in his distinction between central and axial growth.[5]
More recent studies have shown that all three descriptions contribute to the total pat-

---

[1] Ernest W. Burgess, "The Growth of the City," in The City, ed. R.E. Park,
E.W. Burgess, and R.D. McKenzie (Chicago: University of Chicago Press, 1925).

[2] Homer Hoyt, The Structure and Growth of Residential Neighborhoods in
American Cities (Washington: Federal Housing Administration, 1939), p. 114.

[3] Several interesting criticisms and evaluations of the Burgess-Hoyt hypotheses
are available. See, for example, the prefatory remarks by Don Martindale on the
ecological view of the city in Max Weber, The City (New York: Collier Books, 1962),
pp. 9-70; and the discussions and references in A.H. Hawley, Human Ecology (New York:
Ronald Press, 1950), chapters xiii and xiv; James A. Quinn, "The Burgess Zonal
Hypothesis and its Critics," American Sociological Review, V (April, 1940), 210-218;
Lloyd Rodwin, "The Theory of Residential Growth and Structure," The Appraisal Journal,
XVIII, No. 3 (July, 1950), 295-317; Walter Firey, Land Use in Central Boston
(Cambridge: Harvard University Press, 1947); Hans Blumenfeld, "On the Concentric
Circle Theory of Urban Growth," Land Economics, XXV, No. 2 (May, 1949), 209-212;
and M.R. Davie, "The Pattern of Urban Growth," in Studies in the Science of Society,
ed. G.P. Murdock (New Haven, 1937), pp. 133-161.

[4] Harris and Ullman, op. cit., p. 13.

[5] Hurd, op. cit., p. 58.

terning of residential neighborhoods, and that variations of socio-economic characteristics over space exhibit systematic gradients from the city center and along major axes
of transportation.[1] As suggested by Burgess, variables such as population density, land
values, age and type of structure, and family size (defining physical growth and family
structure) decline with distance from the city center. Superimposed is an axial variation
in residential quality as measured by social status and income. Localized concentrations
of ethnic groups are then added as a third pattern based on segregation.

In addition to generality, one of the principal limitations of the concentric-
sectoral interpretation of urban structure and the emphasis on density gradients as
Harris noted, is the assumption of a single center. As useful as the general conceptual
framework is, recent trends suggest that growth forces may be based on an increasing
number of alternative centers, as cities become larger and more dispersed. These new
centers may in fact follow the axial pattern, but not necessarily in the sense of strict
interaction with the city center. Many students of urban structure, for example those
of the Berkeley planning "syndrome," contend that this will be the pattern of the future.[2]
The trade-offs between centrifugal and centripetal forces influencing the urban pattern
have been substantially altered.[3] In this analysis of recent redevelopment trends, as one
aspect of structural change, the degree to which the city center still exerts control and
orientation over the direction of change is therefore of critical importance.

Another point of departure is the criticism directed at deterministic interpretations of the traditional models of urban structure. Implicit in these generalizations are
the inevitable effects of age and deterioration. For example, these theories suggest that
the wealthy are on the periphery of the city because that is obviously the only area where
new construction is possible. They were pushed there it is argued, by the aging and
obsolescence of existing dwellings, which are in turn abandoned to groups of lower
income. Alonso takes issue with this historical determinism, and, voicing the opinions
of others, suggests that the wealthy may move to the suburbs because they want to be

---

[1]For a review and summary of urban density gradients and the theories of urban
socio-economic patterning see Brian J.L. Berry, "Internal Structure of the City," Law
and Contemporary Problems, XXX, No. 1 (Winter, 1965), 111-119.

[2]See, for example, Catherine Bauer Wurster, "The Form and Structure of the
Future Urban Complex," in Cities and Space, ed. Lowdon Wingo, Jr. (Baltimore: Johns
Hopkins Press, for Resources for the Future, Inc., 1963), pp. 73-102; and John
Friedman and John Miller, "The Urban Field," Journal of the American Institute of
Planners, XXXI, November 4 (November, 1965), 312-319.

[3]See the initial formulation of this concept in C.C. Colby, "Centrifugal and
Centripetal Forces in Urban Geography," XXIII, No. 1 (March, 1933), 1-20.

there, not because they have nowhere else to go.[1] In other words, space preference rather than age or accessibility is the strongest factor, with accessibility acting as an inferior good.

A very intriguing question can be posed at this point which in effect holds the age factor constant. Assume that a city were to develop quickly enough that no significant obsolescence of the structural stock could take place: what would be the spatial pattern of land uses and residential stratification? Of course it is impossible to answer this question. Alonso's view, however, suggests that the pattern should be much the same. This does not mean that age is unimportant as a factor in urban spatial structure, but rather that it may operate somewhat independently of other processes. As cities are built for the present and not the future, and are a response to the technology and demands of the time, the primary importance of age may well be in the conditions under which the basic structure developed. Many of the differences between cities, as Winsborough[2] adds, may be explained simply on the basis of time of construction.

The implication of Alonso's argument for renewal purposes, is that space rather than centrality or new construction is the critical factor in attracting new residents.[3] The importance of space or land availability, which of course implies cost, in urban locational decisions is clearly shown by Voorhees[4] for manufacturing, and Frieden[5] for the location of new housing construction. If these relationships hold, it should be possible to explain a significant portion of the pattern of private redevelopment in terms of the amount or average size of spatial unit available. This point will be developed in more detail in this and the following chapters.

Land Use Succession

Ecologists refer to changes in the pattern of land uses and social areas in the

---

[1] William Alonso, "The Historic and the Structural Theories of Urban Form: Their Implications for Urban Renewal," Land Economics, XL, No. 2 (May, 1964), 229. Note also the strong emphasis given to lower density in suburban development in Edgar M. Hoover and Raymond Vernon, The Anatomy of a Metropolis (Cambridge: Harvard University Press, 1959), p. 169.

[2] Hal H. Winsborough, "City Growth and City Structure," Journal of Regional Science, IV, No. 2 (Winter, 1962), 45.

[3] Alonso, op. cit., p. 231. Renewal programs may in fact be employing the wrong basic assumptions, namely central location and accessibility, as the basis for attracting suburban residents back into the central city. Instead some combination of attractions deriving from both the traditional and the "space" oriented approaches is needed.

[4] Alan M. Voorhees, "Urban Growth Characteristics," Urban Land, XX, No. 11 (December, 1961), 4.

[5] Frieden, op. cit., especially chapter iv, "The Economics of New Housing in Old Neighborhoods," pp. 73-103.

city as a process of <u>invasion and succession</u> in neighborhoods and of <u>filtering–down</u> in housing. With time, and increasing demands for space, each land use zone expands into an area of less intensive use immediately adjacent to and further from the city center. In effect, the more intensive uses outbid the existing uses for the locational advantages of that area. The central business district expands at the expense of the surrounding low income and industrial–warehousing zones, which in turn expand into adjacent residential zones, and so on. Residences are generally not capable of outbidding other uses, unless protected by zoning, and therefore bear the brunt of most such expansions.

In this change, the center and each outlying zone undergo a process of <u>selective adaptation</u> to those functions for which they are most suited.[1] Figure 2 provides an example of the nature of distributional change that takes place in different functions with increasing city size.[2] The city center first loses its dominance in food and industrial concentration, followed by general retail and department store functions. It retains dominance in the major office category and, at least up to the size of metropolitan Toronto (1966 population: 2,100,000), in high-rise residential developments. The rate of decline in each category with increasing city size does not necessarily reflect migration from the city center, for example in the case of department stores, but rather the differential rate of growth of these activities in suburban areas.

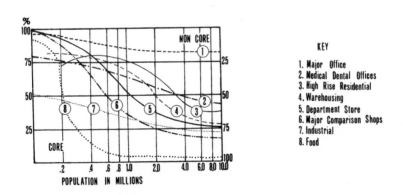

KEY

1. Major Office
2. Medical Dental Offices
3. High Rise Residential
4. Warehousing
5. Department Store
6. Major Comparison Shops
7. Industrial
8. Food

Fig. 2.--Distribution of Functions Related to City Size

---

[1] For example, Hans Blumenfeld, "The Urban Pattern," <u>Annals of the American Academy of Political and Social Science</u>, CCCLII (March, 1964), 79; and Vernon, <u>op. cit</u>.

[2] Larry Smith, "Space for the CBD's Functions," <u>Journal of the American Institute of Planners</u>, XXVII, No. 1 (February, 1961), 40.

The concept of a succession of land uses focussing on the changes in occupancy of a given site in developed areas of the city through time is not well formulated. Fisher and Fisher[1] suggest a theoretical sequence through which such changes might occur. The first stage involves a change in the size of the spatial unit, for example, an alteration of a single-family house to multiple family, but without any change in the type of use. The second involves a change in the type of use without the demolition or modification of the structure and within a designated physical unit. Succession may come about in this case through the conversion of residential to commercial use or from one type of commercial use to another. These changes are undoubtedly the most widespread, but as no structural modification is involved, no records are kept and their significance is difficult to assess. On the other hand, the authors suggest that these changes do seem to anticipate the direction of major structural change and new construction.[2] The third form is land use succession which occurs as a result of demolition and replacement of existing structures.

This interpretation of succession was obviously formulated with land use change in mind.[3] It does, however, bring together the types of changes that occur in both land and building. Were the emphasis on structures, the second stage involving no modification to the structure itself would be placed first. Furthermore, it would be useful to add one and possibly two stages to this sequence to account for variations in intensity of use. An attempt will be made in this direction in the following chapter.

Real Estate and Real Property

The two principal characteristics of urban land and structures as real estate resources are durability and immobility.[4] In contrast to most other economic goods, buildings represent long-term investments which once constructed remain for considerable periods of time.[5] The average physical life of units within the standing stock of a

---

[1]Fisher and Fisher, op. cit., p. 338.

[2]Ibid., p. 339.

[3]As this formulation treats only those sites with existing structures, the conversion of rural land to urban use is not included.

[4]Fisher and Fisher, op. cit., p. 160.

[5]For example, Hoyt pointed out that in 1930 that of 500,000 buildings constructed within the present city limits of Chicago since 1830, over 400,000 were still standing. Homer Hoyt, One Hundred Years of Land Values in Chicago (Chicago: University of Chicago Press, 1933), p. 286.

community has been estimated at between 50 and 60 years, and within specific land use categories may be even higher.

The result of this durability factor is that in the short-run the supply of real estate resources is essentially fixed. Unlike most other commodities, the yearly flow of units into and out of the market has only a minor quantitative effect on the character and volume of the existing inventory. Precisely because changes are costly and slow, extensive alterations to existing units are infrequent. This does not mean that wide-spread improvements in the existing stock do not occur, as is certainly the case in housing in recent years.[1] Rather, it means that major structural modifications of buildings to accommodate new demands and quite often different uses, have not been sufficient to influence the aggregate character of the standing stock.

In terms of additions to and subtractions from the inventory, new construction generally tends to supplement rather than replace existing units. Thus, established patterns persist and the inventory accumulates rather than replaces itself. In the short run then, replacement units do not drastically affect the market as they do in, for example, the clothing and shoe industries, where units are quickly discarded and removed from the market. Where removal from the market or demolition does occur in real estate inventories, it results primarily, as Grebler comments, from a succession of land uses, in other words, an external economic pressure for change, rather than from obsolescence or physical deterioration.[2] The rate of provision of new units is also subject to considerable variations over time following major business cycles and shifts, and is limited by the capacity of the construction industry at any point in time.

The second important consideration in understanding the operation of the real estate market is that of fixed location.[3] Every parcel of real estate has one, and only one, location, and therefore occupies a somewhat unique hierarchical position in the urban spatial structure. Obviously, only one building can occupy a site at one given time, and although the use of a building may vary, in the aggregate the locational distri-bution of the inventory is static. As a result, real estate resources cannot escape the

---

[1] For example, Anderson, The Federal Bulldozer, p. 200 and Table 13.1; and the discussions of housing quality in Grigsby, op. cit.

[2] Grebler, op. cit., p. 28. This comment is in line with Maisel's criticism of housing market analyses based on the assumption of a life cycle in structures as a function of age and deterioration, and it agrees with the argument employed in this study as developed in this and the following chapter.

[3] In fact, Weimer and Hoyt define the study of real estate as " . . . the study of income and income producing potentials at fixed locations." Weimer and Hoyt, op. cit., p. 10.

characteristics of the environment in which they are located. Whether these characteristics be social, economic, physical, or political, the fortunes of any one site and struc
ture are intimately dependent on those of its neighbors. Furthermore, and again in
contrast to other types of economic markets, when the commodity becomes inadequate
for whatever reason the owner or tenant may abandon it, then move himself to another
location.

Two additional characteristics of real estate resources warrant brief comment
here.[1] First, buildings are not standardized units or products compared to other commodities, thus adding considerable complexity to standard demand and supply analyses.
Second, by definition, the real estate market is strongly influenced by ownership and
legal restrictions. As virtually every property is subjected to different controls and
agreements, the responsiveness to change varies widely. Moreover, the real estate
market as a whole operates under considerable legal and social constraints, in the form
of municipal codes, taxing and development policies, which act to limit the scope of the
market and to compartmentalize transactions into submarkets.[2] Zoning is probably the
critical factor in this control, as it essentially limits the locational choices available to
each type of land user.

Real property, therefore, is characterized by fixity of location, permanence of
building investment, durability through time, and variability of product and ownership.
Because of this heterogeneity, and the existence of a large and widely distributed body of
buyers and sellers, the real estate market for structural uses approximates the classical
model of determination of supply and demand more closely than most other markets for
economic goods.

Differential Between Land and Building Values

Through time, buildings have a tendency to depreciate in value, while land tends
to appreciate.[3] With age and abuse, the value of any building as measured by net returns

---

[1] Detailed summaries of the characteristics of the real estate market are contained in: Raleigh Barlowe, Land Resource Economics. The Political Economy of Rural
and Urban Land Resource Use (Englewood Cliffs, N.J.: Prentice-Hall, Inc., 1958),
p. 202; N.L. North and A.A. Ring, Real Estate Principles and Practices (5th ed.;
Englewood Cliffs, N.J.: Prentice-Hall, Inc., 1960); Richard U. Ratcliff, Real Estate
Analysis (New York: McGraw-Hill Book Co., 1961); Weimer and Hoyt, op. cit., pp. 404-
405; and Fisher and Fisher, op. cit., pp. 215-274, which is undoubtedly the best general
reference.

[2] Nelson and Aschman, op. cit., p. 82. Whether the real estate market is more
or less influenced by government controls than other economic markets has been a subject of much debate. Nelson and Aschman express one interpretation in this section.

[3] For example, see the arguments in Ratcliff, Urban Land Economics, p. 356;

on investment, or net capitalized income, declines steadily following an initial period of increase and equilibrium (Fig. 3). In contrast, urban land values tend to increase as the city grows and land use zones expand into areas of less intensive use. Although wide variations do occur in land values over time, and recent events suggest that in many areas of the city absolute declines have been recorded,[1] the theoretical argument for an increasing tendency still holds.[2] For any individual structure, whether the "rent" for land increases or remains relatively constant, as a proportion of total property value, it normally increases. As these two costs comprise the basic costs of redevelopment, the relative importance of each is critical to an understanding of the factors influencing such change.

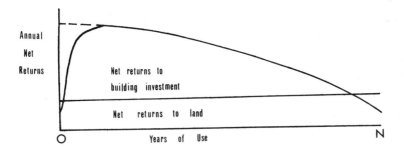

Fig. 3--Expected Net Returns from Investment in a New Building
(After Barlowe)

---

and conversely in Maurice Seldin, "Does Land Depreciate," Appraisal Journal, XXIX, No. 3 (July, 1961), 345-351.

[1]The tendency for land values to increase is by no means consistent or clearly understood. For example, see Wendt's study of central area land values in both San Francisco and Oakland in which he contrasts the increasing values in the former area and the declines in the latter. Paul F. Wendt, The Dynamics of Central City Land Values, San Francisco and Oakland (Research Report No. 18; Berkeley: Real Estate Research Program, University of California, 1961).

[2]The contention that land appreciates with time because of the inelasticity of supply is not valid for urban land as a whole. The land area available for most urban areas is essentially unlimited, given technological innovations. The tendency for land to appreciate can be attributed to generally increasing demands for land at given locations within the city. The amount of land at any location or for particular types of use is essentially limited.

In addition to the increasing divergence between land and building values for a particular property, there is the important question of <u>rent differentials and gradients</u> and the relative rates of change in different properties and between areas. Earlier in this chapter, the relationship between accessibility and transport costs, and the spatial patterns of new construction and "position" rent were discussed and evaluated. This discussion can now be related to the potential for redevelopment at any location through relative variations in rent through time. The effects of increasing land values on the feasibility of redevelopment depends on the relative increases in value of properties in competitive positions. An increase in the value of one parcel of land will of course, decrease its attractiveness relative to all others.

Returning again to the individual property, the importance of the value of the land compared to the building in influencing the feasibility of redevelopment will tend to increase over time. However, this will only be a major consideration if all other properties undergo similar changes such that there is no shift in locational advantages. The effect of a rise in the cost of land on an investment in redevelopment will be to encourage the developer to substitute capital for land and thus to increase the intensity of use.

Economics of Redevelopment and Replacement

In economic theory, the replacement of structures can be defined by a set of cost-profit relationships. It can be assumed that property is held primarily for profit, and as Ratcliff comments, the individual owner is aware of " . . . the possibility that some new use for his land may yield a greater return than the continued operation of the present use."[1]

The profitability of redevelopment is a function of the cost of redevelopment relative to the value of the property after redevelopment. The rationale for redevelopment depends on the individual owner's estimate of the anticipated income from a new structure, compared to the cost of that structure, the costs of removing or demolishing the existing structure, and the income that would be lost by removing that structure. In other words, demolition and replacement will occur, <u>ceteris paribus,</u> when anticipated income exceeds the cost of replacement and original investment lost.[2]

These conditions can be summarized as follows:

Let V_1 = the market value of the existing property before redevelopment, consisting of S_1 the value of the site (land) and B_1 the value of the building.

---

[1] Ratcliff, <u>Urban Land Economics,</u> p. 403.

[2] Schaff, <u>op. cit.</u>, pp. 4-7.

Let V_2 = the market value of the existing property after redevelopment representing the most profitable use of that site. This also may be broken down into S_2 the value of site, and B_2 the value of building.

If the existing building represents the "highest and best" use then, of course,

$$V_2 = V_1$$

Moreover, let C_2 = the cost of constructing this theoretically optimum building B_2

D_1 = the cost of demolishing the original building on the site B_1

Then $S_1 = V_1 - B_1$

But if the building was fully depreciated, i.e., $B_1 = O$

Then $S_1 = V_1$

If V_2 exceeds V_1 by more than the cost of demolition and new construction $(D_1 + C_2)$, it will pay to demolish the building. In other words, redevelopment will be economically feasible for a <u>given property</u>, when V_2 is greater than $V_1 + C_2 + D_1$. The most efficient course of action, in terms of the amount, type, and location of redevelopment, will be that which maximizes the difference between the two, or that which maximizes profits. All other things being equal,[1] replacement will occur at the point of the cost-profit relationship which just compensates the owner for removal of the building. Generally, in a competitive market, V_2 will equal $S_1 + C_2$ if the developers profits are included in C_2.[2]

In many cases, however, the analysis is complicated by the differential reaction of individual owners to the possibility of greater profits from a given site. An owner may not redevelop his property even though it offers higher net returns in the long-run because of the prospect of higher development costs.[3] Others may hesitate to write off the current market value of their existing properties, and some may lack the financial means to do so. This is particularly true for small operators because of the high costs of capital formation and the necessity of long-term financial commitments. Nevertheless, even though the operator may lose income, at least potential income, if he refuses to redevelop his property, his cost-profit situation allows him to continue on a profitable

---

[1]For example, we are ignoring completely the effects of variations in interest and mortgage rates, construction costs, and the like, which would commonly enter into an economic analysis.

[2]Turvey argues that the division between land and building value, as is common in American assessment practices, is meaningless, except in the case of long-run equilibrium, as " . . . no ordinary building is ever sold floating in the air. . . ." Turvey, <u>op. cit</u>. p. 23.

[3]Barlowe, <u>op. cit</u>., p. 224.

basis through the remaining economic life of the structure. These conditions slow urban change by adding to the difficulty of property conversion, and emphasize the conflict between fixed real estate resources and constantly shifting demands for space and location.

Thus, within an economic context, replacement can be explained as a function of the balance between the market value of the present property and the market value less the cost of the new use for that property. The critical difference between the economics of land use succession in urban areas compared to undeveloped rural or suburban areas is the complex problem of increased costs resulting from the inherent value of the land and existing improvements,[1] and the costs of demolition.

Filtering and the Housing Market

Urban housing research is one of the few areas of urban studies generally in which the character of the structural stock froms an integral part of the analysis,[2] and where explicit reference is made to the dynamics of change and the process of replacement within this stock.

How does this inventory change, what generalizations have been developed to describe these changes and to analyze the mechanism by which such changes occur? Inventory changes are usually defined as consisting of additions, replacements, and demolitions. Additions are further subdivided into permanent new construction, conversions, re-classifications, and new mobile homes.[3] For present purposes, only the new construction category is of direct importance. Furthermore, the distinction between new construction and replacements is not based on whether the new building replaces an existing one as in this study, but rather on the relationship of the provision of new units to the growth of the population. Replacements refer only to new housing units added in excess of those required by population increase alone.

---

[1] Ratcliff, Real Estate Analysis, p. 132.

[2] For example, in Canada a constant source of information on new construction is maintained by Central Mortgage and Housing Corporation, Canadian Housing Statistics 1964 (Ottawa: The Central Mortgage and Housing Corporation, 1965). A thorough review of trends in the U.S. housing supply are contained in H.H. Lansberg, L.L. Fischman and J.L. Fisher, Resources in America's Future (Baltimore: Johns Hopkins Press, for Resources for the Future, Inc., 1963); and in Leo Grebler, D.M. Blank, and L. Winnick, Capital Formation in Residential Real Estate: Trends and Prospects (Princeton: Princeton University Press, 1956), p. 329; and in United States Census of Housing, 1960, chapter iv, Part 2, "Components of Inventory Change" (Washington: U.S. Bureau of the Census), p. 20.

[3] J.R. Borchert, E.E. Stewart, and S.S. Hasbrouck, Urban Renewal: Needs and Opportunities in the Upper Midwest (Urban Report No. 5, Upper Midwest Economic Study; Minneapolis: University of Minnesota, 1963), pp. 3-9.

As mentioned earlier, the existing inventory of structures in a city tends to act as a constraint on the volume and nature of new construction. The evidence commonly quoted to substantiate this theory of the dominance of the existing stock, is that new units, for example in housing, amount to only about 2 per cent of the total inventory annually. As Grigsby points out, however, this comparison is misleading. Dominance is not derived from quantitative comparisons alone, but rather in the operation of the market itself, and here the importance of the existing stock is appreciably less.[1] He estimates that of all single-family homes sold in the United States about 45 per cent on the average are new. Moreover, in the higher price range, where most new construction is generated and dependent of course on variations in the business cycle, as much as 60 or 70 per cent of the market consists of new units.[2] This results from the fact that in the real estate market individual owners and structures enter into market exchange for sale or purchase very infrequently.

The importance of the relationship between new construction and the existing stock becomes more apparent for our purposes when the factor of location is included. For some time it has not been economically feasible for private industry to provide new housing for lower income groups. In part this may be explained by the economics of construction, but it also derives from locational constraints on new housing. In most cities the cost of land, restrictive zoning, and the economics of replacement have all but limited new construction to the suburban periphery. This location is generally farthest from the sources of employment, as well as the present residential location, of these lower income groups.

Thus, the vast majority of new units added to the existing stock are beyond the financial means of a large proportion of the urban population. Estimates of the size of this proportion range from 40 to 60 per cent.[3] Within this proportion, those who desire to improve their housing standard have no recourse other than the purchase of a second-hand unit. Such movements are only possible when new units are added, and the unit occupied by any move is usually that directly above the abandoned unit in terms of quality.

---

[1] Leo Grebler, "The Housing Inventory: Analytical Concept and Quantitative Change," American Economic Review, XLI, No. 2 (May, 1951), 563.

[2] Grigsby, op. cit., p. 180. For a critical review of Grigsby's analysis of the housing market and the traditional emphasis on the structural stock, see A.H. Schaaf, Review of William C. Grigsby, "Housing Markets and Public Policy," in Journal of the American Institute of Planners, XXXI, No. 1 (February, 1965), 76.

[3] Sherman J. Maisel, "Policy Problems in Expanding the Private Housing Market," American Economic Review, XLI, No. 2 (May, 1951), 599-611.

The mechanism by which these changes take place is the <u>filtering</u> process.[1] In its broadest definition, filtering pertains to a change in the relative position of a housing unit in the "matrix" of prices and rents of similar units within an urban area.[2] The concept does not include·a change in the type of activity in any unit, nor the composition or structure of the unit itself. Ratcliff defines it more explicitly as " . . . the changing of occupancy as the housing that is occupied by one income group becomes available to the next lower income group. . . ."[3] With age and deterioration, a house usually becomes less desirable for the original occupant and it is then abandoned in favor of a newer unit. In effect, the dwelling unit filters down, and the owner or occupant filters up.

Considerable confusion still surrounds the conceptualization of this process because, as Grigsby comments,[4] filtering is used to describe not one but several processes and it has been subjected to a variety of interpretations. Among the different interpretations involved are those based on changes in occupancy, housing values, housing standards, and various combinations of income and rent ratios. Lowry attempts to broaden these definitions, which are essentially dependent on the aging and deterioration of housing, to include the factor of <u>obsolescence</u>.[5] He associates filtering with four types of obsolescence; technological, style, site, and locational, which act to alter the nature and rate of change in addition to the effects of depreciation.

The importance of this process in understanding urban change in general, is that the majority of social movements within a city conform to this theory, and that <u>filtering</u> <u>in turn is conditioned by the character and location of new construction</u>.[6] To a degree,

---

[1] Fisher and Fisher, op. cit., p. 348; Wallace F. Smith, <u>Filtering and Neighborhood Change</u> (Research Report No. 24; Berkeley: Center for Real Estate and Urban Economics, University of California, 1964), offers an interesting empirical examination of the filtering process in Oakland; E.M. Fisher and L.B. Winnick, "A Reformulation of the Filtering Concept," <u>Journal of Social Issues</u>, VII (1951), 47-85; and probably the most comprehensive review is contained in Grigsby, op. cit., pp. 84-130.

[2] The concept of filtering has also been applied to sequential movements in other forms of occupancy, for example, in the use of office and industrial space.

[3] Ratcliff, <u>Urban Land Economics</u>, p. 321.

[4] Grigsby, op. cit., p. 98.

[5] Ira S. Lowry, "Filtering and Housing Standards," <u>Land Economics</u>, XXXVI, No. 4 (November, 1960), 362-370.

[6] The question of whether filtering improves housing quality is another problem. Although this is not one of the basic assumptions of any of the definitions, it has been implicit in much of the thinking on the subject. In fact, filtering need not imply an improvement of housing quality. Individual movements to improve accommodation may occur continuously whether aggregate housing quality is increasing or not. Quality increases will occur, however, if the process operates efficiently, when the rate of filtering exceeds the rate of deterioration, allowing for the removal of older units at the lower end of the scale.

Lowry's factors dictate the incentive to move, and the economics of construction dictates the range of possibilities of where to move.

The locational constraints that influence the owner-occupied and predominantly single-family market, however, do not apply to apartments and other forms of rental accommodation.[1] Apartment construction need not take place on vacant land, and in fact usually does not. Because of the scale of such projects and the nature of the occupants, apartments can afford to locate almost anywhere within the developed areas of cities. On the other hand, given that the high cost of land in central areas prohibits all but high density construction, and given that most new housing is added at the highest quality level, the economic rationale for the predominance of luxury apartments in private redevelopment is well established.

Urban Renewal and Redevelopment Research

As a result of its close ties to the public sector, renewal research has been primarily concerned with organized efforts by municipalities directed at improving urban conditions. Within this general context, some specific orientations are apparent from published reports.[2] One includes a wide range of research in the analysis of financial productivity in public renewal programs. Another research orientation involves detailed examinations of urban slums and the factors responsible for limited private investment in these areas. An enumeration of these factors should provide insight indirectly into the factors that are conducive to change.

Where private renewal processes are operative two factors are present irrespective of the characteristics of the properties affected. First, the possibility of putting the land to a more profitable use exists, and second, the means are at hand to permit

---

[1] Two of the more interesting treatments of this subject are Louis P. Winnick, Rental Housing: Opportunities for Private Investment (New York: McGraw-Hill Book Co., 1958); and C. Rapkin and W. G. Grigsby, Residential Renewal in the Urban Core (Philadelphia: University of Pennsylvania Press, 1960).

[2] A useful cross section of discussions and evaluations of the obstacles to private renewal efforts and their effects on slum formation is contained in: Hemdahl, op. cit.; Victor Gruen, The Heart of Our Cities The Urban Crisis: Diagnosis and Cure (New York: Simon and Schuster, 1964); Fred Kramer, "The Role of Private Enterprise in Urban Redevelopment," The Mortgage Banker, XI, No. 1 (October, 1950), 3-8; Ross H. Thurston, "Market Significance of Declining Neighborhoods," Appraisal Journal, XXIII, No. 2 (April, 1955), 203-211; John R. Seeley, "The Slum: Its Nature, Use, and Users," Journal of the American Institute of Planners, XXV, No. 1 (February, 1959), 7-14; Wilbur S. Smith, "Traffic and Rebuilding Cities," Traffic Quarterly, XII, No. 1 (January, 1959), 156-168; Donald H. Webster, "Urban Redevelopment and Urban Renewal," chapter x in Urban Planning and Municipal Public Policy, pp. 489-548; A. M. Weimer, "Investors and Downtown Real Estate-Opinion and Comment," Urban Land Institute, Technical Bulletin No. 39 (November, 1960); and the classic statements on the subject by

realization of this possibility.. Thus, not only must redevelopment be economically feasible, it also must be socially and politically practical and acceptable. In areas where private redevelopment has not occurred, primarily in the older central areas of cities outside of the commercial core, it must be concluded that either or both of these conditions are not present. Among the most frequently cited obstacles to private redevelopment, although rarely empirically validated, are the following:

1) The units of ownership are too small in most central areas for present redevelopment uses. The acquisition and assembly of a suitable parcel of land becomes more difficult as property size decreases.

2) The physical and social environments in many areas are unattractive as both centers of employment and residence. Environmental deficiencies range from simple age and deterioration to obsolescent streets and buildings, congestion and pollution, and the concentration of low income groups and various social pathologies.

3) Land values are extremely high and in fact are excessive in terms of realistic possibilities for the use of the land. In part, market values are inflated by historical persistence, over-optimism on the part of the owners, taxation, or inappropriate zoning.

4) Various legal and financial constraints act as obstacles to renewal either directly through the difficulties of securing zoning changes, financing, and land titles in certain areas, or indirectly in the form of property and building codes.

5) In any given area, individual properties vary considerably in the stage of their economic life often making it difficult and costly to undertake redevelopment because of the value remaining in these properties.

6) Not only are ownership units small, but their titles are often dispersed, delinquent, obscure, or otherwise unavailable.

7) Neighborhood and community resistence to change is often sufficiently strong to delay or prevent proposed renewal schemes.

8) The housing shortage for lower income groups combined with the complex problem of racial segregation in central areas, have acted to hinder the progress of efforts to remove existing deteriorated housing.

The most apparent catalyst for government intervention, given such obstacles, is the presence and persistence of extensive areas of structural deterioration and blight. In a general context, blight is defined as the absence of growth, the persistence of a condition of real property depreciation which by community standards is unacceptable.[1] On a more specific level, definitions and interpretations of blight as a continuous and functionally derived phenomena are rare.

Colean, op. cit.; M.L. Walker, Urban Blight and Slums: Economic and Legal Factors in Their Origin, Reclamation, and Prevention (Harvard City Planning Studies, Vol. XII; Cambridge: Harvard University Press, 1938).

[1] Gerald F. Berger, "TheEconomics of Urban Blight and Economic Guidelines for Urban Renewal," (Unpublished Ph.D. dissertation, University of Arkansas, 1964). For an early definition of blight see The Chicago Plan Commission, Master Plan of Residential Land Use of Chicago (Chicago: The Chicago Plan Commission, 1943), particularly pp. 67-91, and the sections on Blighted and Near-Blighted Areas.

Probably the most useful classification and empirical analysis of blight, based on the actual processes involved, was suggested by Berry in Chicago.[1] Four distinct types of blight were defined on the criterion of the attractiveness of a site or structure as a place to do business. The four included: functional or technological blight, reflecting changes in the demand or supply conditions and resulting in obsolescence of that site; physical, which may occur as a result of misuse or simple aging; economic, reflecting a decline in the demand situation itself; and environmental, in which neighborhood changes reduce the general amenities of the area. The value of this classification for present purposes is that it summarizes and clarifies the types of factors and processes of change which must be investigated in an analysis of urban redevelopment.

Synthesis: Dynamics of Urban Structural Change

From these general spatial models, the relationship between urban structural change and redevelopment is by no means clear. Reference to buildings is only implicit, the effects of the standing stock on urban change tend to be ignored, and the process of replacement as reflected in the spatial pattern of new construction, is left untouched.[2] Given the emphasis on age and obsolescence in the historical theories of growth, the replacement process should be concomitant with land use succession, and the spatial pattern should be readily apparent. We might expect a wave-like progression of new building outward from the city center following the original pattern of growth like rings in a pool of water. The central area should receive the largest proportion of this change, with a continuous decline outward as the buildings become more recent, and densities decline. Wallace Smith,[3] for example, relates the tendency for new apartments to concentrate near the city center to the age and obsolescence of the structures that are replaced in the process. On the other hand, Raymond Vernon[4] points out that outside of

---

[1] Brian J.L. Berry, Commercial Blight. A Review, Report to the Community Renewal Program of the City of Chicago, February, 1962; and Commercial Structure and Commercial Blight, Department of Geography Research Paper No. 85 (Chicago: University of Chicago Press, 1963), p. 179.

[2] Moreover, the traditional theories of spatial patterning as devised by Burgess and Hoyt, are presently nearly 40 years out of date. The enormous changes that have taken place during this time are reviewed briefly by Homer Hoyt in "Recent Distortions of the Classical Models of Urban Structure," Land Economics, XL, No. 2 (May, 1964), 199-212, in an attempt to reformulate these concepts.

[3] Wallace F. Smith, The Low-Rise Speculative Apartment (Research Report No. 25; Berkeley: Center for Real Estate and Urban Economics, University of California, 1964), p. 79.

[4] Raymond Vernon, "The Myth and Reality of Our Urban Problems," in City and Suburb: The Economics of Metropolitan Growth, ed. Benjamin Chinitz (Englewood Cliffs, N.J.: Prentice-Hall, Inc., 1964), p. 104.

the central area, redevelopment is almost negligible. Evidence thus far suggests that redevelopment is not a simple function of aging and deterioration, but neither is there empirical or theoretical evidence from the above to support Vernon's hypothesis.

The ecological concepts of invasion and succession suggest that the areas of expansion and greatest change within the city are those where one concentric zone is expanding at the expense of its neighbor. If replacement occurred concomitantly with land use succession and in direct response to the rate and magnitude of change, structural change would be greatest at the margins of these expanding zones. But this does not seem to be the case. In the past, the only notable exception has been the expansion of the central business district into the surrounding zone of mixed uses. However, more recently the center has tended to expand up and not out, or center functions have migrated to distant outlying points more convenient to the suburbs.[1]

Bernard Frieden attempts to identify the major structural features of change which influence the location of new construction from existing theories of urban spatial structure.[2] Apart from the obvious relationship between suburban housing construction and the availability of land and accessibility, there is little that can be said about the location of new construction within central areas. He concludes, quoting Hoyt,[3] that only high rent apartments can afford the costs of site acquisition and demolition of existing properties, but that the inhabitants generally object to living in these surroundings.[4] This represents only one aspect of redevelopment, however, and the relative importance of this aspect and the factors which are said to influence the resulting spatial pattern have not been adequately assessed.

The overriding factor in urban structural change in almost all of the previous research discussed is accessibility, in some cases to the exclusion of all other factors. There is little doubt of the validity of this relationship, but as many of the studies point out, it is by no means all. Accessibility factors vary widely for different uses, as well as over space and through time. Furthermore, the question is raised of accessibility to what. Evidence suggests that new construction does tend to occur in areas with a

---

[1] Edward L. Ullman, "The Nature of Cities Reconsidered," Papers and Proceedings of the Regional Science Association, IX, (1962), 21.

[2] Frieden, op. cit., Appendix C, pp. 173-196.

[3] Hoyt, One Hundred Years of Land Values in Chicago, p. 355.

[4] Frieden, op. cit., p. 188.

relative access advantage, but not in all such areas.[1] A much wider range of variables must be considered if this approach is to provide a broader explanatory basis.

In summary, it appears that the basic processes being addressed here can be summarized under the headings of succession, filtering, and replacement.

The term succession was developed by plant and animal ecologists, and later borrowed and modified by sociologists.[2] In urban research, succession has been used to describe two interrelated processes, one referring to sequential occupance of a given site by different land uses and the other by different social groups. In the latter usage, succession refers to the culmination of an ecological process of invasion whereby one social group invades and occupies the residential space of another. In terms of land use, succession means the conversion of an area from one type of use to a different type. In fact, Ratcliff has described land use succession simply as parcel by parcel redevelopment.[3]

Filtering on the other hand, refers explicitly to the sequential occupance of urban housing units by groups of succeeding lower incomes. This process is reflected spatially in the movement of lower income groups into areas abandoned by groups of higher income usually immediately adjacent to and further from the city center. Thus, in contrast to succession where emphasis is placed on social groups and area, filtering is concerned with changes in the relative position of housing units within the hierarchy of housing units in the city. A quality factor, furthermore, is introduced in which the housing unit filters down and, if the rate of filtering is greater than that of deterioration, the occupants filter up.

Replacement has several distinct meanings in the current literature, but most commonly is applied to the physical clearance and rebuilding. In economics, replacement is a static term in general investment theory referring to the costs of various courses of action derived from evaluations of current and potential returns from a given capital investment. In housing research, however, replacements refer to the surplus of new housing units over net family formation. In this study, the redevelopment connotation is employed and reformulated such that replacement becomes a continuous process, and an integral part of urban structural change. More specifically, succession is limited to land use change and replacement to changes in individual structures or groups of structures.

---

[1] Homer Hoyt, "Expressways and Apartment Sites," Traffic Quarterly, XII, No. 2 (April, 1958), 263-268.

[2] Dictionary of the Social Sciences, p. 701.

[3] Richard U. Ratcliff, Private Investment in Urban Redevelopment (Research Report No. 17; Berkeley: Real Estate Research Program, University of California, 1961), p. 2.

CHAPTER III

REDEVELOPMENT AS A SPATIAL PROCESS

At first glance, concepts derived from research in urban spatial structure appear to be of only limited value in assessing the location and impact of redevelopment. The closest approximation to a theoretical framework for the process of replacement within the building stock is found in land use theory.

Land Use and Structural Change

Land use is traditionally defined in terms of activities performed and is measured in units of land area. Reference to buildings and structures is of course implicit in these theories.[1] Structures provide the permissive space for the activities which serve to identify and classify land use types. Moreover, one of the critical differences between rural and urban land economics is that to earn income from urban land, it is usually necessary to construct a building. Yet the effects of the variable character of the structural inventory are largely ignored. As a result, the coincidence between our understanding of the processes of change operative in land and those in buildings is not sufficiently close to permit free substitution of land use theories for structural theory.

This has been one of the principal criticisms of such theories. Pendleton, in his generally favorable critique of Alonso's Location and Land Use,[2] argues that he can put little faith in a theory of urban residential spatial structure which completely ignores the standing stock of buildings.[3] There are fairly obvious reasons why the stock of buildings in a city is assumed uniform or irrelevant. Essentially these reasons can be reduced to two: complexity, and the lack of basic information. The structural surface[4]

---

[1] This may include either the type of structure, the activity for which the structure was originally designed, or the dominant activity at present (as in the Toronto data).

[2] William Alonso, Location and Land Use Toward a General Theory of Land Rent (Cambridge: Harvard University Press, 1964).

[3] W.C. Pendleton, Review of W. Alonso, "Location and Land Use," in Journal of the American Institute of Planners, XXXI, No. 1 (February, 1965), 78-79.

[4] The term "surface" is used to emphasize the three-dimensional view of the structural stock of the city implied throughout this text.

39

of a city is extremely complex, containing structures of diverse physical condition and economic value. The inclusion of structures in existing theories necessitates consideration of such factors as vested interests, fixed assets, depreciation rates, and so on, which may act to accelerate, slow, or repulse major changes. Moreover, the total inventory of buildings implies a consideration of volume and the variable nature of this volume through time. This inventory is constantly being added to, subtracted from, and replaced within, while the land inventory remains relatively fixed and more readily delimited.

Land use theories thus represent a simplification of what in effect should be a structure-land-activity theory of urban change. Ideally, this more comprehensive theory would treat the city as a complex surface rather than an area, it would incorporate the duality of processes in both land and buildings, and it would assess the spatial linkages between activities, all in a temporal setting. Much has been said about land and activities, but little about structures. In effect, we are arguing for the inclusion of structural change as a spatial process, for a third dimension in theories of land use and spatial patterning, and for consideration of the effects of quality and age factors in urban change.

Defining the Basic Concepts

The Development-Redevelopment Continuum

The distinction between urban development and redevelopment has been drawn in this study on the basis that redevelopment involves replacement. To this can now be added the factor of location and the relationship to distance from the city center. As a growth process, development and redevelopment may be thought of as a spatial continuum, extending from redevelopment in the central areas of cities to new development on the suburban fringe. At the central end of the continuum, all building activity involves the replacement of one structure by another. The relative proportion of new construction thus classified declines steadily outward from the center as densities decline and vacant land becomes more widespread. At the opposite end of the continuum, all new construction takes place on vacant or agricultural land.[1] Between these two extremes are areas of relative structural stability.

In this context, central and suburban growth become part of the same process.

---

[1] This definition excludes the demolition and replacement of farm buildings and other non-urban structures in the expansion of suburban areas. One could argue that such demolition represented a form of rural redevelopment. But as its relative impact in the urban context is negligible, and the conditions under which it occurs are quite different, such replacement can reasonably be ignored.

They act as complements in the same way as investment alternatives. The factors that influence the choice between alternatives will change in the same continuous manner with distance from the city center and the character of the existing structural stock. This distinction is basic to an understanding of the transformation of experience and concepts in suburban and aggregate development patterns to central area redevelopment.

An idealized representation of this building continuum is shown in Figure 4. The proportion of total construction involving redevelopment declines steadily toward the margin of the built-up area, while the proportion affecting vacant land increases. In all areas but the extremes of the scale, considerable mixing of the two occurs. The volume of construction activity, however, as the previous review of the literature suggests, shows no such uniform pattern, but is concentrated in the city center and the suburbs. Figure 5 attempts to represent this hypothetical gradient. This illustration suggests that redevelopment as part of this construction activity is not a spatially continuous phenomenon in terms of impact. Rather than exhibiting a systematic decline with distance it is restricted to the area within or immediately adjacent to the central core. If building replacement occurred solely as a function of age and obsolescence, a more consistent distribution paralleling that of age of structure and area would be expected.

Guttenberg[1] offers a relevant generalization based on his interpretation of changes in "economic density gradients" through time. From a simple comparison of two density profiles (Figure 6), he attempts to isolate variations in the "potential" for change. Although his argument is primarily concerned with regional density changes, we can translate the discussion to include the potential for redevelopment at varying densities and distances from the city center.

In this illustration, if CS represents the economic density gradient in time T, C_1S_1 represents the same gradient in time $T + 1$, the pressures for changing existing densities would be greatest at O, the city center, and at P, the suburban margin of time T. Moreover, the potential for change would show a decline from O to X, and in both directions from P to R and X. At point X, in theory, the existing structure would be in equilibrium, but only in the period from T to $T + 1$.

If we were to graph the spatial variation of this potential from points O to R, that is the difference between the two lines in the profile, the result would closely approximate the curve in Figure 5, with one exception. That is, the drop-off in redevelopment from the city center is more rapid than potentials would suggest. Thus, in effect, there are two distinct locations of growth in the city, the core and the periphery. Over time, the margins of these zones shift outward but by no means at the same rate.

---

[1] Albert Z. Guttenberg, "Urban Structure and Urban Growth," Journal of the American Institute of Planners, XXVI, No. 2 (May, 1960), 109.

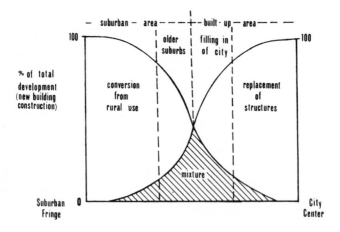

Fig. 4--Idealized Development-Redevelopment Continuum from City Center to Suburbs

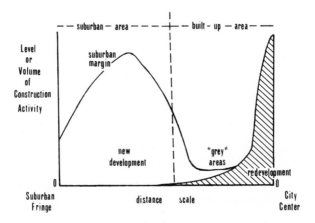

Fig. 5--Idealized Profile of the Volume of Construction Activity from City Center to Suburbs

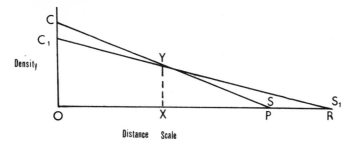

Fig. 6--Urban Economic Density Gradients (After Guttenberg)

The Adaptation Process in the Structural Stock

The standing stock of buildings in a city represents the "physical space" for urban activities. Both the stock and the demands placed on this stock are undergoing continuous change. Most demands for change are accommodated within the existing stock by a change in location or in the amount of space consumed, or both. This constant "ebb and flow" of activities within the standing stock is facilitated by the wide range of uses for which most buildings are suited. Only when the demand for change reaches a certain level is there economic justification for physical modification of the structure to suit its new function. Even less frequently is the economic basis sufficient to warrant demolition and replacement of the structure.

From the viewpoint of the individual structure, the process of adaptation to change tends to be gradual and to fall into a series of distinct stages. First, the original function for which the building was designed, the equilibrium[1] situation, is replaced by another function, but with only slight modification of the structure.[2] This new function usually represents a different and more intensive kind of activity, or an increase in intensity of use by the same activity. The next stage results in the partial conversion or

[1]Equilibrium situation is used here to refer to a theoretical point, at which the function occupying a structure represents the optimum or "highest and best use" for that structure in traditional economic terms. If the forces of supply and demand in urban physical space were to operate simultaneously, that is if buildings could change with the activities that use them, there would be no maladjustments between present and optimal use, and there would be no adaptation process excepting that in response to age.

[2]As the questions posed here relate to structures and groups of structures, it will not be possible to examine changes in the amount of space devoted to particular urban functions in detail. What it will be possible to say, however, is that as an expression of the provision of new buildings and the replacement of one land use type by another, certain trends are indicated in the demand for new space for different activities and that certain of these activities are expanding at the expense of others.

modification of the structure to better accommodate its new occupant. The final stage in this process, which is the most apparent and well recorded, but the least widespread, is the physical replacement of the old building by new construction. At this point a new equilibrium situation has been established, and the cycle begins again.

In total, these stages represent the process of adaptation in the structural stock of a city to accommodate new demands. Obviously, not all structures or areas fulfil this sequence, nor do similar structures or areas appear at the same stage. The standing stock is much too diversified and complex, with each unit differing not only in design, location, and use, but also in quality, age, and value. Change does not and in fact could not, take place in all units at the same time or in equal degree.

Redevelopment, in this context, then, becomes one facet of a larger complex process of structural response to change. It can be defined as part of the supply and demand mechanisms attempting to maintain or achieve an equilibrium between present and optimum use of land and physical space. This concept is applicable both to the processes of change in different areas of the city at one point in time, and for the same structure or area over successive time periods. By adding the time dimension, one can then argue further for repetitive or cyclical variations in structural change.

Concepts of Cyclical Change

Miles Colean, in his study for the Twentieth Century Fund, [1] argued that the redevelopment process was a cyclical phenomenon. He thought of urban change as a cycle of development in structures which included original construction, a period of increased or sustained value and utility, a period of increasing maintenance and deterioration, finally culminating in the replacement of the building.

It would seem worthwhile to extend this generalization to more fully account for both the life cycle of structures[2] and the apparently consistent structural changes that occur in different neighborhoods. Figure 7 represents one view of the sequence of change in the structures occupying a particular site through time. In effect, this sequence follows from Figure 3 in the previous chapter. Here we have simply superimposed additional curves of net returns on replacement investments. Clearly, the diagram is highly simplified and distorted, without scale dimensions, and is intended only for illustration.

---

[1] Colean, op. cit.

[2] The length of time required to repeat this cycle, because of the durability of buildings as investments, may however be considerable. Average building lifespans may be 50 or more years. Empirically it would be most difficult to examine this process, and within the data on hand it is impossible. An approximation may be obtained however by comparing several buildings at different stages of their life cycle.

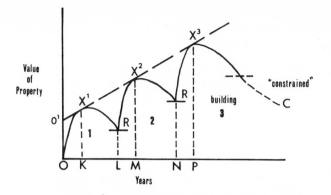

Fig. 7--Idealized Replacement Cycle for Individual Structures

With: O representing time of original building construction
L, N redevelopment by new construction
K, M, P time of theoretical optimum net returns on
original investment
R representing the level at which replacement occurs
C continued deterioration beyond the theoretical point
of replacement

Line X^1 -X^2 -X^3 representing the theoretical increase
in total property value with replacement by more
intensive uses

Following initial construction of a building, O, the value of the property usually
increases to some optimum point, X^1 within a relatively short period of time, K. The
actual time taken to reach this point and the duration of the optimality condition of course
depend on local conditions, competition, and financing arrangements.[1] Thereafter occurs
a long period of depreciation and declining returns on investment as the structure
becomes economically or physically obsolescent (K to L years). The decline continues
until the demand for changes makes it economically feasible to replace the structure
(point R at time L). Usually the new structure represents a different and more intensive
or "efficient" type of land use.

The reasons why such cycles exist are reasonably obvious. The stock of
buildings in a city represents an aging and declining asset. Thus, not only is the present
structure increasingly unsuited for the demands placed on it by the market, it is
becoming physically less suited through age and abuse, as reflected in declining values

---

[1] If we were to argue that a structure achieves its maximum net return in the
first year, all that would be changed in the diagram is to have the curve rise vertically to
points X^1, X^2, X^3, and decline from there. The origin of the curve would then appear on
the vertical axis not at O but at O^1.

and rates of investment return. This decline in value is relevant in this discussion both to the costs of acquisition and replacement and to the potential income that is lost with removal of the old structure.

The relevant concept in replacement is <u>obsolescence,</u> both physical resulting from deterioration, and economic or functional obsolescence relative to market demands.[1] Either of these may appear dominant in any particular circumstance, and in most cases replacement occurs as a function of some <u>composite form</u>.

Cycles of Structural Change in Neighborhoods

The precise nature of cyclical successions has been considered in some detail in neighborhood studies. Ideas of growth areas and cycles are, of course, not recent. Hoyt pointed to the concentration of construction activity in the commercial core and on the periphery, and the static condition of areas in between, in his study of Chicago land values in the 1930's.[2] Blumenfeld described this process as the "tidal wave of urban expansion,"[3] in which zones of rapid population growth migrated outward from the city center. Hoover and Vernon[4] modified this growth wave concept to take account of the two widely separated rings of residential growth, pointed out earlier by Hoyt, one marked by single-family housing and the other by apartments.[5]

Hoover and Vernon carried the analogy further as a refinement of the concentric zonation concept and postulated a series of <u>evolutionary stages for neighborhoods</u>. This interpretation of the process is relevant here because it refers explicitly to the redevelopment of areas and the replacement of structures. The stages are as follows:

---

[1] The tendency to interpret replacement as a function of depreciation is common in housing research. Maisel, in his analysis of residential construction starts, contends that it is unlikely that such a cycle exists, at least one based on depreciation resulting from age and deterioration, because the life span of housing is more a function of economic rather than physical conditions. Sherman J. Maisel, "A Theory of Fluctuations in Residential Construction Starts," <u>American Economic Review</u>, LIII, No. 3 (June, 1963), 359-383.

[2] Hoyt, <u>One Hundred Years of Land Values in Chicago</u>.

[3] Hans Blumenfeld, "The Tidal Wave of Urban Expansion," <u>Journal of the American Institute of Planners,</u> XX, No. 1 (February, 1954), 3-14. Blumenfeld found that he could measure the rate of migration of these zones. Movement outward from the center takes place at a rate approximating .83 of the percentage growth of the population during a given period multiplied by the mileage distance of the zone from the center at the beginning of the period. See also Hans Blumenfeld, "Are Land Uses Predictable," <u>Journal of the American Institute of Planners,</u> XXV, No. 2 (May, 1959), 63.

[4] Hoover and Vernon, <u>op. cit</u>., p. 183.

[5] To an increasing extent, the current pattern of suburban expansion involves mixtures of housing types, particularly characteristic of recent growth in Toronto.

1) The initial period of single family construction, characterized by low density, general uniformity of age and condition.

2) Apartment construction, representing a transition stage, as population density increases and new construction fills in vacant land and, less frequently, "replaces" older single-family housing.

3) A stage of downgrading and deterioration, with limited new construction but with increasing densities as widespread conversion of structures takes place. In later stages of this process increasing densities may be offset by removal of existing structures.

4) A thinning out process, in which densities begin to decline as dwellings are abandoned or occupied by non-residential uses, and as household size declines. New construction is limited, and is largely non-residential.

5) A renewal stage,[1] involving the eventual replacement of obsolescent and deteriorated housing, both multi-family and single-family, by high density apartments. Densities increase considerably for individual sites and small areas but may in fact continue to decline overall because of the expansion of non-residential uses. Generally, this stage takes two forms, private luxury apartments and subsidized medium and low income public housing.

Obviously, not all residential areas go through this cycle of structural change, and its interpretation as a cycle,[2] requires explicit assumptions about long-term trends. It could be pointed out that some areas skip certain of these stages while in others the cycle is arrested by renewal before the full sequence is completed. In fact, the reasons behind the variability of this process in different areas, especially the persistence of stage four, is precisely the problem confronted by renewal programs.

Nevertheless, these ideas do suggest a framework for organizing thoughts on urban structural change and for bringing together changes conditioned by time and growth that occur in both individual structures and areas. For example, the argument suggests that replacement itself is a cyclical phenomenon, that there is more than one point in

---

[1] Hoover and Vernon's interpretation of the renewal phase as only the last and most recent stage of neighborhood change is unfortunately restrictive. The second phase, that of low-density multi-family, is as much a renewal phase as the latter. According to this sequence, and referring to the previous diagram of change in individual structures, this theoretical neighborhood has reached its second cycle of demolition and replacement.

See, for example, the interesting discussion on cycles in real estate in Hoyt, Hundred Years of Land Values, chapter vii, "The Chicago Real Estate Cycle," pp. 368-423. The concept of neighborhood cycles similar to that of Hoover and Vernon, but with emphasis on the social implications of residential turnover, is well developed in the ecological literature. For example, E. Gordon Erickson, Urban Behavior (New York: MacMillan Co., 1954), pp. 215-216. Erickson describes the cycle of change in a sequence of six steps from the period of equilibrium prior to the invasion of a new social group through to the eventual succession and dominance of this group and the establishment of a new equilibrium.

time of concentrated redevelopment activity, and that redevelopment need not involve an increase in overall densities. In addition, for any given area, there appear to by systematic variations through time in population density (Figure 8), the rate of replacement, and new construction (Figure 9), which do not necessarily coincide either in time or location.

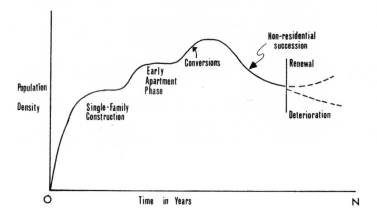

Fig. 8--Idealized Neighborhood Population Density Cycle Related to New Construction and Structural Change

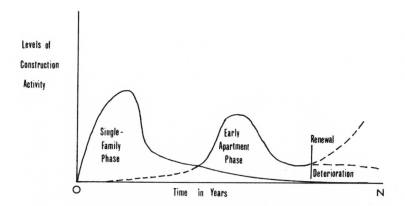

Fig. 9--Idealized Neighborhood Construction Cycle

CHAPTER IV

EMPIRICAL BACKGROUND AND FORMULATION: TORONTO

All cities are unique, but within the North American economic context, extensive research has revealed a variety of common denominators in the spatial patterns and
processes of urban growth. As one objective of the present study is to draw general
implications for theory, some attempt must be made to acknowledge and assess particular factors in the Toronto example which might act to disturb the operation of traditional
processes.

This chapter shifts the discussion from the general theoretical level to the
specific case study of Toronto. Following on a brief introduction to the city and a description of its historical evolution, the chapter outlines the basic data source, and definitions
and procedures for the empirical analysis.

Empirical Base

A wealth of current research in Toronto offers a broad empirical background
for an analysis of structural change. Studies have been completed of the evolution of
Toronto's morphology,[1] the patterns of change in the commercial structure,[2] the

---

[1] Donald Kerr and Jacob Spelt, The Changing Face of Toronto-A Study in Urban
Geography (Memoir 11, Geographical Branch, Department of Mines and Technical
Surveys; Ottawa: The Queen's Printer, 1965); and a preliminary article by Jacob Spelt,
"The Development of the Toronto Conurbation," Buffalo Law Review, XIII, No. 3 (Spring
1964), 557-573. Considerable historical evidence is also available in N.A. Hooper,
"Toronto, A Study in Urban Geography" (Unpublished Master's dissertation, University
of Toronto, 1947); in Rae Corelli, The Toronto That Used to Be (Toronto, 1964); and
D.C. Masters, The Rise of Toronto 1850-1890 (Toronto: University of Toronto Press,
1947).

[2] James W. Simmons, Toronto's Changing Retail Complex: A Study in Growth
and Blight, Department of Geography Research Paper No. 104 (Chicago: University of
Chicago Press, 1966).

changing social geography,[1] and the evolving governmental organization.[2]

Additional studies have been undertaken on transportation, land use, and employment change in both the city and metropolitan area of Toronto in recent years, providing a valuable source of basic information.[3] Housing inventories and evaluations have been completed for small areas of the city as part of a continuing residential improvement program.[4] The downtown area has received extensive treatment, particularly in terms of present and future development trends in new construction and employment.[5] These studies provide a comprehensive inventory of the structural character and distribution of physical space for the downtown area in 1960 with projections to 1980. With this material available, more emphasis can be placed on the aggregate pattern of structural change and the dimensions of redevelopment ouside the central area. Finally, in terms of the effects of public policy constraints, and the relationship of the present study of private redevelopment to public renewal and redevelopment efforts, the results of the recently-completed Urban Renewal Study provide a meaningful complement.[6] Given this descriptive and analytical base, no attempt will be made to replicate this material prefatory to the analysis. However, we will draw extensively on the findings as the analysis proceeds.

---

[1] Brian J.L. Berry and Robert A. Murdie, "Socio-Economic Correlates of Housing Conditions," A study prepared under contract for the Urban Renewal Study of The Metropolitan Toronto Planning Board (Toronto: The Metropolitan Planning Board, 1965). A more extensive treatment of this subject is being prepared as a doctoral dissertation in the Department of Geography at the University of Chicago by Robert Murdie, and will appear in the Research Series of the same department in 1967.

[2] Ontario Royal Commission on Metropolitan Toronto, Report of the Royal Commission on Metropolitan Toronto, H. Carl Goldenberg, Commissioner (Toronto: The Royal Commission, 1965); and Albert Rose, "A Decade of Metropolitan Government in Toronto," Buffalo Law Review, XIII, No. 3 (Spring, 1964), 539-556.

[3] In large part these studies have been prepared under the auspices of the Metropolitan Toronto Planning Board and its consultants.

[4] City of Toronto Planning Board, Improvement Programme for Residential Areas (Toronto: The Planning Board, 1965).

[5] City of Toronto Planning Board, Downtown Toronto Background Studies for the Plan (Technical Series No. 1; Toronto: The Planning Board, 1963); and Plan for Downtown (Toronto: The Planning Board, 1963).

[6] Metropolitan Toronto Planning Board, Urban Renewal Study, Interim Report (Toronto: The Metropolitan Planning Board, 1965). Of particular relevance among the various reports submitted to the Urban Renewal Study is that of "Urban Renewal Policies and Practices," prepared by Murray V. Jones and Associates Ltd., Toronto. The study focusses on Ontario-Federal government legislation in urban renewal and on administrative procedures which might encourage private entrepreneurs to participate in public renewal programs. The final recommendations of the study are contained in The Role of Private Enterprise in Urban Renewal (Toronto: The Metropolitan Planning Board, March, 1966).

Toronto: Population

The Toronto conurbation is relatively young, and its emergence to metropolitan status has been recent and rapid. It was not until 1900 that the population of the city and suburban communities passed 200,000 (Table 1). By the end of 1945 the total urbanized area population reached 1,000,000 and by 1965 it was over 2,000,000.[1] The City of Toronto contained the overwhelming proportion of this growth until the 1920's after which time the legal area of the city was essentially built-up annexation ceased, and development spread increasingly to the suburbs.

The population of the city, following the last major annexation, levelled off in the 1930's at slightly over 600,000, reaching a peak of 690,000 in 1946, and thereafter declined slowly to 670,000. Throughout the period under study then, the population of the city may be considered as relatively stable, but of course, stable only in number and not composition. As a proportion of total "Metro" population the city has declined steadily from over 80 per cent in the 1920's to under 40 per cent in 1965, and to only 33 per cent of the total urbanized area population. As with most other central cities, the City of Toronto has been assuming an increasingly different role as a place of work and residence as the size of the metropolitan community expands.

In the contemporary context, the fact that Toronto is one of the fastest growing urban areas in North America is likely although not necessarily to be reflected in a higher rate of renewal and redevelopment. The average annual growth in population totalled 30,000 in the 1940's, almost 40,000 in the 1950's, and 50-70,000 in the 1960's. This high rate of growth, about five per cent annually, will certainly be translated into considerable space and location shifts in the central city area, both as a result of absolute physical expansion and changing functional composition.

Within the limited study period, significant shifts in the spatial distribution of the population within the city have taken place (See Figure 10 and Appendix C for Zones of Analysis.) In Figure 11 major population declines are apparent in the area adjacent to the central business district and along the older railroad and industrial concentrations. The overall pattern of declining population is reasonably concentric as might be expected with the expansion of non-residential uses around the central area. However, three large areas of declining population also appear on the margins of the city quite removed from the central core. With these three exceptions, increases in population have been recorded in the middle and outer zones of the city, and particularly in a few selected

---

[1]Dominion Bureau of Statistics estimates. The limits of the metropolitan area prior to 1951, correspond with the present boundaries of the municipalities of Metropolitan Toronto.

TABLE 1

POPULATION GROWTH: CITY AND METROPOLITAN TORONTO
1900-1965

Year	City of Toronto	"Metro" Toronto	Census Metro Area	City as o/o of "Metro Census Area"	
1900	200,000	–	220,000	–	91
1921	522,942[a]	–	605,000	–	86
1931	627,231	–	810,000	–	78
1941	655,751	–	910,000	–	72
1946	696,555	–[b]	980,000	–	71
1951	675,754	–	1,117,470	–	60
1956	667,706	1,358,028	1,478,000	49	45
1961	672,407	1,618,000	1,825,000	41	37
1965	670,000[c]	1,800,000[c]	2,050,000[c]	37	33

[a]Last major annexation 1913

[b]Municipality of Metropolitan Toronto formed in 1953

[c]Estimates, Dominion Bureau of Statistics

locations, such as Deer Park, Parkdale and Rosedale (See Figure 10).

The distribution of population over time has shown the same density trends documented in other cities (Figure 12). With the exception of the area immediately adjacent to the central core, densities have been increasing throughout the metropolitan area. The extensive suburban expansion of the 1950's is evident in the considerable increase in density beyond the city boundary. However, in the period under study, densities increased as well throughout most of the central city. Much of this increase is a function of residential redevelopment and particularly apartment construction, but the degree of correlation is obscured by widespread conversion and non-residential succession in lower density areas.

Evolution of the Existing Spatial Structure

The existing spatial structure of Toronto represents the cumulative inheritance from past periods. Change in this structure is conditioned both in form and direction, not only by the form existing at any point in time, but also by past directions of growth. To establish a rationale for redevelopment as a process of change in Toronto, we need to examine very briefly the evolution of the present urban form and the factors affecting this form.

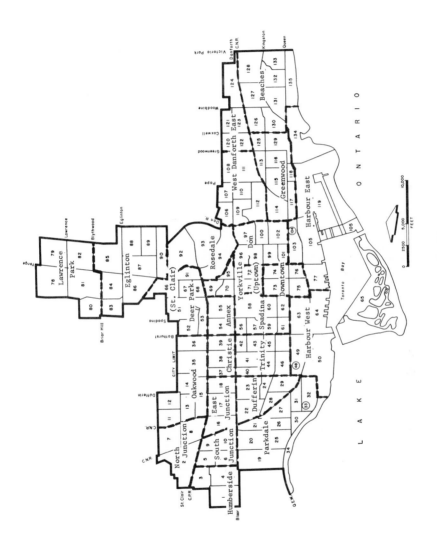

Fig. 10--Zones of analysis: Census Tracts and Planning Districts

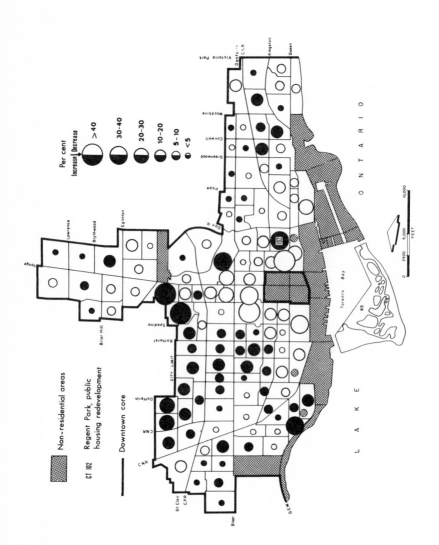

Fig. 11--City of Toronto Population Change 1951-1961

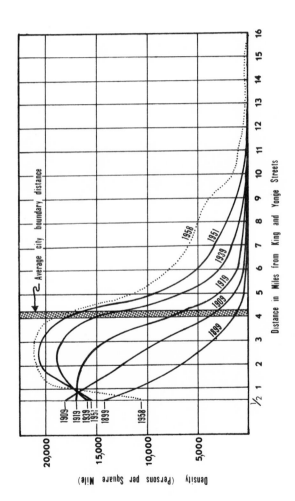

Fig. 12--Metropolitan Toronto Population Density Gradients 1899-1958 (Metropolitan Toronto Planning Board)

The physical growth of Toronto from its inception east of the present city center was constrained by ravines and attenuated by regional ties. The principal axes of growth, representing transportation connections to the hinterland, accelerated urban development east and west along the lakeshore and north along Yonge Street. The Don ravine to the east acted as a total barrier to the spread of settlement for the first half century. As a result, development turned west and northwest, creating a form that has persisted to the present day (Figure 13).[1]

Despite the eventual bridging of the Don and later the Humber ravines, the north-west orientation has continued. Because of its age, the more central portion of this sector contains most of the deteriorated and crowded housing in the city. In contrast, the area east of the Don developed rapidly following the turn of the century, creating a more uniform and younger dwelling stock. Railways penetrated from both the east and west, focussing on the central waterfront, and formed a wide arc across the city. The higher income residential suburbs developed as far from these areas as possible, around High Park and the lakeshore to the west and in the Rosedale-Yorkville-Deer Park areas to the north of the old commercial core (See Figure 10 and Appendix C).

The commercial core migrated from its original King Street East location in parallel with the major development axes. Expansion occurred first westward to Yonge Street, then northward to Queen, and subsequently further north along Yonge. More recent secondary concentrations have appeared at Bloor Street and on Eglinton Avenue extending this linear growth. These developments, with many comparable and competitive central area activities, have been stimulated by the construction of the Yonge Street subway.

The implications of this history for present purposes rests in the solidification of the basic pattern of land uses and structures.[2] There is a discernible relationship between recent redevelopment patterns and those suggested above. Development axes, centers of growth, transportation orientations, and quality distinctions between neighborhoods, are quite apparent. There is a measure of consistency in the areas where pressure to accommodate change has been greatest. Moreover, the inertia of sunk capital in the physical plant renders the character of historical inheritance a critical factor in an analysis of change.

---

[1] See Donald Kerr and Jacob Spelt, "The Morphology of the Nineteenth-Century City," The Changing Face of Toronto chapter iv, pp. 53-73; and J.R. Seeley, R.A. Sim, and E.W. Loosley, Crestwood Heights (New York: J. Wiley and Sons, 1963), Part I, "Structure and Context," particularly pp. 26-41.

[2] Another interesting and related line of research is presently underway at the University of Chicago by Peter Goheen. This study is concerned explicitly with the problem of the evolving spatial structure of Toronto in the nineteenth century.

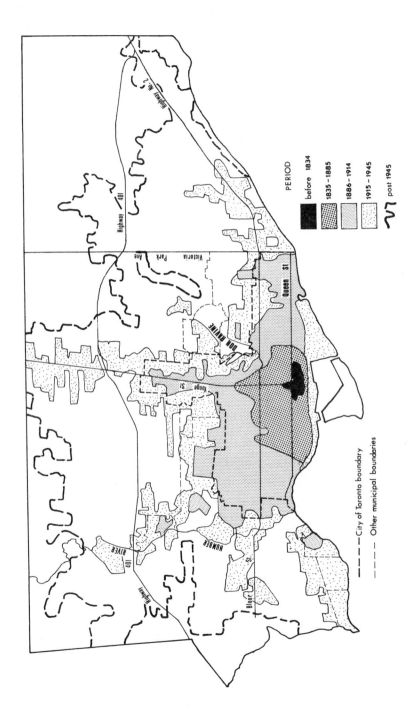

Fig. 13--Patterns of Historical Development: Metropolitan Toronto

Special Considerations: The Toronto Case

Over and above the fact that the city is Canadian, some contrasts with most American cities arise from recent historical occurrences.[1] For example, Toronto has experienced the influx of over one-half million European immigrants in the last two decades,[2] a scale not witnessed by American cities since the early years of this century. This has considerably altered urban life and outlooks in the city, and has contributed substantially to Toronto's rapid post-war growth (Table 1). On the other hand, Toronto does not have a large Negro minority and thus is not faced with the same kind or degree of social constraints on change common to most American cities.

Further, one might cite the effects of the creation of a metropolitan area government in 1953.[3] Although it is difficult to assess the direct implications of "Metro" on the spatial structure of the city, there is little doubt from current evaluations that it has facilitated orderly growth and reduced the cost of municipal services.[4] More important for this analysis, the improvement and stability of the community's financial position, resulting from the merger of city and suburban efforts, has given Toronto a higher credit rating for municipal financing and improved its business climate for private investment, a particularly strong factor in redevelopment activity.

A third consideration would certainly be planning controls and enabling legislation, and the direct impact of public investment. Brought down to the municipal level,

---

[1]It should also be noted that urban and industrial growth in Canada is more recent than in the United States. Canadian cities such as Toronto, did not experience to the same extent what Lewis Mumford refers to as a "palaeo-technic" period of industrialization. As a result they usually do not contain extensive areas of tenements and standardized industrial housing. See Humphrey Carver, "Community Renewal Programming," Habitat, VIII, No. 3 (May-June, 1965), 7.

[2]H. Husain, "Components of Population Change in Metropolitan Area of Toronto 1951-1961," Plan Canada, V, No. 1 (1964), 16-21.

[3]Reference to the Metropolitan Toronto experiment is now almost standard in American textbooks on city government, planning, and geography. As an indication of this interest and for a cross section of evaluation, apart from studies of Toronto per se, see W.S. Fiser, "The Lesson of Toronto," in Mastery of The Metropolis (Englewood Cliffs, N.J.: Prentice Hall, 1962), pp. 117-124; J.C. Bollens and H.J. Schmandt, "Metropolitan Toronto: Federation in Action," in The Metropolis--Its People, Politics and Economic Life (New York: Harper and Row, 1965), pp. 477-490; and Raymond E. Murphy, The American City An Urban Geography (New York: McGraw-Hill, 1966), pp. 429-431. Probably the most comprehensive review and evaluation of the Toronto experience is contained in Frank Smallwood, Metro Toronto: A Decade Later (Toronto: Bureau of Municipal Research, 1963).

[4]For example, see Albert Rose, "A Critique of Metropolitan Government in Toronto, 1953-1965," Planning 1965 (Chicago: American Society of Planning Officials, 1965), pp. 5-34, for a review of Metro's expectations and achievements in political, physical and social planning.

enactment of this legislation in Canada is translated into slightly firmer controls on
urban sprawl, transportation, redevelopment, and other metropolitan problems, than is
generally the case in the United States. This of course is a very recent factor. On the
other hand, the magnitude of government participation in urban renewal and expressway
construction in Canada, has been considerably less than that in the United States.[1]

One major exception to this has been in rapid transit construction. The Yonge
Street subway line, for example, constructed with provincial assistance in 1954, was one
of the first transit systems initiated in a North American city after the initial decade of
this century. Although its effects have not been systematically assessed, all available
evidence suggests that its influence on the location preferences expressed by new construction has been substantial. As a variable in the pattern of accessibility, there is
only a limited basis for evaluating its impact by comparison with older systems, because
of its recent introduction.

The question of differences in the effects of government policy on urban development, particularly in financing,[2] is more difficult to assess. In both countries, national
residential mortgage terms have stimulated the construction of single-family suburban
dwellings to the disadvantage of existing dwellings in central areas. Recent revisions to
the National Housing Acts both in Canada and the United States, however, will permit a
wider range of investment in existing properties and rental units.[3]

Despite recent developments, however, Toronto appears to be subjected to most
of the pressures of metropolitan growth typical of other cities. More important, the
conditions under which the present structure evolved were not basically different than
those operative throughout North America, with the result that generalized spatial patterns are much the same. Blumenfeld's[4] study relating population and land use

---

[1] For example, the increase in Federal government spending in the United States
following the National Housing Act of 1949, and the amendments of 1954 and 1961, and the
Interstate Highway Program of 1956. In Canada, in the fields of public housing and
renewal for example, until recently few cities have participated in federal and provincial
programs, and even these have been meager efforts. See Stanley H. Pickett, "Canadian
Experience in Urban Renewal," Planning 1965, Selected Papers from the Joint Conference
of the American Society of Planning Officials and the Community Planning Association of
Canada, Toronto, April, 1965 (Chicago: American Society of Planning Officials, 1965),
pp. 139-147. In the same issue see A. Adamson, "Physical and Social Planning," pp.
185-193; and H. Carver, "CRP: The Canadian Experience," pp. 200-206.

[2] A comparison of Canadian and American mortgage markets is contained in:
Central Mortgage and Housing Corporation, Insured Mortgages as Investments (Ottawa:
The Central Mortgage and Housing Corporation, 1963).

[3] W.M. Illing, Housing Demand to 1970 (Staff Study No. 4, Economic Council of
Canada; Ottawa: The Queen's Printer, 1964), p. 20.

[4] Blumenfeld, "Are Land Uses Predictable?" loc. cit., pp. 61-66.

distributions in Toronto to those in Philadelphia is a good example. Simmons'[1] study of the changing commercial structure of Toronto; Kerr and Spelt's[2] historical examination of metropolitan expansion; Murdie's[3] analysis of the changing social geography of Toronto; and the metropolitan transportation studies,[4] produced essentially the same results as earlier studies in American cities. This does not mean that we can ignore the differences that exist, but rather we have some idea of the direction of deviation that is likely to appear in the results of the present analysis.

The Data

The data requirements for a detailed examination of structural change and specifically of the replacement process in the standing stock of a city are comprehensive and exacting. First, the analysis requires a relatively complete building inventory of the city in a form that is directly usable, and comparable through time.[5] Second, all new construction and major structural modifications must be rigidly defined and isolated from other property transactions for a specified time period. Third, past records must be available so that comparable characteristics of the properties affected by change can be established prior to redevelopment. The last of these requirements is the most difficult to achieve, but the most critical in assessing the exact impact of redevelopment on the existing structural stock in the city.

We have available in an appropriate form a thorough real property[6] inventory of the building stock of the City of Toronto in 1962, and a summary of all structural

---

[1] Simmons, op. cit.

[2] Kerr and Spelt, op. cit.

[3] Berry and Murdie, op. cit.

[4] Metropolitan Toronto Planning Board, Report on the Metropolitan Toronto Transportation Plan (Toronto: The Metropolitan Planning Board, 1964).

[5] In fact, probably the critical factors in limiting previous studies of this nature are that such inventories are seldom available in a manageable form and, more important, because of changes in the methods of compilation and the classification procedures, seldom is there comparability in these inventories through time.

[6] In its most general sense, property implies ownership, or the thing owned. Property objects themselves may be divided into two categories, real and personal. "The land and all things permanently attached to it are considered to be realty, and all other things are personalty." Weimer and Hoyt, op. cit., p. 57. A comprehensive glossary of terms and techniques in urban real estate, planning, and assessment practices is contained in Fisher and Fisher, op. cit., pp. 473-491.

changes that took place from 1952 to 1962. A "change" in this context is defined as including all new construction, major building modifications, and demolitions.[1] For each property involved in change and conforming to this definition, statistics similar to those in the master inventory were compiled for 1951 from past assessment records by the City of Toronto Planning Board.[2] The changed properties were then deleted from the 1962 master inventory for the city and replaced by the pre-redevelopment characteristics for these properties, thus creating a complete (within the definitional constraints) structural inventory for the city in 1951. The resulting information can be thought of as four data arrays, one each for the properties that changed before and after redevelopment, and one each for the entire city in 1951 and 1962.

The descriptive information includes general assessment and property statistics for both land and building. In total, there are twenty four data items for each property,[3] including assessed value of building and land, age and condition of structure, ground and total floor area, dwelling units and population, and a land use classification of 99 categories (see Appendix B). Problems arise with this classification precisely because of the emphasis on structural types rather than functional differentiation.[4] Furthermore, there is no definitive method of determining the original use for which the building was intended. Original use is implied, but not rigidly incorporated into the analysis, from the use existing in 1951.

The procedures employed in compiling the information, and specifically of achieving "one-to-one" comparability between properties in 1951 and 1962, were both

---

[1] For a detailed explanation of the definition of change and the procedures used in compiling the original data source, see Appendix A.

[2] This information was gathered by the City of Toronto Planning Board as part of an analysis of changing land uses in the city. Magnetic tapes containing the resulting data summaries were loaned to the author with the consent of the Commissioner of Planning. Preliminary analyses and tape preparation were performed on the IBM 1401 of the City of Toronto, and all succeeding operations were performed on the IBM 7094-7040 computing system of the University of Chicago Computation Center.

[3] Some confusion may result from the interchangeable use of property and lot in the terminology of the Planning Board study and definitions. In common usage, a lot means the basic unit of subdivision in the land survey system. A parcel is a particular land holding represented by single ownership, and may include one lot or any part or combination of parts of lots. A property on the other hand, consists of a parcel of land as well as the physical improvements that occupy that land. In this study the basic unit of measurement is the property including both land and building, but to conform to the terms used in the data sources, the term lot will appear consistently to refer to the land area connected with a property or structure.

[4] For example, the classification records nineteen types of residential use but only one general retail commercial category.

costly and complicated (see Appendix A). In many of the 9,000 cases of changes cited earlier the property dimensions and identification changed, as is inherent in the complexity of the real estate market. The critical links in locating the same property in both years were the property ledger number and lot area. The area of the 1962 property was located and its ledger number derived from 1951 assessment records and maps, whether this area represented a single property holding or not.[1]

Because of widespread amalgamation of properties concomitant with redevelopment, the number of properties involved declined from about 9,000 in 1951 to 5,600 in 1962. The nature of property change is considerably more complex than suggested by simple amalgamation. Although less frequent, property splits, and partial demolitions of structures also had to be examined and accounted for. To achieve systematic comparability for a given parcel of land through time, it was necessary to split individual properties to the lowest size denominator in either year. For example, in the case of a split of a 1951 property, each part is treated as a percentage of the whole in 1951. Each part has the dimensions of the 1962 property, and the assessments are divided proportionately. Lot area then becomes the control criterion in the analysis, and the property statistics are allocated accordingly.

The Analysis

Specifically, structural change in the City of Toronto is examined from the following points of departure:

1) A description of the nature of changes in the period under study, in terms of the amount, type, density and general distribution of new construction within the city.

2) A description of the relative rate of change among and between different activities and areas.

3) An examination of the degree of correlation between structural change and the economic, physical, and social characteristics of the areas affected by change.

4) An examination of the characteristics of individual properties before and after redevelopment to analyze the replacement process in structures and to establish a succession of land uses through time.

Following the initial description of structural change in Toronto, an attempt is made to account for spatial variations by employing a multiple regression framework of analysis. The relative amount and composition of new construction and major building modifications in any area of the city is hypothesized to be a function of the environmental

---

[1] In actual fact, the property statistics are for 1949, the last major reassessment in the City of Toronto, although all changes date from 1952.

qualities of that area, the character of the existing stock of buildings, and the relative position of the area within the metropolitan spatial structure. In selecting variables for the analysis the rationale is not to find factors that correlate with structural change over time, such as population or dwelling units, but rather to test whether the potential for change in an area can be deduced from conditions apparent before the change took place. In this case, the "before change" situation is provided by assessment, land use, and census statistics for 1951. The variables postulated as influencing the spatial distribution of structural change within an urban area include: the composition of the existing stock of buildings the age, value, and condition of these structures as qualitative measures of the environment; the income level and social status of the area; and accessibility to the commercial core and to the metropolitan population as a whole. Because of the problem of comparability of data sources at this level of generalization, census tracts provide the most suitable unit of area measurement.[1]

The second level of analysis is concerned with the individual property. For each of the approximately 9,000 properties affected by change in the study period, the characteristics of the building and property before redevelopment can be compared directly on a one-to-one basis with the same property following redevelopment. In this way is it possible to assess the impact of redevelopment on the structural stock, the character of the areas receiving redevelopment, and the regularities in the replacement cycle.[2]

In addition, spatial variations in the succession of land uses resulting from redevelopment can be examined by totalling the number of properties and amount of land area of each type of use that changed to some other type of use. The resulting matrix would contain on the diagonal all properties which remained in the same land use category between 1951 and 1962, with all off-diagonal elements measuring the frequency of conversion from one type to another. For each subarea in the city, in this case census tracts, similar matrices can be prepared and then converted directly to proportions.

---

[1] It is well documented that correlations between areally distributed data are strongly affected by the size of the unit employed. This problem, commonly referred to as that of modifable units, is likely to appear in this study not only because of the use of census tract data, but also in the collection and summarization of data for both the city and the metropolitan area. At present the only solution to the problem is to be aware of its consequences and to reduce its effects when possible by maintaining certain variables as controls throughout the analysis, and by testing the results with spatial units of different sizes.

[2] As the analysis deals with a straight "before and after" situation, only one conversion is possible for each site during the study period. The development of a longer perspective in land use succession will therefore be based on cross-sectional patterns for different properties at various stages in their life cycle.

Thus, not only will the analysis answer precisely the question of "what replaces what" in redevelopment and land use succession, it is possible to attach probabilities to this conversion, and measure the scale in land area. This approach provides a direct means of translating the regression estimates allocating redevelopment to subareas of the city into the nature of the impact on individual properties within these areas.

Measurement of Structural Change

In the previous chapter there is implicit reference to two distinct dimensions of urban structural change, one involving land and the other building space. It is not clear whether these dimensions exhibit similar patterns of variation in redevelopment, and the implications of different trends in both aspects are still to be determined. The following analysis is designed to assess the degree of consistency in the relationship between land and floor area for each type of use involved in redevelopment.

The results show considerable differences in the correlation between land and floor area for each use, from almost perfect for single-family residential to very weak for commercial uses. The former derives from the obvious homogeneity of the product and the latter occurs because commercial uses appear both as high-density activities in the central core and as low-density uses scattered throughout the city. For most uses, however, the correlations are above .700 (Table 2).

Off-diagonal correlations are small indicating that the spatial variations of land and floor area involved in change are largely independent between land use categories. As expected there is some association between single-family and low-density mixed residential, between industrial and warehousing, and between those commercial functions concentrated in the core, but these are relatively minor. The degree of independence provides the rationale for treating each category as a separate and additive contribution to the aggregate pattern of redevelopment in the following analysis.

Although the correlations for a single use are generally strong, the variation is sufficient to suggest that both floor and land area statistics should be carried through the entire study. Even at this level of generalization, and certainly below this level, it will not be possible to predict with reasonable accuracy the change in one knowing the change in the other.

The two basic sources of information on structural change and redevelopment in a city are assessment records and building permits. The following comparison relates total assessment added by new construction and the value of building permits issued over a six year period to test their comparability as data sources. Table 3, based on ratio rather than absolute values because of different definitional bases, shows a wide discrepancy in this relationship through time. Since 1959, total assessed value as

TABLE 2

SIMPLE CORRELATIONS BETWEEN THE FLOOR AND LOT AREAS OF PRIVATE[a] PROPERTIES INVOLVED IN CHANGE, BY MAJOR TYPE FOR CENSUS TRACTS, CITY OF TORONTO, 1952-1962

Floor Area	Lot Area											
	1	2	3	4	5	6	7	8	9	10	11	12
1 Single Family	.980	.420					.605					
2 Multi Family		.968										
3 Transport: Auto, Truck			.911									
4 Apartments				.905							.443	
5 Warehousing					.891	.711						
6 Industry					.486	.822						
7 Other Residential							.763					
8 Offices								.735		.480		
9 Commercial General									.634			
10 Hotel-Motel								.410		.606		
11 Parking Garages, Lots											.439	
12 Commercial Automobile											.440	.085

Sample size 127   Null error 0.089   Data are untransformed

[a]Includes only those land use groups defined as private in Appendix B.

Notes: The property types are ranked according to the strength of correlation between lot and floor area. The table does not include lot area to lot area, or floor area to floor area correlations for each type of change.

The sample size excludes eight census tracts in the city total of 135, representing parks, cemeteries, hospitals, and other public institutions and services. A detailed list is included in Appendix C.

a proportion of permit value has varied from 13.5 to over 27 per cent for any one year, from 20 to 60 per cent for residential, and from 7 to 25 per cent for commercial and industrial construction. For a variety of reasons, only some of which are obvious by definition (see footnotes to Table 3), these two measures are not directly comparable, at least at this level of generalization, and with the available data, and will therefore be treated separately in the analysis.

TABLE 3

COMPARISON OF VALUE OF BUILDING PERMITS AND ASSESSMENT ADDED
BY NEW CONSTRUCTION, CITY OF TORONTO, 1959-1963
(in 000's dollars)

Year	Residential		Commercial Industrial		Totals		Total Assessed as % of Permit Value
	Assessed	Permit	Assessed	Permit	Assessed	Permit	
1964	13,743	37,651	7,645	108,966	22,937	167,667	13.7
1963	5,576	33,304	14,179	65,457	20,162	121,772	17.4
1962	6,732	15,171	7,958	64,939	14,894	107,353	13.5
1961	6,973	16,840	13,280	77,837	22,462	108,065	20.8
1960	13,890	18,244	12,959	71,832	29,095	107,471	27.1
1959	9,970	24,611	13,844	72,320	24,401	106,561	22.9

Sources: City of Toronto Buildings Department
City of Toronto Planning Board

Note: A building permit is a means of public control on private construction . . ."
designed to ensure that the proposed structure or use conforms to
existing zoning and other municipal standards." All physical improvements, demolitions, and new construction require a building permit. A
building permit is simply a statement of intent, and although most permits
are realized they may not be completed for some time, and may represent only a part of the structure or project. The value attached to any
permit is the developer's estimate of total costs, for which he pays a
nominal fee, usually insufficient to discourage renewal of the permit.
Assessment added includes: (1) new construction--completed new
structures ready for occupancy; (2) additions--floor area added to
existing structures; and (3) changes--partial assessments prior to
completion of an entire project.

Delimiting the Study Area: Rationale

The purposeful limitation of the detailed analysis to the City of Toronto rather than the metropolitan area, or some economically-defined subarea, represents a compromise between available data sources and necessary preliminary assumptions. The basic source of information, largely because of the cost and complexity of compilation, is only available for the central city.

The preferable study area would include that part of the metropolitan area which by 1951 was completely built-up or developed. Figure 4 in the previous chapter suggests where this theoretical line would fall between city center and periphery. It could then be assumed that all new construction in this area involved the replacement of an existing building, and therefore by definition, redevelopment. Without this assumption, the analysis is complicated by the inclusion of new construction on vacant land in suburban areas, which do not take place under a similar set of economic constraints.

In Toronto, the city boundary offers one political approximation to the outer limit of what could be called "pure" redevelopment. By the late 1940's, and in fact in most areas by the late 1920's, urban development had spread far beyond the city limits (see Figure 13). Within the city itself, less than three per cent of the land area was classified as vacant in 1958.[1] At this point, this figure is not sufficiently large to violate the above assumption, although considerable attention will be given later to the importance of vacant land.

Inclusion of the suburban communities would add further complications in dealing with different municipal policies pertaining to redevelopment. It is generally agreed that the character and location of new construction are strongly affected by public regulations, and the degree of enforcement of these regulations, and that both of these vary considerably between municipalities even within the same metropolitan area. There is ample evidence of the effects of such procedures on the location of new construction in Toronto.

The disadvantages of this delimitation are obvious. Specifically, it ignores extensive areas of redevelopment activity that appear outside of the central city, for example, in Forest Hill, East York, and York Townships. The latter particularly has witnessed extensive apartment construction in selected areas since the early 1950's.

---

[1]Later in the analysis the argument will be put forward that even new construction on scattered vacant properties within a built-up area can be thought of as redevelopment. The reasoning is based on the fact that land left vacant in the initial wave of urban expansion plays a different role in the urban setting and is suitable for more limited uses than vacant land on the periphery.

More generally, it ignores the fact that with few exceptions central city boundaries have little meaning in economic and functional terms, and that economic activity in any part of the city cannot be logically examined apart from its metropolitan context.

To counter these disadvantages, the general analysis is set within a metropolitan context, in which the discussions and derivations of factors relating to redevelopment in the city are based on metropolitan data and trends. This two-level approach will enable the analysis to satisfy both the assumptions of "pure" redevelopment and the absence of variations in municipal policy, while recognizing and incorporating the continuum of growth from suburban development to central city redevelopment.

CHAPTER V

LOCATION FACTORS IN STRUCTURAL CHANGE

Investment, the basis of structural change, is the most volatile element in the national economic mix. Net real investment is synonymous with growth, and gross investment with economic activity. In a competitive economy investment decisions are linked to changing levels of national income and productivity,[1] as well as to the alternatives available for capital financing. Although a detailed discussion of national investment conditions is beyond the scope of this study, a few general observations are relevant to the question of capital investment in new construction.

This chapter falls into two distinct sections. The first provides a brief introductory context for redevelopment investment in Toronto examining national construction activity and the relative balance of public and private expenditures. The second relates the theoretical discussion of location factors in redevelopment in preceding chapters to specific operational hypotheses to be tested in the Toronto case study.

National Construction and the Urban Investment Mix

The distribution of investment funds among different kinds of construction activity and other investment opportunities varies widely with the availability of capital producing wide swings in the industry as a whole and in each of its subdivisions.[2] The addition of new units to the building inventory by new construction exhibits much greater volatility than the repair and maintenance of the existing stock. In Canada, business investment expenditures, which are probably most sensitive to changing conditions, have varied from less than 7 per cent of the total gross national expenditures in 1933 to a high of 27 per cent in 1957.[3] This erratic behavior over time is to be expected considering

---

[1] J.W. Dyckman and R.R. Isaccs, Capital Requirements for Urban Develoment and Renewal (ACTION Series in Housing and Community Development; New York: McGraw-Hill Book Co., 1961), p. 114.

[2] See C.D. Long, Building Cycles and the Theory of Investment (Princeton: Princeton University Press, 1940); P. Schrumpter, Business Cycles (New York: McGraw-Hill Book Co., 1964); and M. Colean and R. Newcomb, Stabilizing Construction (McGraw-Hill Book Co., 1952).

[3] G.W. Wilson, S. Gordon, and S. Judek, Canada: An Appraisal of its Needs and Resources (Toronto: University of Toronto Press, 1965), p. 305.

that such expenditures are usually made on a speculative basis, and thus are deferable in a way that other outlays are not. However, once a project is completed the costs of construction become "sunk" costs in the sense that they are committed at one time yet in anticipation of a long period of returns and cannot be withdrawn. Because of these variations, long-term generalizations cannot be based on the level of construction activity, in Toronto or in any other city.

The allocation of capital investment to different types of redevelopment activity in any city is closely related to national investment in different sectors of the economy.[1] About one-third of all new investment goes into machinery and equipment and the rest into new construction. Of the construction total, about 15 per cent represents government outlays, almost all of which is non-residential, while the private sector accounts for 50 per cent, of which 30 is non-residential. When machinery and equipment are excluded, the proportion of private investment rises to about 75, and private non-residential construction totals about 50 per cent. The three largest sectors in terms of capital formation in 1947, manufacturing, utilities, and housing, declined from 60 to 50 per cent of the total by 1961 in the face of rapid growth in government, and services in general.[2] (Public non-residential construction, for example, increased from 12 to 18 per cent between 1946 and 1961).

Table 4 shows that public investment in housing has been extremely low, usually less than one per cent of all housing construction, and it has declined. Housing as a whole has not kept pace with the national construction level, particularly relative to the private non-residential category. Of the value of private residential construction, over 90 per cent is represented by new dwelling units as opposed to all other costs including major alterations and improvements.[3]

To draw these findings together: the public sector accounts for 25 per cent of investment in new construction; government and services have received most of the investment growth in recent years, while manufacturing and housing have declined relative to the former.

---

[1] For a general review of recent construction activity in Canada, see The Financial Post, "Construction '66," A Special Report, February 19, 1966, pp. 49-64.

[2] Ibid., p. 310. See also R.E. Caves and R.H. Holden, The Canadian Economy: Prospect and Retrospect (Cambridge, Mass., 1959), p. 335.

[3] These figures are derived in large part from publications by the Central Mortgage and Housing Corporation. The most recent and comprehensive of these is: Canadian Housing Statistics 1965 (Ottawa: Central Mortgage and Housing Corporation, 1966), published annually since 1955. The most useful reference for all construction activity is: Dominion Bureau of Statistics, Private and Public Investments in Canada (Ottawa: Queen's Printer, 1959).

TABLE 4

PUBLIC AND PRIVATE EXPENDITURES ON NEW CONSTRUCTION IN CANADA, 1949-1964

(in millions of dollars)

Year	Public	Private	Total	Per Cent Private	Public	Private	Total	Per Cent Private	All Construction Total
1949	28	794	822	96.7	424	920	1,344	68.5	2,166
1950	40	883	923		488	1,042	1,530		2,453
1951	52	895	947		654	1,270	1,924		2,871
1952	38	933	971	96.2	897	1,566	2,463	63.4	3,434
1953	23	1,166	1,189		848	1,719	2,567		3,756
1954	11	1,227	1,238		828	1,671	2,499		3,737
1955	19	1,378	1,397		924	1,848	2,772		4,169
1956	21	1,526	1,547	98.8	1,137	2,589	3,726	69.5	5,273
1957	21	1,409	1,430		1,251	3,103	4,354		5,784
1958	19	1,763	1,782		1,237	2,811	4,048		5,830
1959	18	1,734	1,752		1,368	2,589	3,957		5,709
1960	13	1,443	1,456	99.3	1,420	2,577	3,997	64.0	5,453
1961	9	1,458	1,467		1,368	2,683	4,051		5,518
1962	10	1,577	1,587		1,562	2,638	4,200		5,787
1963	6	1,707	1,713		1,609	2,835	4,444	67.3	6,157
1964	7	2,020	2,027	99.9	1,640	3,344	4,984		7,011

Source: Central Mortgage and Housing Corporation

Given this general picture of national construction, we can now turn to the specific factors influencing the location of redevelopment construction <u>within an urban area</u>. To provide a thorough explanatory base for the hypotheses to be tested and for relating redevelopment to other processes of change demands that one first understand the framework provided by the existing stock, the changing character and location of economic activity, and the effects of public policy restrictions on locational patterns.

The Changing Economic Structure: Spatial Dimensions

Probably the most common and direct index of community health and economic growth is the changing character of employment. Despite obvious and well–documented shortcomings,[1] employment statistics do provide a useful and meaningful measure of the contribution of different industries and areas to the total urban economy. In this study, employment serves as one means of isolating <u>locations of economic growth</u> within the city, and of relating economic demands for change to the spatial pattern of new construction and investment.

As in most central cities in recent years, the City of Toronto lost employment both absolutely and relative to the metropolitan area. Between 1956 and 1964 employment in the city declined from 460,214 to 432,350 while metropolitan employment rose from 630,197 to 711,748.[2] During this eight year period the city lost jobs at the rate of 3,000 a year, and its proportion of Metro's employment declined from 73.2 to 60.7 per cent (Table 5). Thus, while employment fell some 28,000 in the city and rose 82,000 in the metropolitan area, the real increase for suburban areas outside the city was nearly 110,000 persons.

The decline in employment in the city was by no means consistent for different

---

[1] Economists argue, for example, that employment itself is not an accurate measure of productivity and therefore of the contribution of an industry to the economy. The preferred method, earned income, is generally considered to be more sensitive to economic fluctuations and more suitable for comparative analysis. Employment is not nearly as responsive to change as personal income, and the assessment of trends is complicated by part-time employment, moonlighting, unemployment, variable hours, and the like.

[2] The 1956 statistics were derived from a sample of employers while both 1960 and 1964 surveys were relatively complete enumerations. Because of the introduction of a large sampling error and the use of a different industrial classification, the 1956 data will only be used for general comparisons. Statistics for earlier periods are not available because the census did not publish employment by census tract, and for the city as a whole the figures are given by place of residence rather than place of work.

TABLE 5

RELATIVE EMPLOYMENT SHIFTS IN TORONTO, 1956-1964
BY MAJOR SUBAREAS OF THE CITY

	1956[a]	1960[b]	1964[b]	Change 1960-64	Change 1956-64
Metropolitan Toronto	630,197	674,651	711,748	+37,097	+81,551
City of Toronto	460,214	444,512	432,350	-12,162	-27,864
City as o/o of Metro	73.2	65.9	60.7	-5.2	-12.5
CBD Total[c]	146,224	158,518	156,383	-2,135	+10,159
o/o of City	31.8	35.7	36.2	+0.5	+4.4
o/o of Metro	23.2	23.6	22.0	-1.6	-1.2
CBD Downtown[d]	121,702	122,179	117,748	-4,431	-3,954
o/o of City	26.4	27.6	27.2	-0.4	+0.8
o/o of Metro	19.3	18.2	16.5	-1.7	-1.8
CBD Uptown[e]	23,224	34,998	36,502	+1,504	+13,278
o/o of City	5.0	7.9	8.4	+0.5	+3.4
o/o of Metro	3.7	5.2	5.1	-0.1	+1.4
CBD Lower Uptown[f]	14,707	21,403	24,559	+3,156	+9,854
o/o of City	3.2	4.8	5.7	+0.9	+2.5
o/o of Metro	2.3	3.2	3.5	+0.3	+1.2
Eglinton-Yonge[g]	8,596	15,093	19,120	+4,027	+10,524
o/o of City	1.9	3.4	4.4	+1.0	+2.5
o/o of Metro	1.4	2.2	2.7	+0.5	+1.3
St. Clair, Yonge, Avenue Road[h]	6,493	8,063	7,900	-163	+1,407
o/o of City	1.4	1.8	1.8	+0.0	+0.4
o/o of Metro	1.0	1.2	1.1	-0.1	+0.1

[a] A sample of employers within planning districts from the records of the National Employment Service, undertaken by the Metropolitan Toronto Planning Board.

[b] Both of these surveys used identical formats and procedures, and represent complete censuses.

[c] Includes census tracts 70, 71, 72, 73, 74, 75, 76, 69, and 95.

[d] Includes census tracts 73, 74, 75, and 76.

[e] Includes census tracts 70, 71, 72, and 95.

[f] Includes census tracts 71 and 72.

[g] Includes census tracts 84, 85, 86, and 87.

[h] Includes census tracts 51, 66, 67, and 91.

(see Figure 10 in text for map of zones of analysis)

Source: Metropolitan Toronto Planning Board, Employment Surveys, 1956, 1960, and 1964.

industrial groups and among areas. In the metropolitan area the principal growth industries were the retail and service groups, followed by finance, manufacturing, and
government (Table 6). In the city, somewhat similar but lower growth rates appear for
these groups with the exception of manufacturing (Table 7). Employment growth was
greatest in the city in government, totalling over 3,100 persons or a 4.7 per cent
increase, and in personal service with a 4.3 per cent change. In the declining sector,
wholesaling and construction registered the largest percentage declines, while wholesaling and manufacturing showed the greatest numerical declines.

Although a reduction in employment need not exclude new construction in that
category or area, employment growth is generally associated with non-residential floor
space expansion. The expansion of land intensive functions such as commercial offices,
and the decline in land consuming industries such as manufacturing, wholesaling, transportation, and construction, follows similarly documented trends elsewhere. The fact
that the government sector is growing most rapidly in the central area holds important
implications for the city's evolving economic organization, as well as for the distribution
and impact of private new construction.

The spatial pattern of employment concentration and change is most relevant to
this analysis as an indicator of growth centers (Figure 14). Within the city three major
concentrations of employment growth are apparent. One is the "Uptown" portion of the
commercial core, the second includes the area around the intersection of Eglinton and
Yonge Streets, and the third is the northwest industrial area of the city (also see Figure
10). The coincidence of these areas with existing centers of localized employment concentration, suggests that the distribution of employment is becoming more agglomerated
in selective foci outside the older central business district.

Within the "Downtown" area itself, employment declined from 122,000 to
118,000 in the eight years following 1956, but at a slower rate than for the city as a
whole. Referring back to Table 5, it can be seen that the proportion of city employment
in this area remained stable at 27 per cent despite the overall decline, while the Uptown
area increased from 5 to over 8 per cent. The entire central business district actually
increased its share of the city's employment while dropping slightly relative to the
metropolitan area. The bulk of the growth stimulus has derived from government and
finance sectors of the economy.

The Eglinton-Yonge area has witnessed substantial office and apartment development in recent years as the northern terminus of the first subway line. As a measure of
the importance of this expansion, employment increased from 8,596 to 15,093 in the
four census tracts involved between 1956 and 1960, and further to over 19,000 by 1964.
The increase consisted primarily of finance and business service establishments,

TABLE 6

EMPLOYMENT CHANGE: METROPOLITAN TORONTO 1960 -1964
(by Major Categories)

Standard Industrial Category	1960	o/o	1964	o/o (2)	Diff. No.	1960-64 o/o
1. Primary	4,209	0.6	3,749	0.5	-460	-10.9
2. Manufacturing	211,199	31.3	228,401	32.1	+17,202	+8.1
3. Construction	43.354	6.4	35,989	5.1	-7,365	-17.0
4. Transportation	53,930	8.0	54,901	7.7	+971	+1.8
5. Wholesale	49,904	7.4	45,412	6.4	-4,492	-9.0
6. Retail	92,548	13.7	104,917	14.7	+11,369	+12.3
7. Finance	73,345	10.9	79,669	11.2	+6,324	+8.6
8. Pers. Service	44,873	6.8	50,353	7.1	+5,480	+12.2
9. Government	100,289	14.9	108,357	15.2	+8,068	+8.0
TOTALS	674,651	100.0	711,748	100.0	+37,097	+5.5

[a] A rough index of the degree of employment concentration in the City, obtained by subtracting the percentage employed in each category in the City from that in the metropolitan area.

traditionally described as "central business district" activities. Despite the increase, however, employment in the area represented less than 5 per cent of the total for the city and less than 3 per cent of the metropolitan total, hardly as yet a major revision of the spatial distribution of economic activity.

From these general directions of growth it is easy to generalize about a northward shift in central area employment. Whether this growth in fact represents a migration of employment opportunities from the Downtown area or more likely, geographic differentials in the rate of growth, is not clear at this point. It is apparent, however, that employment growth is taking place in the area immediately adjacent and to the north of the old core, and in proximity to the subway terminus at Eglinton Avenue two miles further north. This northward pull of employment is in keeping with the historical interpretation of principal axes of growth in the city and the traditional emphasis given to the role of Yonge Street. Furthermore, the development of Eglinton-Yonge as a small but expanding nucleus for office functions testifies to the increasing locational freedom of these functions in the modern metropolitan context.

TABLE 7

EMPLOYMENT CHANGE: CITY OF TORONTO 1960-1964
(by Major Categories)

Standard Industrial Category	1960	o/o	1964	o/o	Diff. No. (1)	1960- 1964 o/o	Concentration in City[a] (1) - (2)
1. Primary[b]	3,389	0.8	2,416	0.6	-973	-28.2	+0.1
2. Manufacturing	120,955	27.2	114,866	26.6	-6,089	-5.0	-5.5
3. Construction	14,836	3.3	12,244	2.8	-2,592	-17.4	-2.3
4. Transportation	45,133	10.2	43,315	10.0	-1,818	-4.0	+2.3
5. Wholesale	30,116	6.8	23,062	5.3	-7,054	-23.2	-1.1
6. Retail	64,541	14.5	64,638	15,0	+97	+0.2	+0.3
7. Finance	65,470	14.7	67,208	15.5	+1,738	+2.7	+4.3
8. Pers. Service	32,779	7.4	34,178	7.9	+1,399	+4.3	+0.8
9. Government	67,293	15.1	70,423	16.3	+3,130	+4.7	+1.1
TOTALS	444,512	100.0	432,350	100.0	-12,162	-2.7	

[a]A rough index of the degree of employment concentration in the City, obtained by subtracting the percentage employed in each category in the City from that in the metropolitan area.

[b]Includes some employment connected with mining offices and suppliers in the city as well as the standard primary industries.

Source: Metropolitan Toronto Planning Board. The employment classification is based on the Dominion Bureau of Statistics, Standard Industrial Classification Manual for 1948

The Standing Stock: Framework for Change

The standing stock of buildings in a city can be viewed as a physical space, divided among different activities,[1] and used with differing degrees of intensity. In 1962 the City of Toronto included nearly 400 million square feet of floor space, divided into

[1]This land use classification, employed by the City of Toronto Planning Board, represents an aggregation of the original 99 categories used in the basic assessment survey.

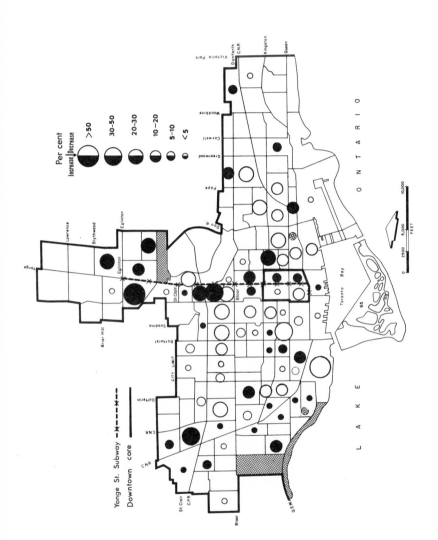

Fig. 14--Employment Change in the City of Toronto 1960-64

130,000 structures covering 19,500 acres of land,[1] and housing 641,000 persons.[2] Of the total number of structures, some 109,000 were residential, containing about 180,000 dwelling units.

As expected, wide variations occur in the scale, intensity and distribution of both physical space and land area among different urban functions. Residential uses, for example, account for over 84 per cent of all structures in the city, but less than 50 per cent of the total floor area and land area. Commercial functions occupy almost 20 per cent of the floor space, but less than 10 per cent of the land area and structures. The contrast is greatest among the major uses in the office and industrial categories. Office functions, for example, represent almost 8 per cent of the city's building space, but affect only 1.4 per cent of the land area and one per cent of all structures. Industrial activity, at the other extreme, comprises more than 5 per cent of all land, 13 per cent of the floor area, and similarly about one per cent of all structures.

Table 8 groups and classifies this stock into public and private, defined on the basis of the land use classification,[3] and excluding all undeveloped areas. By this definition, private uses account for 98 per cent of all structures, 73 per cent of the total developed land area, and 88 per cent of the city's floor area. As a proportion of total private developed land and buildings, residential uses account for 66 per cnet and 56 per cent respectively. Commercial and industrial uses each represent about 19 per cent of the total private floor area, and approximately 9 and 11 per cent of the land area. The government category, excluded in this analysis, accounts for slightly more than 10 per cent of the land and building area of the city.

The degree of turnover and instability in the building stock is suggested by the 1,600 structures occupying some 545 acres, classified as vacant in 1962, and the 155

---

[1] The total land area was obtained by summing all assessed properties (170,000) in the city, and is therefore somewhat less than the actual land area of the city, which includes all non-assessed land.

[2] The difference between this figure and the quoted census total of some 670,000 persons is the result of assessment procedures, and is in line with similar differences noted elsewhere (3 to 5 per cent lower). This differential was examined in more detail for each of 135 census tracts in the city, and was found to be generally consistent and within an acceptable range.

[3] Public uses were defined as including all schools and universities, places of amusement, assembly, and worship, all hospitals and institutions, government offices, and utilities. Also, in order to exclude large areas of land without structures, and the extensive holdings of the government-owned railroad, the categories of Other Transportation and Open Space are eliminated. It should be pointed out as well, that these designations represent the dominant use in each structure, and not all types present within any given structure.

TABLE 8

COMPOSITION OF PRIVATE STRUCTURAL STOCK, PROPORTIONAL TO
TOTAL STOCK AND TOTAL DEVELOPED LAND
CITY OF TORONTO, 1962

Major Use[a]	Structures[b] Numbers	o/o	Lot Size[b] Acres	o/o	Floor Area X1000 sq ft	o/o	o/o of Total Private[c] Lot Area	Floor Area
Residential	109,078	84.1	8,006.75	48.1	196,723.4	49.2	66.2	56.0
Commercial Office	1,507	1.1	267.38	1.6	30,544.0	7.6	2.2	8.7
Commercial General	8,953	6.7	616.18	3.7	34,016.5	8.5	5.1	9.7
Other Commercial	2,926	2.1	575.65	3.4	11,541.7	2.8	4.8	3.3
Total Commercial	13,386	9.9	1,459.21	8.8	76,102.2	18.9	12.1	21.7
Warehousing	1,321	1.0	892.01	5.4	23,723.3	5.9	7.4	6.8
Industrial	1,648	1.2	1,015.47	6.1	53,314.3	13.3	8.4	15.2
Total Industrial	2,969	2.2	1,907.48	11.5	77,037.6	19.2	15.8	22.0
Transport: Auto, Truck	34	–	14.58	.1	328.1	.1	.1	.1
Vacant	1,673	1.3	544.89	3.3	68.9	–	4.5	–
Under Construction	528	.4	155.49	.9	873.7	.2	1.3	.3
TOTAL PRIVATE DEVELOPED	127,668	97.9	12,088.40	72.6	351,133.9	88.0	100.0	100.0
Public, Institutional	1,251	.9	1,174.50	7.1	33,949.3	8.5	–	–
Government Offices	103	.1	64.64	.4	5,678.9	1.4	–	–
Utilities	126	.1	419.89	2.5	2,857.7	.7	–	–
Total Public	1,480	1.1	1,659.03	10.0	42,485.9	10.6	–	–
Other Transportation	563	.4	1,041.02	6.2	3,810.0	1.0	–	–
Other[d]	512	.4	1,865.49	11.2	1,472.4	.5	–	–
TOTAL PUBLIC AND PRIVATE DEVELOPED	130,223	100.0	16,653.94	100.0	398,905.5	100.0	–	–

[a] For a complete description and breakdown of each land use type see Appendix B.

[b] Per cent of total city developed area.

[c] Per cent of total city private developed area.

[d] Includes open space, both commercial and public, but excludes undeveloped areas such as water, waste land, agriculture, and forestry.

acres under construction. The former, representing 3 per cent of the city's area, provides a rough measure of the degree of disequilibrium between supply and demand in the standing stock. The area involved in new construction at this one point in time, comprised less than one per cent of the city's developed area.

Spatial Variables in Urban Redevelopment

New construction occurs to meet demands that cannot be met within the existing stock. Because of the numerical superiority of this stock it dominates the market for urban space, and thus one would expect the distribution of additions to be directly related to the geography of this stock. Prevailing prices of both land and building space influence the rate and location of new construction, and the allocation of investment among competitive types of urban activities.

Levels of Spatial Analysis

The operation of these economic forces, however, is disturbed by a variety of social, political, and historical constraints. The resulting spatial pattern of new construction represents the cumulative effects of this bundle of interrelated factors. As location factors, furthermore, these may operate to influence the feasibility of a site for redevelopment at different levels of spatial analysis. Three levels are suggested: site, neighborhood, and relative location. Site factors are those which derive from the individual property, such as building condition, depreciation, and ownership. Primarily, these relate to the costs and ease of acquiring and preparing a site for redevelopment. Neighborhood factors[1] include the relative amenity advantages of an area, the immediate social and physical environment, and the external economies that accrue through proximity to related uses. The third level involves the relative location of a given site or area within the metropolitan area as a whole and is usually measured in terms of accessibility.[2]

One way to summarize how these different levels of factors relate in conditioning the pattern of redevelopment is the following. Redevelopment is primarily an economic

---

[1] The term neighborhood contains no explicit sociological connotation in this context. Instead, it refers to the geographic area surrounding a site or set of sites which acts as the environmental framework for change.

[2] It is recognized that these levels are not mutually exclusive, nor can the levels be sharply defined in all cases. This approach is introduced here as a means of organizing the explanatory discussion around general themes of locational analysis that occur repeatedly but in rather vague terms in the literature.

process, which occurs when there is economic benefit to be gained. The potential for economic gain in redeveloping a site usually depends on its relative location within the urban complex and an immediate neighborhood context. Investing in urban land also means investing in a portion of a neighborhood, as is the case in real estate. The immediate environment may act to prevent the realization of situations where redevelopment is feasible, or it may act to accelerate the process.

However, this still leaves wide latitude for choice of location. The primary effects of site factors then appear to influence the selection of individual properties within a given range of locations. The final selection is based on the cumulative assessment of the attractions of alternate parcels of land. The relative influence of each of these sets of factors will vary widely between land uses and areas as well as over time.

In this study, variations in redevelopment activity among areas of the city is hypothesized to be related to the character and distribution of activities and the existing stock, the social and physical amenities of these areas, relative accessibility to the urban population and distance from the city center, and the size and cost of individual parcels. Looking at the city in 1951, prior to the period of change analysis, it is possible to assess the "potential" of different areas and locations for new construction?

Relative Location and Environmental Factors

Accessibility and Transportation Facilities. --Accessibility, as it is commonly used in urban research, refers to a number of measures of distance and spatial association. In its broadest form, accessibility may include the summation of all actual or potential opportunities for interaction, or specifically it may include only distance in time or money costs between different points of interest. This study is concerned only with the effects of accessibility that derive directly from transportation facilities.

The impact of transportation facilities on the spatial structure of the city has two aspects--the effects on mobility and movement patterns and thus on the locational advantages of all areas; and secondly, the direct effect on the physical plant by road and transit construction. In the first case, there is an abundant literature both theoretical and empirical, which treats the question of the relationship between accessibility and the location of urban land uses.[1] However, in the case of transportation construction considerably less insight is available from existing research.

In the following analysis, the effects of location and accessibility on redevelopment will be assessed with three largely independent distance measures: distance from

---

[1] For example, Walter G. Hansen, "How Accessibility Shapes Land Use," Journal of the American Institute of Planners, XXV, No. 2 (May, 1959), 73-76; William L. Garrison et al., Studies of Highway Development and Geographic Change (Seattle: University of Washington Press, 1959); Wingo, Transportation and Urban Land; and Mitchell and Rapkin, op. cit.

the city center and from the geographic center of metropolitan population, and proximity to mass transit. These measures may appear shallow in light of the extensive research into this topic in recent years, particularly in reference to the units of measurement and the points from which accessibility should be measured. Yet it appears that distance from the city center, although significantly weaker than in the past, is still the most meaningful measure of many urban structural phenomena.[1]

There is also considerable evidence to support the conclusion that the relative effects of accessibility improvements on mobility and urban spatial structure have declined. The ubiquity of the automobile, improved road networks, and a greater variety of transportation alternatives, has reduced the dependence of an area on any given facility. Greater uniformity in access advantages and increasing space consumption have been the obvious results of these trends.

In Toronto, accessibility differentials over space were altered by the completion of the Yonge Street subway line in 1954.[2] This line, following one of the traditional axes of growth, has acted as a stimulant to redevelopment around major intersections on Yonge Street. Another commonly cited explanation of the continued importance of this axis is the northward migration of the center of population.[3] If accessibility means distance to the urban population as a whole, then a marked spatial shift in this distribution will change all location relationships in the city.

In the second case, the recent increase in expressway and other public construction has had a direct impact on the urban physical plant through the demolition and clearance of extensive areas of the city. Lowdon Wingo,[4] for example, asserts that destruction of buildings under the urban expressway and related programs is the only source of large scale replacement and land use conversion in American cities. As the

---

[1]Measuring accessibility as distance from the city center more than simple access is being considered. Areas of roughly similar time distance will have been constructed at much the same time and will reflect conditions prevailing at that time.

[2]The coincidence between the opening of the subway and the beginning of the study period enables us to assume a somewhat uniform accessibility pattern throughout the entire period. The major east-west expressway was not completed until after the period of study.

[3]As is true for all lakefront cities, with time and increasing size the central business district becomes increasingly off-center in reference to the aggregate distribution of population. In most cases this may be compensated for by transportation improvements, but the changing distance relationships cannot be altered. For an interesting discussion of the relationship between the form of a city and strength of C.B.D. retail dominance, see: R.R. Boyce and W.A.V. Clark, "The Concept of Shape in Geography," Geographical Review, LIV, No. 4 (October, 1964), 561-572.

[4]Lowdon Wingo, Jr., "The Use of Urban Land," in Land Use Policy and Problems in the United States (Lincoln: University of Nebraska Press, 1963), p. 242.

results of this study will show, this is somewhat of an exaggeration, nevertheless the impact has been substantial. In Toronto, it is estimated that expressway construction, along with parks and schools, will result in the clearance of nearly 500 acres and the removal of 6,000 dwellings by 1980.[1] From preliminary estimates, if present trends continue, this rate of demolition will account for approximately one-third of all estimated replacements in the stock of dwelling units. Although this study excludes public redevelopment of all types, it is essential to evaluate its relative impact in the succeeding analysis.

Environmental Amenity Factors and Externalities.--The critical importance of the environment in determining the feasibility of site redevelopment has already been established. From several aspects of urban research,[2] empirical documentation is available to support this contention. The character of the environment, whether measured in terms of structures, land use, socio-economic status, or physical attractiveness,[3] may act to hinder or accelerate property conversion and redevelopment investment. For example, in the central areas of many cities, the activities for which these areas are becoming increasingly suited, and for which redevelopment is economically feasible, are often in conflict with the present character of these areas.

Where adverse effects are considerable, new activities will probably be unwilling to locate within these areas even when the costs of land and property acquisition are competitive with other locations. That is, unless the new development is of sufficient magnitude to generate its own environment separate from that presently in existence. A paradox may result from the influence of the environment, such that rebuilding may be profitable on a large scale for an entire area, but not for any individual property within that area. Some authors have taken this as the real problem of blight. Davis and Whinston,[4] for example, suggest that blight exists whenever ". . . strictly individual action does not result in redevelopment," and where ". . . the coordination of decision-making . . . would result in redevelopment."

---

[1]City of Toronto Planning Board, The Changing City. A Forecast of Planning Issues for the City of Toronto 1956-80 (Toronto: The Planning Board, 1959), p. 26.

[2]For example, note the earlier references in real estate, renewal and land use research in chapter ii to the effects of the environment.

[3]This refers to the whole range of physical environment considerations such as congestion, pollution, and deterioration, which act to reduce the attractiveness of an area for new investment. See the discussion in Colean, op. cit., p. 69.

[4]Otto A. Davis and Andrew B. Whinston, "The Economics of Urban Renewal," Law and Contemporary Problems, XXVI, No. 1 (Winter, 1961), 105.

Two of the most common measures of neighborhood character are social status and structural condition.[1] In this study an approximation to these conditions is made by employing census tracts as neighborhood or environmental units, and income, population density, and age and condition of housing as "quality" measures.

The spatial distribution of social characteristics in Toronto exhibits similar patterns to those of other major cities. Income, as a proxy for social status, appears highest in three distinct sectors separated by areas of middle and lower income, paralleling industrial and railroad uses (Figure 15). The most prominent of the higher income sectors follows the Yonge Street axis north from the central business district, while the two additional areas are located in the extreme east and west of the city along the lakeshore. Underlying these sectorial patterns, there is a generally consistent concentric variation. The zero order correlation between median income and distance from the city center is +.600 for the City of Toronto and +.532 for the metropolitan area.

There is likewise a close correlation between income and building age and condition (Figure 16), but with two major exceptions. First, concentrations of older housing extend much farther to the west following the original orientation of growth along the Dundas-CNR route. Second, some areas of higher income, particularly those immediately to the north of the central area, show a much younger structural stock than might be expected for that location, presumably because of widespread demolition and new construction.

These cumulative distributions are indicative of the scale of variations in overcrowding, property size, structural deterioration, and social amenities, all of which will influence the attractiveness of an area for redevelopment. It is then hypothesized, that variation of redevelopment activity among areas of the city will show a strong positive relationship with income and property size and an inverse relationship with structural age and deterioration.

Site Factors

The Cost of Land. --It is often suggested that the central economic problem of urban rebuilding is the cost of land. Throughout most older areas of central cities, certainly those outside the central business district, the cost of land assembly and preparation of sites for rebuilding far exceeds the economic value for most potential redevelopment purposes. Whether these values are in fact inflated is of critical importance in the solution of renewal problems, but for our purposes it is sufficient to say that they exist.

---

[1] For example, the role assigned to neighborhood amenities in Eugene F. Brigham, "The Determinants of Residential Land Values," Land Economics, XLI, No. 4 (November, 1965), 325-334. Brigham employs income and overcrowding in different sectors of Los Angeles as measures of amenity.

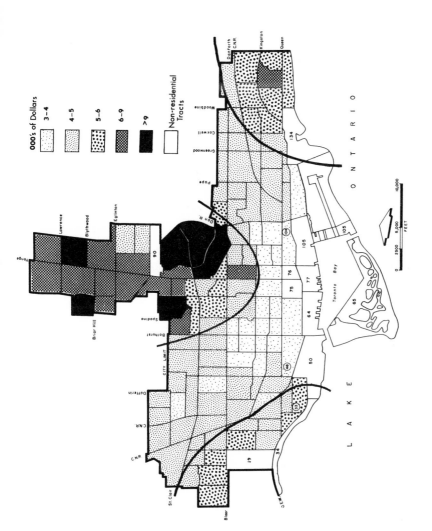

Fig. 15--Residential Sectors in Toronto Family Income, 1961

88

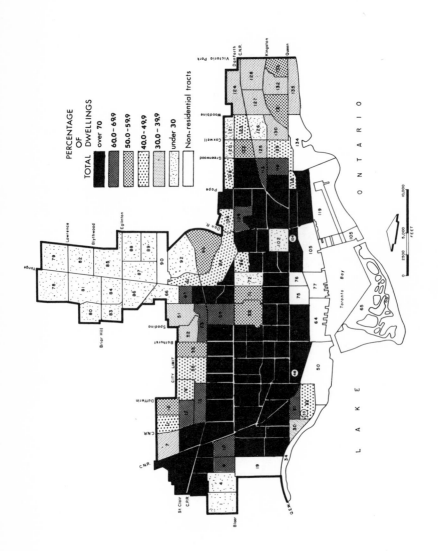

Fig. 16--Age of Residential Buildings Pre 1920

Land is important as a cost component from two points of view. First, as a proportion of total construction and investment costs, it exerts a strong effect on redevelopment feasibility, and second, because of variations within the city its effects on redevelopment will vary from one area to another. The effect of the latter as a locational determinant is the most difficult to assess, especially in cities such as Toronto where comprehensive land value data are not available. In general terms at least, a measure of the former effect is available from national housing statistics and the latter from assessment records.

In Canada, land costs comprise almost 18 per cent of the average cost of new bungalows in 1964 (Table 9). Out of a total cost of $15,800, the price paid for individual lots amounted to over $2,800. In Toronto, average land costs are considerably higher, and are in fact the highest of any urban area in Canada. Land accounted for 31.5 per cent of all construction costs in Toronto in 1964, compared to 20.2 in Ottawa and 14.2 per cent in Montreal.[1] Although similar figures are not available for Toronto, land costs as a proportion of total construction costs in Canada have increased by almost 70 per cent since 1952.

An approximation to market value of land in Toronto is available in the form of assessed values for each property.[2] Although there is widespread caution in the conversion of assessed to market valued, the critical factor here is not the size of the difference in ration, but variations in this ratio from place to place. These difficulties are not as serious however, as they might appear.

It is generally agreed that considerable variations occur in the rate of assessment for different land use types but as the markets for each use are largely independent it is possible to ignore these differences. In addition, by limiting the analysis to the city of Toronto the problem of differences between municipalities is avoided. In reference to variations within the city, preliminary results from the Ontario Royal Commission on Taxation suggest that these are considerably smaller than expected.[3]

---

[1] Central Mortgage and Housing Corporation, Canadian Housing Statistics 1964, p. 73.

[2] In Toronto, assessments are based on an approximation to 110 per cent of the 1940 market values. The entire city of Toronto was reassessed in 1949 just prior to the period of study.

[3] As part of its review of property and municipal taxing systems in Ontario, the Commission undertook a study of the relationship between assessed and market values in Metropolitan Toronto. From a stratified sample of recent property sales, conversion factors for individual types of use were developed from least squares regression analysis. The resulting fit was relatively close, indicating only minor variations in the relationship among individual properties.

TABLE 9

ESTIMATED COST OF LAND AND CONSTRUCTION OF NEW BUNGALOWS
TORONTO AND CANADA, 1962-1964

	1962	1963 (in dollars)	1964
Toronto			
Total Cost[a]	17,009	17,096	18,105
Land Cost[b]	5,416	5,480	5,706
Cost/Sq. Ft.	9.37	9.31	9.78
Land Cost as o/o of Total Cost	31.8	32.1	31.5
Canada: Urban			
Total Cost[a]	14,648	15,068	15,807
Land Cost[b]	2,535	2,692	2,813
Cost/Sq. Ft.	10.56	10.68	11.01
Land Cost as o/o of Total Cost	17.3	17.9	17.7

[a]Includes land, construction, and other costs, but not mortgage insurance.

[b]Price paid for lots – these prices vary with the proportion fully or partially serviced or unserviced.

Source: Central Mortgage and Housing Corporation.

Average Size of Lot. --Adding to the cost of land, one of the overwhelming barriers to private redevelopment is the extremely fragmented ownership of real estate resources.[1] The relatively small units of private property characteristic of the older areas of cities adds considerably to the difficulty of land assembly. In most cases, new construction in built-up areas requires larger units of land than the present property subdivision provides. Developers are inclined to seek out areas of larger individual lots, or areas where consolidation has already taken place for other purposes, rather than face the difficulty and expense of assembling the necessary parcel.

This points to the dilemma facing developers in rebuilding the central areas of cities. Because of the generally unattractive physical and social environments of these

---

[1]For example, the discussions in Colean, op. cit., pp. 69-99; and Hemdahl, op. cit.

areas, the developer must create his own environment if the project is to attract investment. In order to improve this environment, however, requires increasingly larger
areas of land. The more unattractive the area the greater is the need to shield the new
development from its surroundings by enclosing a larger area. Thus, land requirements
for redevelopment increase precisely in those areas where the size of the individual
property declines.

Average size of lot is not, however, an independent factor. Preliminary analyses for Toronto show that lot size is inversely correlated with population density and
age of structure, and directly correlated with income and rent levels.[1] The spatial
distribution of lot sizes in Toronto, for single-family residential uses, shown in Figure
17, is remarkably like that for population density and income. Thus lot size is synoptic
of, and in part responsible for, the environmental conditions prevailing in these areas.
It could then be hypothesized, for the area outside the cnetral business district, that the
spatial pattern of redevelopment activity, specifically office and residential uses, will
show a strong positive correlation with the average size of lot in that area.

Effects of Public Policy on the Location of Structural Changes

All too often in research, assumptions are made to hold constant factors thought
to be overly complicating in the core of the analysis, without any reference to the
possible to explain. In Chapter I, the direct impact of public construction and investment
on the structural stock was purposefully excluded from the analysis. At this point, it is
further assumed that the aggregate pattern of private redevelopment will not be drastically altered or at least altered in the same direction by the effects of public policy through
the enforcement of codes and covenants.[2] Although no attempt will be made to assess
these effects empirically, it is possible to evaluate the assumption generally by referring
to the available literature. Two factors are singled out for discussion, real property
taxation and assessment procedures, and zoning.

As the most comprehensive form of public control of the private land market,

---

[1]This applies only to the City of Toronto. One study of the relationship between
lot size and price of home, for example, concluded that for suburban locations lot size
cannot be used to predict selling price. J. G. Coke and C. S. Liebman, "Political Values
and Population Density Controls," Land Economics, XXXVII, No. 4 (November, 1961),
347-361.

[2]It is recognized that these are only a few of the types of public action which
directly or indirectly influence the building stock of the city. Obviously, the municipal
road and service systems provide the basic infrastructure for urban development, and
major alterations to either of these systems will alter locational preferences within the
city. Of more immediate interest, however, is the direct competitive effect of public
demands for land and building space, particularly government office construction which
is competitive with office space in the private market.

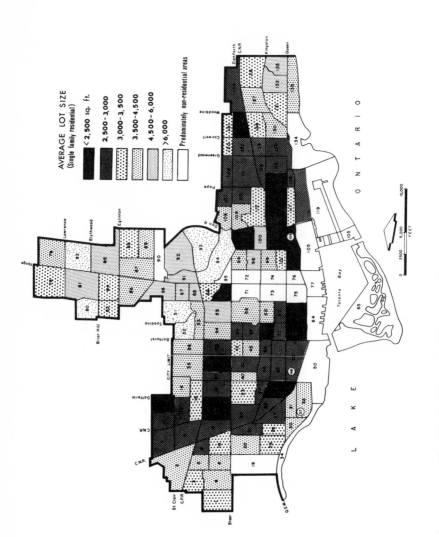

Fig. 17--Land Fragmentation: Average Size of Residential Properties

zoning would appear to be of critical importance in the location of new construction. Briefly, zoning designates the most "appropriate" use and density for all locations in the city,[1] on the notion of separating "incompatible" land uses and the desire to preserve property values. Because zoning post-dated the development of older central cities, and because the existing knowledge of land use distributions and the desired form of future cities was meager indeed, zoning could do little more than reflect the land use pattern of the time. By adding administrative barriers to the process of change, zoning has acted as a negative form of control, tending to preserve the present and prohibit change. In fact, zoning is really only of importance in its present form, when there is pressure for change. Redevelopment, by definition, involves a change in structure, usually accompanied by a change in the type and density of use, and therefore necessitates a change in zoning.

Isolating the specific effects of zoning from other factors in urban redevelopment is difficult if not impossible, and has not been done on a comprehensive scale. Vernon comments that zoning came too late to have any appreciable impact, and that today most developers are successful in securing zoning revisions because of the pressures of economic "efficiency."[2] In light of the lack of positive alternatives for development this is not surprising. Justement[3] concludes that zoning has only been capable of preventing some of the more glaring abuses of the real estate market. In reference to land values, Alonso[4] contends that in the long run zoning will have little effect on the prices of individual parcels,[5] but in the short run, by limiting the amount of land available for each use, it encourages the operation of independent markets for each type of land use.

Probably the most important considerations in zoning and the most difficult to

---

[1]Detailed descriptions of zoning practices are contained in: Donald H. Webster, Urban Planning and Municipal Public Policy (New York: Harper and Row, Publishers, 1958), pp. 362-435; F. Stuart Chapin, Jr., Urban Land Use Planning (Urbana: University of Illinois Press, 1965), pp. 356-362; and Charles M. Haar, Land-Use Planning, A Casebook on the Use, Misuse, and Re-use of Urban Land (Boston: Little, Brown and Co., 1959), p. 744.

[2]Vernon, "The Myth and Reality of Our Urban Problems," loc. cit., p. 99.

[3]Louis Justement, New Cities for Old (New York: McGraw-Hill Book Co., Inc. 1946), p. 28.

[4]Alonso, Location and Land Use, p. 117.

[5]In a study of Rogers Park in Chicago, Yeates was able to allocate only 20 per cent of the spatial variations in land values to the effects of zoning. See Maurice H. Yeates, "An Estimation of the Effect of Zoning on the Spatial Distribution of Land Values in Rogers Park, Chicago, 1960" (Paper presented at the 60th Annual Meeting of the Association of American Geographers, Syracuse, New York, March 20-April 1, 1964).

measure, are the <u>degree of enforcement</u> on the part of the municipality, and the degree of <u>neighborhood resistence.</u>[1] Wide variations exist between cities, even within the same metropolitan area, in the rigidity of zoning by-laws. This differential in itself may account for a significant proportion of the variation in redevelopment activity between municipalities within Metropolitan Toronto. Although it is not possible in this study to assess these differences with the data available, their presence must be kept in mind.

The effects of real property taxation on structural change are equally difficult to evaluate.[2] Assessment practices tend to encourage an imperfect equity of assessment between different kinds of property within the city. Moreover, as land values and uses are closely interrelated, taxation must affect both but presumably not in an identical fashion.

It is generally agreed that the existing property tax system in most cities has a deterrent effect upon the improvement and replacement of structures in older areas. With the improvement of any property the assessed value and tax level increase. The owner in a sense pays twice for his incentive, the cost of the improvement, and the increased tax assessment.[3] As with zoning, variations between municipalities may prove to exert a stronger influence on redevelopment than the differential among land use types, within the same metropolitan context.

Summary

The distribution of redevelopment activity among subareas of the city is con-

---

[1] Community opposition to change is often a critical obstacle in redevelopment in both high and low income areas. The former areas of course are the most successful in these efforts. See, for example S.M. Willhelm, <u>Urban Zoning and Land Use Theory</u> (New York: Free Press of Glencoe, 1962), which is primarily a collection of dialogues between participants in zoning appeals; Otto A. Davis, "Economic Elements in Municipal Zoning Decisions," <u>Land Economics</u>, XXXIX, No. 4 (November, 1963), 375-386; Stephen Sussna, "Zoning Boards: In Theory and In Practice," <u>Land Economics</u>, XXXVII, No. 1 (February, 1961), 82-87; S.M. Willhelm and G. Sjoberg, "Economic vs. Protective Values in Urban Land Use Change," <u>American Journal of Economics and Sociology</u>, XIX, No. 2 (January, 1960), 151-160; and C. Woodbury and F.A. Gutheim, <u>Rethinking Urban Redevelopment</u> (Chicago: Public Administration Service, 1949), p. 8.

[2] For example: Jerome P. Pickard, <u>Changing Urban Land Uses as Affected by Taxation</u> (Research Monograph No. 6; Washington: Urban Land Institute, 1962), which contains an excellent bibliography on property taxation and its effects on land use, urban sprawl, and urban redevelopment. See also, Edwin M. Rams, "Changing Rights-- Changing Values," <u>The Residential Appraiser</u>, XXVII, No. 10 (October, 1961), 2-10, a study of the implications of public control on real property.

[3] For an interesting discussion of the influence of property taxes on land use patterns and urban development and redevelopment in Metropolitan Toronto, see Bureau of Municipal Research, "The Impact of Property Taxes in Metro," <u>Civic Affairs</u> (Toronto: Bureau of Municipal Research, February, 1964), 10 pp.

sidered to be a function of the potential to attract new investment. This potential is based on the relative position of each area in the urban framework in terms of proximity to related activities, general accessibility, environmental amenities, and the ease and costs of property acquisition and consolidation. Traditionally, the absence of such factors has been associated with the occurrence of deterioration and blight. There has not, however, been a thorough assessment of the relative effects of these factors in determining areas of growth in the city.

The following chapter turns to the detailed examination of redevelopment activity in Toronto. Chapter 7 then relates the above discussion to the results of the Toronto study in a regression model approach, to evaluate the degree to which these factors differentiate the potential for structural change.

CHAPTER VI

STRUCTURAL CHANGE IN TORONTO

Where is the private real estate market and the replacement process operative?
What types of land uses and building construction are involved, and what has been the
impact of these changes on the aggregate spatial structure of the city? What locations
and areas in the city have been affected? Are there regularities in the character, direction, and spatial patterning of redevelopment which provide insight into the processes of
urban structural change? These are the questions to which this chapter is directed as the
basis of the empirical analysis of redevelopment in Toronto.

Historical and Metropolitan Trends in Construction

Redevelopment activity in the years 1952-1962 cannot be properly assessed
without a broader historical and metropolitan perspective. Initially, it is essential to
relate building activity in this period to the experience of past periods. Figure 18 summarizes the volume of construction activity in the City of Toronto since 1925.[1] From a
wartime low of under $6 million, the value of building construction rose to $80 million in
1953, $120 million in 1957, and $167 million in 1964.[2]

The period under study exhibits a generally uniform increase in building activity,
given the usual fluctuations of the construction industry. More striking, however, is the
dominance of the two decades in total construction since 1925 and particularly since 1932.
Demolition figures (superimposed on the same illustration), show similar trends, and
provide one direct means of comparing the historical impact of new construction activity

---

[1] The limitations of building permits as a measure of construction activity, and
the difficulties of relating these figures to those derived from assessment sources, have
been discussed in chapter III. In this chapter we assume consistency within each source,
but no attempt will be made to relate them. These figures include expenditures for
repair and maintenance as well as new construction.

[2] In terms of constant 1949 dollars these figures become $60 million, $87 million,
and $120 million, based on the residential construction cost index.

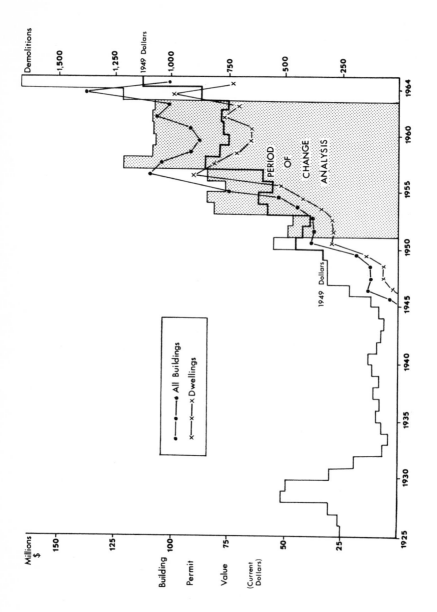

Fig. 18--Value of Building Permits and Number of Dwellings Demolished, City of Toronto, 1925-1964

on the standing stock. Of some 11,200 dwellings demolished between 1940 and 1962, over 80 per cent were recorded after 1951. Thus, the particular narrow slice of Toronto's recent building history under study here is quantitatively more important than the length of the period would suggest.

In Figure 18, the coincidence of trends in the number of demolitions and value of building permits, despite the effects of inflation, should be noted. Also, the impressive rise in the rate of demolition after 1945 and particularly since 1952, is strong evidence, not subject to monetary distortion, of an accelerated rate of redevelopment and replacement within the standing stock.

The low level of capital investment and construction activity typical of the 1930's and 1940's explains in part why most cities are now faced with widespread structural deterioration and obsolescence. Had the rate of new construction, and by definition the rate of replacement, reached in the 1920's continued through to the 1950's, cities would look much different than they do now. The present level of construction is in fact, an attempt to overcome these years of inactivity.[1] In this respect, Dyckman and Isaacs[2] comment, the current construction boom is unusual and probably quite unstable.

Building construction in the City of Toronto is in addition, an integral part of a larger metropolitan framework of development. Table 10 shows trends in total building permits issued in the City as a proportion of the Metropolitan Toronto total, and compares this to changes in the proportions of population, employment, and taxable assessment. In 1951, the city accounted for 25 per cent of all building permits issued in the metropolitan area, a substantially lower proportion than for the other three measures. However, despite a decline in the relative importance of the city as a center of population, from 60 to 38 per cent, as well as employment the proportion of building permits issued actually increased from 25 to 33 per cent.

Although this increase is in part the result of an expanding need for replacement in the aging stock of the central city, particularly in the commercial core, it implies the continued strength of the city in the aggregate distribution of urban investment. By limiting the analysis to the City of Toronto, this study therefore includes from one-quarter to one-third of the aggregate investment in the physical plant of Metropolitan Toronto during the period under study.

---

[1] Part of the construction boom, particularly in housing in the 1950's, can be accounted for by low interest rates and easy mortgage terms. See Grigsby, Housing Markets and Public Policy, p. 268.

[2] Dyckman and Isaacs, op. cit., p. 25.

TABLE 10

CITY OF TORONTO AS A PROPORTION OF
METROPOLITAN TORONTO,[a] 1951-1964

Year	Value of Building Permits[b] %	Population %	Employment (work place) %	Taxable Assessment %
1951	25	60	–	59
1953	28	56	–	–
1956	27	49	73	–
1961	30	43	66	45
1964	33	38	61	44

[a]The municipality of Metropolitan Toronto.

[b]Source: Dominion Bureau of Statistics, Building Permits, 1951-1956 (Ottawa: The Queen's Printer, 1957); and annual reports from 1957 through 1964, City of Toronto Buildings Department.

Notes: Figures are estimates and may not refer to the exact year listed.

The City of Toronto occupies only 14.6 per cent of the land area of Metropolitan Toronto.

Magnitude and Composition of Structural Change

New building construction and major structural modifications in Toronto, have shown a distinct concentration on limited activities in limited areas. Table 11 summarizes the thousands of additions and modifications to the private building stock of the city in the years 1952 through 1962. Although this summary could be considerably more complex, the purpose here is to provide a general impression of relative magnitude.

During this period, what has been defined as private redevelopment resulted in the addition of 45.8 million square feet of building floor space on over 5,100 properties, involving about 1,400 acres of land. In total, these changes accounted for 13 per cent of the aggregate building stock in 1962, and represented the redevelopment of nearly 12 per cent of the developed land area of the city. On the average, approximately one per cent of the city was subjected to this process in each year.[1] As a proportion of total

[1]Obviously as an indication of the rate of redevelopment in the city this measure

TABLE 11

SUMMARY OF PRIVATE STRUCTURAL CHANGES
CITY OF TORONTO, 1952-1962

	Properties		Lot Area		Floor Area	
	No.	o/o	Acres	o/o	Sq. ft. 000's	o/o
Single-family	503	9.7	61.77	4.3	781.9	1.7
Multi-family < 6	922	17.8	82.95	5.9	2,022.6	4.4
Apartments[a]	271	5.3	156.07	11.1	15,121.2	33.0
Other Residential	184	3.6	20.92	1.5	640.7	1.4
Total Residential	1,880	36.4	321.71	22.8	18,566.4	40.5
Offices: Commercial	265	5.1	74.92	5.3	10,709.2	23.4
General Commercial	316	6.1	66.36	4.7	2,810.8	6.1
Automotive Commercial	335	6.5	162.25	11.5	803.0	1.8
Parking	1,127	21.8	186.07	13.2	1,054.6	2.3
Hotel, Motel	9	0.2	3.47	0.3	829.1	1.8
Total Commercial	2,052	39.7	493.07	35.0	16,206.7	35.4
Trans: Auto, Truck	9	0.2	4.14	0.3	91.0	0.2
Under Construction	288	5.6	79.33	5.6	609.3	1.3
Vacant	461	8.9	97.96	6.9	4.0	–
Total Private and Developed	5,166	100.0	1,410.44	100.0	45,829.6	100.0
o/o of total changes	92.1		74.85		85.9	
Total City Public and Private	5,609		1,884.17		53,305.9	

[a]Apartments are defined as consisting of 6 or more dwelling units.

Notes: Includes all new construction and major structural modifications, i.e.,
additions and demolitions equalling 50 per cent or more of the original
building.

Summary for 5,166 individual properties in 130 of 135 census tracts.

Excludes all public buildings, hospitals, churches, schools, institutions,
municipal, provincial and federal offices, parks and open space, railways,
utilities, agricultural and waste land.

See Appendix B for detailed breakdown of land use categories.

redevelopment activity the private sector comprised 86 per cent of the floor area and
75 per cent of the redeveloped land area.

In terms of floor area added, the largest individual category was apartments,
involving over 15 million square feet and 33 per cent of all new construction. Commercial offices were second, representing over 23 per cent or 10.7 million square feet.
Combined, apartments and offices made up over half the aggregate additions to the
physical plant, and more generally, residential and commercial uses represented 76 per
cent of the total.

In terms of the land area affected by this construction, the results are quite
different. Commercial uses dominated with 493 acres or 35 per cent of the total,
followed by warehousing and industrial with 414 acres and residential uses with 322 acres.
Residential and commercial uses, represented only 58 per cent of the land area compared
to 76 per cent of the aggregate floor area. The largest individual categories were warehousing and parking uses, followed by related automotive and industrial uses.

In the aggregate, redevelopment appears concentrated in those uses at opposite
ends of the density scale. Table 12 underscores the contrasting nature of land and
building change by ranking the proportion of total lot and floor area contributed by each
major category of use. Figure 19 then relates these proportions to aggregate floor area
ratios for the properties involved in change. The largest increases in floor area were
recorded by apartments and offices, the most intensive uses, and by automobile and
parking uses, the least intensive. The former group totalled 55 per cent of the floor
area but only 16 per cent of the land area; the latter comprised almost 25 per cent of the
land area, but less than 4 per cent of the total floor area.

The immediate implication of these trends is to suggest an increasing disparity
in the density of redevelopment between uses and areas of the city. Where change has
occurred in the existing structural stock, it seems to have resulted in a marked specialization toward high density construction, or essentially non-structural change. Almost
26 million square feet of office and apartment construction took place on only 500 properties and 230 acres of land, or slightly over one per cent of the developed area of the
city. Commercial automobile and parking uses, on the other hand, seldom involve any
major contribution to total building construction, but are occupying an increasing proportion of the land area in the central portion of cities.

Not only are the most intensive uses dominant in redevelopment, but these uses
are being constructed at even higher densities than comparable divisions of the existing

has little significance. Only if the assumption is made that, in the long run, all new
construction occurs in different areas, does this measure suggest a rate of change.
Similar estimates are given for public renewal efforts in the United States in Gordon,
Sick Cities, p. 388.

TABLE 12

RANKING OF MAJOR TYPES OF USE IN CONTRIBUTION TO
STRUCTURAL CHANGE, CITY OF TORONTO, 1952-1962

Floor Area % of total change		Lot Area % of total change	
Apartments	33.0	Warehousing[a]	17.9
Offices: Commercial	23.4	Parking[b]	13.2
Industrial	14.3	Auto Commercial	11.5
Warehousing[a]	8.3	Industrial	11.5
General Commercial	6.1	Apartments	11.1
Multi-family	4.4	Multi-family	5.9
Parking[b]	2.3	Offices: Commercial	5.3
Auto Commercial	1.8	General Commercial	4.7

[a]Including 1.0 million square feet of municipal warehousing facilities.

[b]Includes both parking garages and lots.

stock. Table 13 compares aggregate floor area ratios[1] for new construction and the existing stock of the city, showing that only two categories of use recorded increases in intensity while all others declined.[2] These two categories, apartments and offices, increased in intensity by 20 and 30 per cent respectively relative to the city averages. Thus, compounding the concentration of redevelopment at the extremes of the density scale, these same uses are clearly becoming more divergent in intensity.

Moreover, these trends toward specialization of type and increasing intensity are accelerating over time. Although the analysis covers only one decade, significant differences appeared when the data were split into two intervals and compared. Approximately the same amount of building took place in the 1959-1963 period as in the earlier five years, 22.1 to 22.7 million square feet, but on 40 per cent less land area (Table 14).[3] With but two exceptions, the actual amount of land area affected by redevelopment within

[1]Intensity of use is measured simply as the ratio of total building floor area to site or lot area for an individual property, or for aggregates of property types, as in this general comparison.

[2]The Other Residential category is too diverse to be meaningful, and the Hotel-Motel category, although reflecting the degree of intensity one might expect, is based on a very limited sample and is relatively unimportant.

[3]Note that these figures are not directly comparable to those in preceding tables because they include both public and private uses, and are limited to new construction.

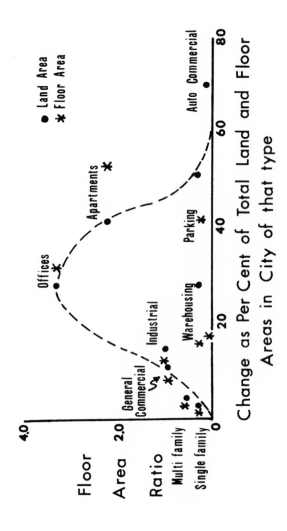

Fig. 19--Relationship Between the Rate of Redevelopment and Intensity of Use

TABLE 13

RELATIVE INTENSITY OF USE: STRUCTURAL CHANGE AND EXISTING STOCK
CITY OF TORONTO, 1952-1962

| | | Floor Area Ratios[a] | |
| | | Changes | |
	Existing Stock	1952-62	Difference
Single-family	0.37	0.29	-.08
Multi-family	0.63	0.56	-.07
Apartments	1.71	2.22	+.51
Other Residential	0.58	0.70	+.12
Offices: Commercial	2.62	3.28	+.62
General Commercial	1.27	0.97	-.30
Auto Commercial	0.48	0.11	-.37
Parking	0.17	0.13	-.04
Hotel-Motel	4.69	5.49	+.80
Warehousing	0.61	0.34	-.27
Industry	1.21	0.94	-.27
CITY TOTAL: Private and Developed Land	0.66	0.75	+.09

[a]See text for definition.

each category declined, including both offices and apartments. Although it was noted
previously that floor area ratios for new construction were below those of the existing
stock, except for apartments and offices, this difference can be explained by a substantial
shift in the composition of redevelopment.

The established dominance of office and apartment construction increased appreciably during the period. In total, these uses accounted for over 74 per cent of all floor
area added in the latter period compared to 51 per cent in the earlier period. On the
other hand, manufacturing construction declined from 21 to 6 per cent of total change,
and warehousing from 7 to 4 per cent. In both cases, the decline in land area involved
was greater than that in floor area, and intensity of use increased.

Implications of Redevelopment Trends

The dominant role of apartment and office construction in private redevelopment
in Toronto documents previous assertions of the changing character of central cities.
In 1962 apartments represented only 7 per cent of the building stock in the city, while in

terms of additions to this stock between 1952 and 1962 over 33 per cent were apartments. Offices accounted for the same proportion of the stock as apartments in 1962, but over 23 per cent of recent additions.

The reasons for this degree of dominance, as suggested in Chapter II, are complex and closely interrelated. Increasing costs of land and site preparation, combined with the decentralization of land-extensive activities, creates the necessity for high density construction at the center of the city. Basic changes in the economy, the increasing role of service functions, and recent shifts in housing needs,[1] have expanded the demand for rental accommodation and commercial office space.[2] This demand has been particularly strong in cities that are rapidly growing and which serve as regional or national centers for retail and service activities. Toronto is clearly a good example.

The need for both rental accommodation and office space can be supplied by high density construction in central areas. In fact, it is optimal for most because of the nature of their operation and the advantages of centrality. Thus, forces working on both the supply and demand sides of the market for urban physical space have merged to accelerate the emphasis in redevelopment on apartments and offices.

The characteristics associated with these uses carry important implications. First, both are highly intensive uses requiring relatively small and decreasing amounts of land area. For renewal purposes, this means that an accelerated rate of investment in new construction need not involve an increase in the portion of the city area affected. As most renewal programs are concerned with a given geographic area, this problem becomes of central concern. Second, as places of work and residence these uses involve only a limited range of the social and economic strata in the city. As pointed out in Chapter II, new residential units added to the inventory in central areas are usually above the price and rent scale of 60 per cent or more of the urban population. Adding further to the importance of this factor, this social composition is in distinct contrast to existing social conditions in most parts of the central city. Third, and most critical for subsequent steps in this study, the locational choices open to both offices and apartments are relatively broad.[3] This implies less rigidity and systematic variation in location,

---

[1] Bank of Nova Scotia, "The Apartment Boom in Canada," Monthly Review (Toronto: October, 1965).

[2] For an interesting discussion of these trends see: Jean Gottmann, "Why the Skyscraper," Geographical Review, LVI, No. 2 (April, 1966), 190-212.

[3] In terms of employment, Toronto is relatively more specialized in service and finance sectors of the economy than most North American cities. See Metropolitan Toronto and Region Transportation Study, Growth and Travel Past and Present (Toronto: MTARTS, April, 1966).

TABLE 14

COMPARISON OF NEW CONSTRUCTION, CITY OF TORONTO
1952-56 and 1959-63

	Total Lot Area (Acres)			Total Floor Area (000 Sq. Ft.)			Floor Area Ratios	
	1959-63	1952-56	Change Index o/o	1959-64	1952-56	Change Index o/o	1959-63	1952-56
Residential (1-19)*	142.4	153.8	92.6	10,111	7,218	140.0	1.63	1.08
Offices (35-39)	32.8	37.3	87.8	6,583	4,764	138.2	4.61	2.93
Commercial (40-44)	25.9	17.1	150.8	1,915	1,010	189.6	1.70	1.35
Auto (46-51)	31.2	27.4	113.6	735	502	146.4	0.54	0.42
Warehousing (55-59)	52.7	88.2	59.7	1,114	1,585	70.2	0.49	0.41
Manufacturing (60-64)	20.9	114.6	18.2	1,500	4,706	31.8	1.65	0.94
Other	14.0	116.5	12.0	723	2,339	30.9	1.18	0.46
Total	319.9	554.9	57.6	22,681	22,124	102.5	1.63	0.92

Source: City of Toronto Planning Board
*Minor Land Use Codes, See Appendix B

Note: Includes both public and private construction.

and therefore <u>less predictability</u> in the spatial pattern that results.

The scale of industrial and warehousing construction is more difficult to explain. Aside from waterfront reclamation areas, involving about one million square feet of floor space on land recently filled by the Toronto Harbour Commission,[1] the magnitude of change is still considerable. To some degree, these figures are exaggerated by the inclusion of modifications and additions to the existing stock within large property holdings.[2] Nevertheless, the figures indicate that industrial migration to the suburbs need not preclude substantial industrial investment in central cities. In the latter half of the study period, however, this rate of change declined substantially relative to other types of redevelopment activity.

The extensive areas of automobile commercial and parking uses seem to conflict with trends toward rising costs and increasing intensity. It cannot be assumed, however, that this is a clear indication of declining re-use value and potential for central locations. In many cases such uses simply represent a transition period between demolition and new construction. Even where no new structures are involved, parking particularly is a complementary function to the higher intensity uses in the central area. Municipal codes to a degree ensure that parking provision is made for high-density office and apartment construction. Here again the data present problems, as many parking areas represent conversion of storage or open areas within properties rather than any form of structural replacement.

The Spatial Pattern of Structural Change

Generalized Patterns of Association

The spatial patterns of lot and floor area added by new construction in this period clearly emphasize limited areas of the City of Toronto (Figures 20 and 21). In terms of building floor space, the commercial core and the northern sector of the city along Yonge Street dominate the pattern. The amount of land area affected by this activity differs appreciably in distribution from that of floor area. In addition to the central and northern areas, outlying concentrations, particularly industrial areas in the extreme east and west and along the waterfront, stand out.

Each of the major types of redevelopment activity shows a quite distinct and

---

[1] These figures are included here as a meaningful part of the total construction and investment picture in the City of Toronto.

[2] In the collection of the basic data, in cases where more than half of the building was added during the study period, the entire building was included as undergoing change. For large warehousing and industrial structures this could represent a significant distortion of the statistics.

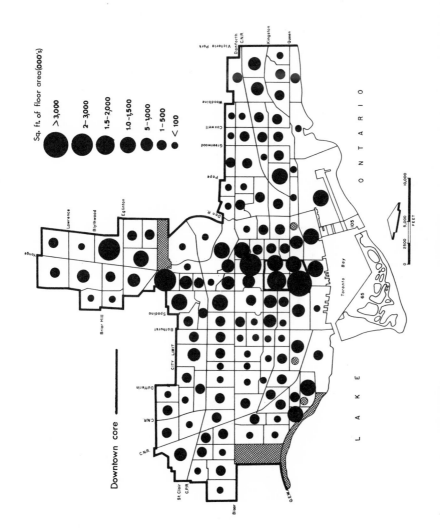

Fig. 20--Total New Construction, Floor Area Added, 1952-1962

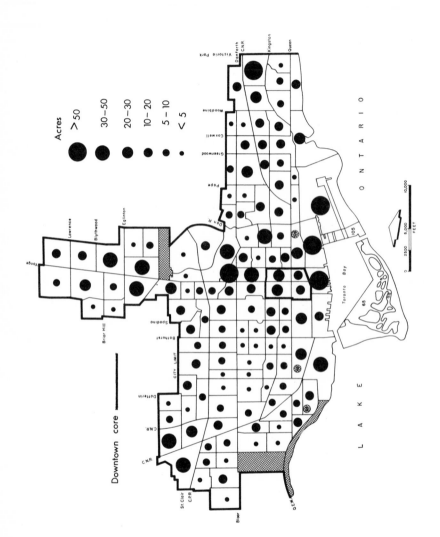

Fig. 21--Land Area Involved in New Construction, 1952-1962

concentrated pattern. Offices (Figure 22), as expected, are most heavily concentrated in the central core, but also appear in a narrowly-defined belt along Yonge Street, following the subway line. Apartment construction (Figure 23), reveals a similar degree of concentration, but in three distinct sectors of the city. The first follows the office sector to the north, while the others occur in the Parkdale and Beaches areas along the lakeshore, each about three to four miles from Downtown. Industrial construction (Figure 24), adds a separate dimension to the aggregate pattern emphasizing the central waterfront and following the railway zones to the northwest. The fourth pattern, auto-motive and parking uses (Figure 25), appears concentrated in both the "frame" area surrounding the central core and in the industrial and warehousing zones.

To assess the degree of association between these patterns and the relative contribution of each to the total spatial variation in redevelopment activity, factor analytic techniques were applied to both lot and floor area statistics.[1] The factor solutions con-sistently isolated the major land use types as might be expected, but with some interest-ing differences. Five underlying patterns resulted, for both lot and floor area, accounting for over 61 per cent of the aggregate variation in redevelopment between census tracts (Table 15).

In the lot area analysis, warehousing and industrial uses appear as factor one, followed by residential uses, two commercial factors, and transportation uses. The clustering of commercial uses in two groups, factors three and four, differentiates between redevelopment downtown and redevelopment in the surrounding fringe. The fourth factor groups office lot area, general commercial, parking, and hotel uses, while the fifth groups offices with automobile commercial. The latter is clearly the pattern in the fringe area to the north of the central core, which has witnessed considerable office construction.

In floor area, the core and fringe patterns for commercial redevelopment sepa-rate completely. Office redevelopment combines with the other core uses to become the dominant factor. Residential redevelopment remains as factor two, but apartments split from the others and appear isolated as a separate dimension.[2] Thus, it seems that only in terms of floor area can apartment redevelopment be treated as an independent spatial pattern. Parking uses, which in the lot area analysis are associated to some degree with each of the other patterns, are strongly correlated with factor one when measured in floor area, as predominantly a core function.

---

[1] Principal components factor analysis was applied to both raw and transformed statistics for lot and floor area separately and in combination. Only the separate analyses of raw statistics are described here.

[2] The vacant floor area category is too small to be of any significance, and its correlation with apartment floor area is spurious.

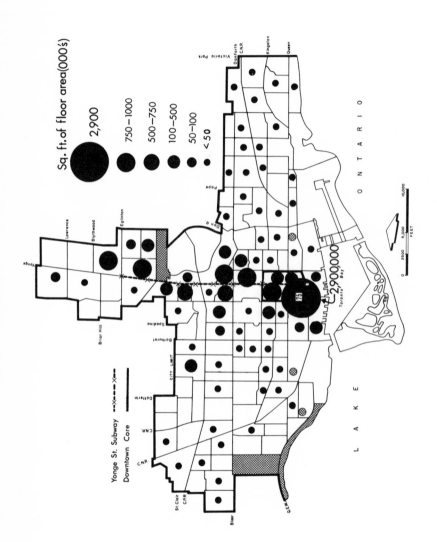

Fig. 22--Office Construction, Floor Area Added, 1952-1962

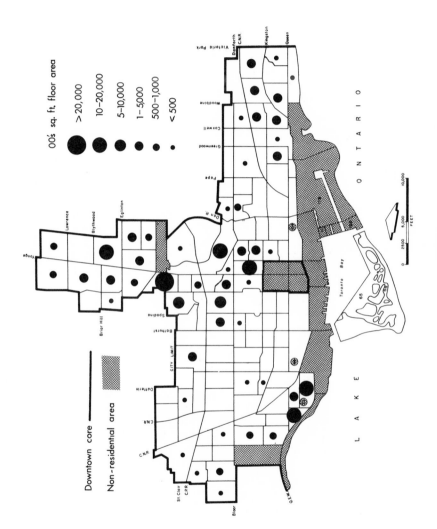

Fig. 23--Apartment Construction, Floor Area Added, 1952-1962

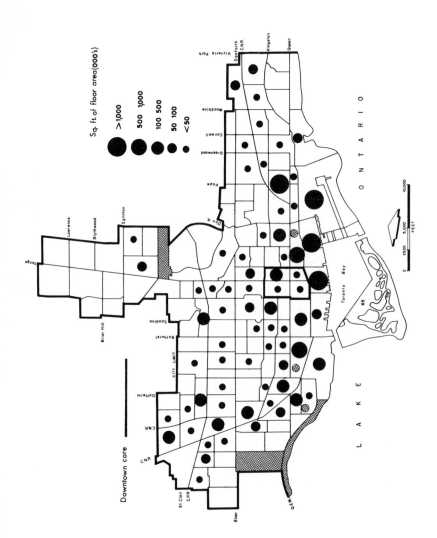

Fig. 24--Industrial and Warehousing Construction, Floor Area Added, 1952-1962

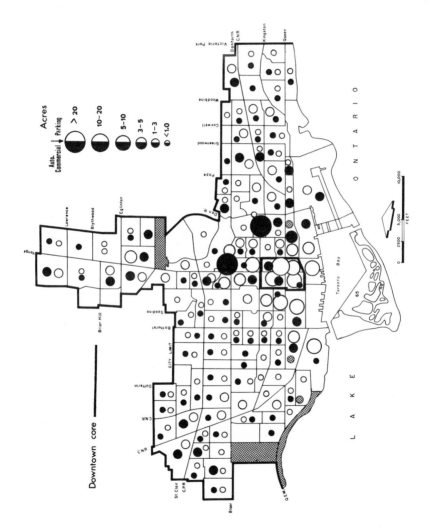

Fig. 25--Commercial Automobile and Parking Changes, Land Area Involved, 1952-1962

TABLE 15

FACTOR ANALYSIS RESULTS, LOT AND FLOOR AREAS INVOLVED IN
CHANGE, BY LAND USE TYPE, CITY OF TORONTO
1952-1962

			Factor Matrix - 5 Rotated Factors				
Sum of Squares		2.061	2.001	1.689	1.394	1.390
Per Cent 14 Factors		14.7	29.0	41.1	51.0	61.0
5 Factors		24.1	47.6	67.4	83.7	100.0

No.	Name	Communality					
1	SING FAM LOT	0.700	0.043	0.829	-0.094	0.033	0.044
2	MULTIFAM LOT	0.369	-0.082	0.597	-0.070	-0.035	-0.012
3	APT LOT AREA	0.465	-0.039	0.490	0.428	-0.097	-0.175
4	OTHER RES LT	0.645	-0.030	0.802	-0.021	-0.013	0.004
5	OFFICES LOT	0.790	-0.031	-0.006	0.577	0.674	-0.033
6	GEN COMM LOT	0.311	0.034	-0.016	0.555	0.024	-0.039
7	AUTO COM LOT	0.844	0.000	-0.035	-0.037	0.917	-0.026
8	PARKING LOT	0.563	0.257	-0.218	0.527	0.278	0.306
9	HOTEL LOT AR	0.541	-0.074	-0.053	0.729	0.010	-0.007
10	WAREHOUSE LT	0.686	0.822	-0.063	0.019	-0.058	0.045
11	INDUSTRY LOT	0.798	0.614	-0.114	-0.018	-0.046	0.636
12	TRANS LOT AR	0.827	-0.067	0.042	-0.026	-0.029	0.905
13	UNDER CONS L	0.580	0.726	-0.050	0.158	0.026	-0.155
14	VACANT LOT A	0.417	0.625	0.031	-0.115	0.041	0.100

Sum of Squares		2.564	1.588	1.582	1.533	1.300
Per Cent 14 Factors		18.3	29.7	41.0	51.9	61.2
5 Factors		29.9	48.5	66.9	84.8	100.0

No.	Name	Communality					
1	SING FAM FLA	0.692	-0.042	0.830	0.020	0.040	0.002
2	MULTIFAM FLA	0.429	-0.084	0.611	0.153	0.014	0.157
3	APT FLOOR AR	0.626	0.117	0.308	0.098	0.035	-0.712
4	OTHER RES FA	0.403	0.010	0.599	-0.061	0.009	-0.201
5	OFFICE FL AR	0.887	0.931	-0.049	0.076	-0.112	0.012
6	GEN COMM FLA	0.698	0.335	0.009	-0.042	-0.709	-0.285
7	AUTO COM FLA	0.797	-0.050	-0.020	-0.215	-0.864	0.021
8	PARKING FLAR	0.848	0.889	-0.071	0.008	-0.184	0.138
9	HOTEL FLOORA	0.778	0.867	-0.010	-0.029	0.034	-0.158
10	WAREHOUSE FA	0.655	0.022	-0.095	-0.788	-0.149	-0.049
11	INDUSTRY FLA	0.738	-0.059	-0.140	-0.840	-0.061	0.071
12	TRANS FLAREA	0.130	0.003	0.085	-0.296	0.084	0.169
13	UNDER CONS F	0.349	0.105	-0.074	0.261	-0.444	0.258
14	VACANT FL AR	0.535	-0.061	-0.151	0.081	-0.037	-0.708

[a]Communalities are the sum of the squared factor loadings and measure the
proportion of the total variance of a variable accounted for by the factors given. Factor
loadings are the direct correlation of each variable with each factor.

Despite low communalities for some uses, there is sufficient stability in the factor loadings to indicate that each of the major types of redevelopment represents an independent and additive contribution to the aggregate pattern. Thus, each can be treated separately as meaningful divisions of the input data for subsequent analyses.

Area Concentrations and Variations in Redevelopment

Supporting the previous conclusion of increasing intensity and specialization in the composition of redevelopment activity, a rather crude index of concentration suggests an equally strong localization factor. The largest contributors to aggregate floor area addition, offices and apartments, are among the least widely distributed. The rank correlation coefficient (r_s) between frequency of occurrence (measured as number of census tracts recording new construction) and total volume of construction by land use type, shows a strong inverse relationship of -.66. Thus, in addition to an absolute decline in the land area affected by redevelopment, the major uses involved are tending toward even greater locational concentration.

The degree of concentration is also apparent among the major areas of growth in the city. The five largest centers of non-industrial redevelopment (Table 16), account for over 41 per cent of all floor area added, over 83 per cent of all office space, and 67 per cent of all apartments. The Downtown area, as commonly asserted in the literature, dominates the pattern with 44 per cent of private office construction. However, the northern sector of the city, including the Uptown, St. Clair and Eglinton areas, accounted for nearly 40 per cent of office space added. Further, this sector also includes over 40 per cent of all apartments and 23 per cent of general commercial construction.[1] Comparable figures for land area with the exception of offices, show similar relative distributions but are slightly lower.

The scale of redevelopment construction outside the central area suggests a

---

[1] One of the more interesting examples of private investment in commercial activity in this sector of the city is the rise of the Yorkville coffee house district just north of Bloor Street between Bay and Avenue Road. Similar collections of artisan and specialty shops have appeared in many other North American cities, for example, the Old Town area of Chicago's Near North Side. Although this activity takes place without major modification to the existing structures in most cases, as a form of rehabilitation, and is thus passed over in the basic data source, the location factors involved are revealing in the context of the present analysis.

Such centers usually develop in or near the commercial core, both for general accessibility reasons and to take advantage of the considerable pedestrian and vehicle traffic attracted to other facilities in the area. Further, they tend to locate in that sector of the central area fringe which is considered most fashionable, because of the nature of their clientele, and away from lower income areas. Within this sector they usually involve areas of relatively old and depreciated residential structures which are in a transitional phase leading to demolition or non-residential use, and which require initially

TABLE 16

DISTRIBUTION OF STRUCTURAL CHANGE BY MAJOR AREAS
CITY OF TORONTO, 1952-1962

Major Area[a]	o/o of Total Floor Area Change				o/o of Total Lot Area Change			
	Total Change	Offices	Apts.	General Comm.	Total Change	Offices	Apts.	General Comm.
Downtown	16.0	44.0	–	15.3	5.5	17.3	–	3.7
Uptown	11.1	19.8	10.4	17.5	10.2	24.4	5.8	11.8
Eglinton	9.7	13.0	11.4	7.4	8.0	20.4	15.8	7.5
St. Clair	8.6	6.6	18.9	0.2	2.6	6.2	13.9	–
Parkdale	5.9	–	16.0	3.6	0.2	–	11.3	3.6
Totals	41.3	83.4	66.7	44.0	26.5	68.3	46.8	26.6

[a]Definitions of Major Areas: Census tract numbers (see Figure 10).

Downtown -- 73, 74, 75, 76.   St. Clair -- 51, 66, 67.
Uptown   -- 69, 70, 71, 72, 95.   Parkdale -- 30, 31, 32.
Eglinton -- 84, 85, 86, 87.

strong trend toward functional and spatial decentralization. In particular, the northern
sector of the city received more office and general commercial construction than the
commercial core itself. In the previous chapter similar patterns were described in the
changing spatial distribution of employment. Between 1956 and 1964 employment in the
Downtown area declined by nearly 4,000 while in the northern sector employment
increased by some 34,000 (see Table 5). This should be contrasted with an overall
decline for the city of 28,000 in the labor force. Unfortunately the data source does not
allow us to say whether this represents a functional "migration," or more likely geo-

low overhead and investment costs. Another interesting feature of these developments
is that they may in turn act as a stimulant to further residential expansion in the
immediate area, even though their clientele are drawn from a far wider range. On the
other hand, because of the low investment costs involved, such areas tend to be unstable,
both in functional composition and location, and are often susceptible to the expansion of
adjacent and more intensive land uses.

The actual impact of such activity on the condition of the aggregate standing
stock in the city is in itself quite small. However, as one form of rehabilitation of
existing structures, which often acts to generate other forms of private investment in
central areas, the secondary benefits to the physical plant may be substantial.

graphic differentials in the rate of change.[1] Nor is our theoretical knowledge sufficient to enable us to predict what these changes might be. Whichever is the case, probably a complex combination of the two, the emerging pattern of additions to the building stock reflects major adjustments in the spatial structure of the city.

The tendency for central area functions such as offices to locate at outlying nuclei has been widely documented.[2] The reasons for this change of course vary widely with the particular circumstance, yet there are certain common threads among location factors. Ullman,[3] for example, in describing the development of the Clayton area in St. Louis as an office center seven miles from downtown, suggests three primary factors. This area is located closer to the geographic heart of the city and to higher income areas than the central business district, and land values are only one-third those of the downtown area.[4] In Toronto all three of these considerations certainly apply, particularly the centrality factor. Previously it was noted that the center of metropolitan population was moving northward in the direction of Eglinton Avenue.

To these broad locational advantages must be added the specific impact of the accessibility offered by the Yonge Street subway line. Location in the northern sector offers greater proximity to the expanding suburban residential areas, particularly those of higher income, while the subway allows for direct and rapid access to the commercial core. Another factor, and one that is stressed throughout this study as a critical location variable, is the environmental attraction of areas such as Eglinton and St. Clair relative to the downtown center.

Relative Concentrations and Variations in Intensity

Many of the above patterns of variation in redevelopment between areas can be

---

[1] One recent but limited survey of the geographic origin of tenants in a major office complex over the Eglinton subway station provides some evidence as to the nature of this change. Of the new tenants only 15 per cent moved from downtown locations, compared to 22 per cent from other areas and 53 per cent from the immediate Eglinton area. A.E. LePage Ltd., "Office Space Market Survey," Toronto, March, 1964. In this case at least, actual migration is of secondary importance to the expansion of activities within the same area.

[2] For example, The Suburbanization of Administrative Offices in the San Francisco Bay Area; Business Week, "Office Center in Suburbs," March, 1954, pp. 138-139; F.P. Clark, "Office Buildings in the Suburbs," Urban Land, XIII, No. 1 (July-August, 1954), 3-10; and Urban Land Institute, "Office Decentralization: A Challenge the Central City Must Meet," Urban Land, IX, No. 2 (October, 1950), 1-3.

[3] Edward L. Ullman, "The Nature of Cities Reconsidered," Papers and Proceedings of the Regional Science Association, IX (1962), pp. 7-24.

[4] For an interesting analysis of the reasons for office decentralization in central London see J.S. Wade, "Office Decentralization: An Empirical Study," Urban Studies, III, No. 1 (February, 1966), 35-55.

summarized by illustration. In Figure 26 the relative contributions to total change of the four most prominent areas of redevelopment are plotted for each of the major categories of use. As the axes of the graph are proportions of total redevelopment lot and floor area, the position of each type of use measures both the relative magnitude and intensity of that use. The median line, joins those points which account for an equal proportion of land area and floor area, and thus separates extensive from intensive uses within each area.

The fact that the points for each area cluster is further evidence of uniformity in the spatial pattern of redevelopment. The merging of points for Parkdale and St. Clair indicates the coincidence in magnitude and character of redevelopment in these areas. The trend lines fitted visually to each cluster show the decreasing intensity patterns to be expected with increasing distance from the city center.

The trend lines can also be interpreted as measures of the response to an increasing scale of construction. For example, in the Downtown area, as expected, those uses representing the largest proportions of floor area added affect relatively less land area. There is a declining rate of land consumption with increasing floor area additions. For other areas the reverse is true. Larger proportions of floor area were recorded among those uses with increasing lower densities.

Spatial Gradients and Spatial Clustering

Given the degree of localization in redevelopment documented above, the magnitude of new construction as expected exhibits a discontinuous gradient with distance from the city center. Redevelopment drops off rapidly from its peak in the Downtown area, and then rises abruptly at major outlying foci. There is not a systematic decline with distance at least in terms of magnitude. The preceding illustration, however, showed that intensity of use in redevelopment did vary more systematically with distance from the center.

On the other hand, redevelopment does exhibit sharp variations between sectors of the city (see Figures 10 and 15). Figure 27 was compiled to illustrate the axial pattern of redevelopment in two different income sectors radiating from the city center. Clearly the level of aggregate construction activity is greater throughout the higher income sector than in the low income sector. In fact, outside the central business district there are no major points of concentrated redevelopment in the latter zone. The same pattern could be repeated for each of the other recognized sectors in the city.

Given the nature of redevelopment activity this sectoral variation is to be expected. For apartments and offices particularly, the higher income sectors provide the environmental amenities attractive for residential location, and the large property

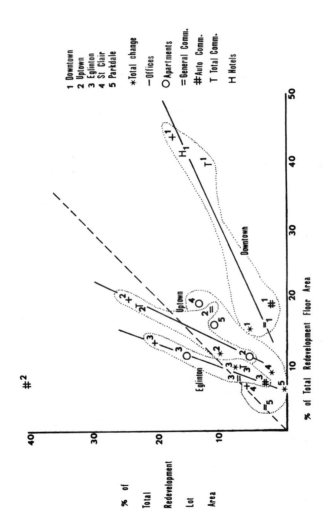

Fig. 26--Relative Concentrations of New Construction by Major Areas of the City

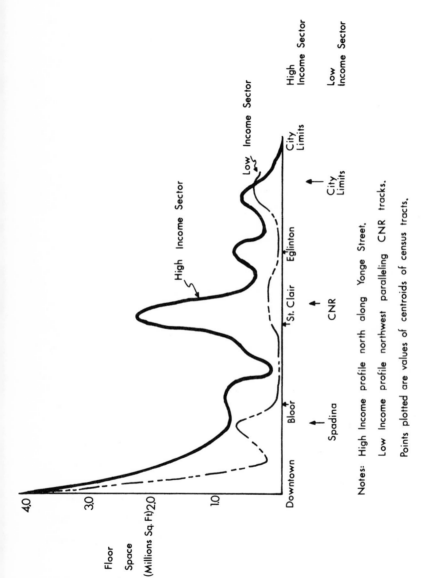

Fig. 27--Sectorial Differences in Spatial Gradients in New Construction

size and low densities which facilitate land assembly and encourage redevelopment. Moreover, as new residential construction is directed at the upper portion of the income scale, it would be expected to locate within existing areas of higher income. Such sectors tend to persist not only in peripheral expansion but in redevelopment as well. This distinction is, however, somewhat blurred in areas immediately adjacent to the central core where site location itself becomes of primary importance. In this area, new apartments, for example, appear outside although usually in close proximity to, and as an extension of the northern sector. As simple extensions, areas such as the Don (Figures 10 and 28) take advantage of the environmental attractions of areas to the immediate north.

The concept of sector variation in effect provides only a broad locational frame-work for redevelopment. The scale of redevelopment in areal extent is sufficiently small and variations within sectors large enough that isolating a sector of intensive construction is inadequate. Detailed plotting of individual properties undergoing redevelopment reveals a greater degree of clustering than is apparent from aggregate statistics for census tracts. Apartment redevelopment, for example (Figure 28), is largely confined in about a dozen specific nodes within the three general sectors previously noted. In fact, within these areas, all construction may be located along one or two streets such as on Jameson Avenue in Parkdale (between tracts 30 and 31). But, more often they are centered in an area of several blocks.

These nodes offer localized advantages over and above the more widespread advantages of the higher income sectors. There are thus two quite distinct levels of factors influencing the location of redevelopment as suggested in the preceding chapter. The sector pattern is mainly the result of environment and relative accessibility consid-erations within which specific nodes are selected on the basis of advantages limited to that site or sites.

Not only does redevelopment exhibit a discontinuous spatial distribution at one point in time, but locational concentrations may change drastically over time. For example, apartment construction in Toronto has apparently shifted in emphasis from Parkdale, Deer Park, and Yorkville areas to Eglinton Park and the Don (Table 17). Examining dates of construction for individual properties in these areas, redevelopment appears heaviest first in Parkdale, then in Deer Park and Yorkville, and in the late 1950's and early 1960's in Eglinton and finally the Don area. Thus, adding to a distinct clustering of redevelopment this table measures the dynamic spatial patterning through time.

This tendency toward spatial clustering and a chain reaction through time is to be expected given the mechanics of the real estate market operation. Economic pressure for new construction builds up in several broadly-defined areas of the city. Once the

TABLE 17

CHANGING LOCATIONAL CONCENTRATION OF NEW APARTMENT
CONSTRUCTION, CITY OF TORONTO, 1959-1964

Planning Districts	% of total apartment floor area		
	1959-63[a]	1960-64[a]	Change
Parkdale	23.4	21.2	-2.2
Deer Park	16.1	13.1	-3.0
Eglinton Park	15.6	22.0	+6.4
Yorkville	11.0	5.1	-5.9
Don	9.2	21.5	+12.3
Beaches	8.2	5.3	-2.9
Annex	5.9	4.2	-1.7

[a]Five year moving averages.

initial zoning regulations, and community resistence efforts, are overcome to permit the
entry of apartments, for example, developers will concentrate on this area or areas
immediately to take advantage of the disruption and to purchase sites and build before
land values rise appreciably. The initial restrictions may disappear in any given area
for a variety of reasons, only some of which are apparent on the surface.

Very rapidly the cost of land in the initial area will rise until there is no longer
an absolute advantage over other areas. Construction will continue until the area has
been redeveloped to its potential maximum, with potential measured in terms of physical
capacity or in costs relative to other areas. Construction activity will then migrate as
resistence is broken in another area and the sequence is repeated. It would seem then,
that within a given range of location alternatives all equally suited to apartment construction, the critical factor initiating redevelopment in one area and not another, in
other words the "triggering" mechanism, may be the ease of breakthrough in zoning and
community resistence.

Shifts in construction activity from one small area in the city to another over
short time periods is further evidence of the degree of fluidity in the locational preferences expressed by such activities as office and apartment activities, and thus the
difficulty of predicting the scale and timing of this activity at the local level. Over one
decade many of these variations average out so that a more meaningful pattern evolves
as documented in the earlier illustrations. The most important question depends on

125

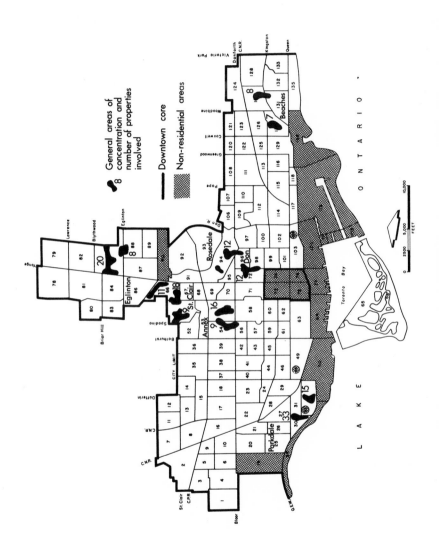

Fig. 28--Locational Concentrations in Apartment Construction

these broader trends and relates to the directions of growth rather than to localized sites.

Spatial Variations in the Rate of Redevelopment

The impact of redevelopment on the existing distribution of building space and land uses in the city varies considerably among areas much as it does among uses. In Figure 29 the amount of land area classified as undergoing redevelopment is plotted as a proportion of the total private and developed land area in each tract, and in modified concentric zones from the central core.[1] These zones provide an alternate to the size and aggregation of geographical units previously employed.

The initial impression of spatial variations in the impact or rate of change is one of distinct clustering, similar to that in previous illustrations. The Downtown area and the surrounding frame, clearly have undergone the most widespread redevelopment of existing land uses. The surprisingly extensive land areas involved in the core area frame, particularly to the north, reflects the cumulative effects of apartments and offices as well as parking and automobile related uses. Outside of the core area local- ized concentrations occur at distances from three to five miles where the rate of change is quite high. The industrial areas in the east and northwest stand out more sharply than the apartment and office clusters in the northern sector, in part because of extensive property holdings.

As these values are proportions, one might expect a somewhat systematic decline with distance from the city center. As the area of each zone expands with the square of the linear distance from the center, the impact of any given amount of new construction will be successively less significant outward. In fact this is only partly the case. The amount of land area affected by redevelopment in the study decade was taken as a proportion of the total land area in six concentric zones around the city center and summarized in graphic form on the same illustration.

The relative impact of redevelopment drops continuously through the first four zones from 25 per cent of the developed land area in the Downtown area to less than 7 per cent in the fourth zone. But then the proportions begin to increase in the outer two zones, rising to 10.8 per cent in zone six. This difference appears even though zone four contains the enormous apartment redevelopments in the St. Clair and Parkdale

---

[1] The concentric zones approximate one mile distances from the peak land value intersection at Yonge and Queen, modified to conform to clearly recognized areas of the city outlined by census tract boundaries. The major exceptions to the distance measure are the Downtown core and the adjacent tier of census tracts forming the core "frame."

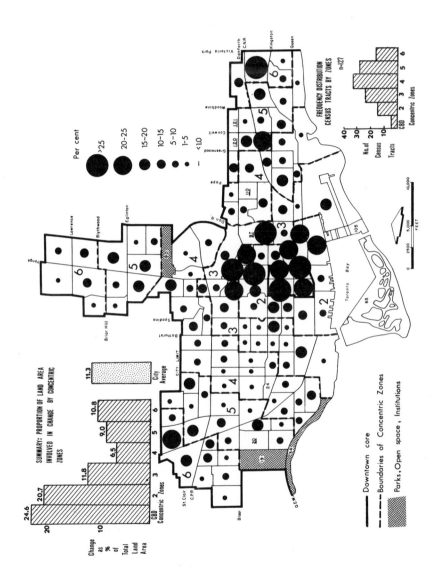

Fig. 29--Impact of Redevelopment: Rate of Change as a Proportion of Total Land Area

areas (see Figure 28). In large part, the upswing from zones four to six can be attributed to the transition from intensive to extensive users of land, with the latter primarily consisting of industrial and warehousing activities.

Relating this discussion to the theoretical framework provided in Chapter III, several points can be clarified. The generalized distribution of the rate of change substantiates the hypothesized gradient in Figure 5. The zones of limited activity within three to five miles of the city center represent the grey area effect commonly referred to in the literature where areas are by-passed in the redevelopment process. The outlying concentrations are the result of considerable conversion of vacant land and a mixing of new development and redevelopment, and reflect quite different processes of change than those of the city center. Finally, the imbalances in the spatial allocation of new construction are sufficiently strong to portray major implications for the analysis of location factors in redevelopment in the following chapter.

Pre-Redevelopment Patterns

What are the characteristics of the areas subjected to redevelopment and what types of land uses are involved? What structures and uses are being replaced in the rebuilding process in the City of Toronto, and how do these areas compare in character and density with the new redevelopment uses? What in the aggregate is the nature of the replacement process?

Table 18 provides the basis for this comparison, summarizing the land and floor area distributions for 8,300 properties in 1951 before they were subjected to redevelopment, and is the means by which the impact of redevelopment can be assessed. Table 19 then compares this distribution with the same properties in 1962 after redevelopment.[1]

The results clearly show a drastic rearrangement of both land use and structural composition in the areas affected. Non-residential uses, particularly commercial, expanded at the expense of low-density residential uses and vacant land. In fact, all but

---

[1] It is assumed that all of the 1,400 acres undergoing redevelopment were cleared and rebuilt in the decade under study. Given this assumption, the nature of change in Table 19 has not been, for example, to reduce single-family acreage by 83 acres as the difference suggests, but rather to remove 145 acres and replace it with 62 acres of new single-family construction. These need not be and likely are not the same acres. In fact, however, the entire building inventory was not removed, as preceding comments on the nature of data compilation have suggested. The assumption is made for argumentative purposes so that the allocation of land to different uses and the patterns of density that appear can be interpreted as reflecting, in their entirety, current demands for rebuilding.

TABLE 18

COMPOSITION OF AREAS AFFECTED PRIOR TO REDEVELOPMENT: TOTAL
PRIVATE LAND AND BUILDING STOCK, CITY OF TORONTO, 1951[a]

	Lot Area (Acres)	o/o	Floor Area (000's sq ft)	o/o
Single-family	145.54	10.7	1,938.4	11.5
Multi-family	80.16	5.9	2,219.6	13.1
Apartments	20.62	1.5	455.9	2.7
Other Residential	79.67	5.9	1,932.6	11.4
Total Residential	325.99	24.0	6,546.5	38.7
Office: Commercial	21.39	1.6	1,286.0	7.6
General Commercial	52.33	3.8	2,280.0	13.5
Auto Commercial	32.75	2.5	406.0	2.4
Parking	36.28	2.7	182.5	1.1
Hotel-Motel	1.57	0.1	145.3	.8
Total Commercial	144.32	10.7	4,299.8	25.4
Warehousing	194.56	14.3	2,508.0	14.8
Industrial	104.66	7.8	3,452.3	20.4
Total	299.22	22.1	5,960.3	35.2
Trans: Auto, Truck	4.00	0.3	58.5	0.4
Under Construction	4.23	0.3	46.6	0.3
Vacant	576.44[b]	42.6[b]	5.5	-
TOTAL PRIVATE	1,354.20	100.0	16,917.2	100.0

[a] Aggregates for 8,300 properties

[b] Includes both public and private areas. See footnote in text

these two categories experienced an expansion in area through redevelopment. At this
point it is not possible to say which uses expanded into areas of a different use, and
particularly into vacant land. These questions will be left to the analysis of individual
properties in the following chapter.

Within the redevelopment areas, the rate of change between categories of use
was greatest at the extremes of the density scale. Similar trends were noted previously
in comparing densities in redevelopment to those of the standing stock for the entire city.
Commercial automobile and parking uses, combined with offices and apartments showed
the largest numerical and percentage expansion.

TABLE 19

CHANGING LAND USES WITHIN REDEVELOPMENT AREAS; CITY OF TORONTO, 1951 and 1962

	Land Area Changes (acres)		
	1951 (acres)	1962 (acres)	Change (acres)
Single-family	145.54	61.77	-83.77
Multi-family	80.16	82.95	+2.79
Apartments	20.62	156.07	+135.45
Other Residential	79.67	20.92	-58.75
Total Residential	325.99	321.71	-4.28
Offices: Commercial	21.39	74.92	+53.53
General Commercial	52.33	66.36	+14.03
Auto Commercial	32.75	162.25	+129.50
Parking	36.28	186.07	+149.79
Hotel-Motel	1.57	3.47	+1.90
Total Commercial	144.32	493.07	+348.75
Warehousing	194.56	253.05	+58.49
Industrial	104.66	161.16	+56.50
Total	299.22	414.21	+114.99
Trans: Auto, Truck	4.00	4.14	+0.14
Under Construction	4.23	79.33	+75.10
Vacant	576.44	97.96	-478.48

Nature of the Replacement Process

Verification of the hypothesis that redevelopment tends toward the extremes of the density scale, does not conflict with the assertion of structural replacement as a process involving, in economic terms, a "higher and better use." Despite the expansion of extensive land uses, the overall ratio of floor to land area increased substantially. Between 1952 and 1962, total building floor area rose from 17.6 to 53.3 million square feet, and private floor area from 16.9 to 45 million. Private building space as a proportion declined, however, supporting the preceding evidence of increasing government employment and construction in central areas. Population likewise increased despite the expansion of non-residential uses, from 24,000 to 41,000, and dwellings increased from 11,000 to 23,000.[1] Residential densities as a result almost doubled, from 76 to 128 persons per net acre.

The largest increases in land area within the redeveloped area were for commercial use (Table 19). Although undoubtedly inflated by the data compilation problems noted earlier, the increase was apparent in all categories. Residential uses remained constant as a proportion of the land area, although such areas usually suffer from the expansion of other uses, because the extensive acreage of apartment redevelopment was sufficient to compensate for the sharp decline in single-family and other lower density residential uses. In total, 142 acres of low-density residential land were replaced by other uses. Warehousing and industrial uses also expanded in the rebuilding process but at a much lower rate than for commercial and apartment uses.

The most critical outcome of this comparison is in revealing the extensive conversion of vacant land in redevelopment. Over 36 per cent of the area undergoing private redevelopment was classified as vacant in 1951.[2] As an indication of the rate of change, the 576 acres of vacant land converted to a new use between 1951 and 1962, is greater than the vacant acreage in existence at the end of the period. In other words, over one-half of all vacant land in the city in 1951, in the areas included in the analysis,[3] was converted in the following decade.

In terms of location therefore, redevelopment is an extremely selective process. Vacant land does not exhibit any marked spatial differentiation among areas in the City of Toronto, but it assumes critical importance in redevelopment when aggregated from individual properties. It seems reasonable to conclude that vacant land acts as a strong positive factor in attracting and orienting redevelopment to specific locations, but over large areas the two spatial distributions do not coincide. It is not possible at this point to say whether vacant areas received new private construction, or more likely were converted to parking and public open space uses. Questions of this nature will be dealt with

---

[1] Indicating a decline in persons per dwelling from 2.3 to 1.8 and reflecting the changing composition of the housing stock. Single-family homes made up 56 per cent of the housing inventory in the redevelopment areas in 1951, but only 2 per cent of the net additions between 1952 and 1962.

[2] It is not possible in these summaries to classify and separate from the analysis public vacant land or vacant land that eventually went into public use. This will be done in the one-to-one property comparisons in the following chapter. Here we are forced to include all vacant land in the context of private redevelopment in dealing with aggregate statistics. The proportions quoted above and in Table 19 represent all vacant land as a proportion of total public and private redevelopment (36 per cent), and as a proportion of private redevelopment (42 per cent). The latter is misleading and thus is not quoted in here.

[3] Again, the analysis excludes some of the large waterfront areas of transportation, industrial, warehousing, and open space uses, which contain larger areas of vacant land.

in the analysis of site succession that follows.

The prominent role of vacant land as a location factor necessitates some reassessment of the assumptions and theoretical formulation of redevelopment as a replacement process, and of the importance attached to different levels of location determinants in the previous chapter. The most interesting feedback to the theoretical discussion of location factors is that site conditions, in this case the relative costs and ease of site preparation offered by vacant land, are considerably more important in redevelopment than previously suggested. This does not conflict with the emphasis given to environmental amenities in defining the range of locations suitable for redevelopment, but simply points to the selectivity of redevelopment within this range. *of the city. As structural replacement is not involved, in this form of*

In effect, this conversion of land classed as vacant can be interpreted as a filling-in process within the older established structural stock change, the concept of physical obsolescence as a factor in redevelopment is inappropriate. Economic obsolescence, and the succession of one use by another, becomes the primary factor generating change.

The argument as to whether construction on vacant land in central areas of cities represents a process of redevelopment or simply development, is of major importance in the following analysis. Previously, the distinction between urban development and redevelopment was drawn on the basis that redevelopment involves replacement of an existing urban use, while development refers to the conversion of land from rural to urban use in the initial wave of urban expansion.[1] The distinction is based not only on the type of conversion taking place, but also on the conditions under which it occurs. Vacant land left behind in the initial wave of urban development and contained within a built-up area represents a different use than vacant or agricultural land on the periphery of the city.[2]

---

[1] In chapter I the entire area of the City of Toronto, with the exception of some waterfront areas, was assumed to be fully developed. It was then possible at the outset to define all new construction in this area as redevelopment on the basis that it must by definition replace an urban use. This assumption is reasonable considering that less than four per cent of the city was classified as vacant in the study period, and that all open space and waste land areas were deleted in the first analytical steps. Without this assumption, the necessary editing and sorting of the data at the beginning would have been extremely complex.

[2] The actual amount of vacant land involved in redevelopment could be substantially reduced by two factors. First, it is not possible to say with the data given whether the land classified as vacant in 1951 has in fact always been vacant. It is likely that much of the area was built on at sometime in the past building history of the city and is thus clearly an urban use. Second, at any one point in time a significant proportion of the land undergoing redevelopment would appear vacant simply in the transition period between demolition and new construction.

It plays a different role in the hierarchy or urban real estate inventories in its location, value, and environmental context. The potential of such properties for new uses is dependent on the same factors, be they neighborhood amenities, costs, or accessibility advantages, as adjacent properties developed long before. Real estate resources cannot escape the environment in which they are located.

For whatever reason the land remained vacatn, it could be argued that this use, or lack of use, represented the optimal condition at that time. Thereafter, conditions gradually changed until the relative advantage of lower costs and ease of site preparation resulted in the selection of this site for redevelopment. Although structural replacement per se is not involved, clearly an existing urban use is replaced in the conversion of vacant land. For these reasons, the inclusion of vacant properties in the following analyses is considered both reasonable and necessary.

Synthesis

Redevelopment in Toronto has been shown to represent a significant but highly specialized contribution to urban growth and structural change. On the average about one per cent of the standing stock and the developed land area of the city underwent some form of redevelopment annually. Moreover, the degree of specialization by type is considerably greater in terms of the impact on the physical plant of the city than in the amount of land area affected. Fully 56 per cent of the floor area added to the standing stock was in apartments and offices, compared to only 16 per cent of the land involved.

Not only is redevelopment specialized in type, but these types are concentrated at opposite ends of the density scale of urban land uses. Offices and apartments are the most intensive uses; parking, commercial automobile, and warehousing uses are among the least intensive. Moreover, these uses are expanding at higher and lower densities respectively than comparable divisions of the aggregate stock. Yet, despite the expansion of land-extensive uses, overall densities are increasing. All of these trends in the rebuilding process are cumulative, and are acting to separate areas and uses in the city into sharply contrasting density zones.

Even within the study period these trends have accelerated. Comparing the first with the last five years of the decade, the contrast between intensive and extensive uses has grown. Compounding this increasing divergence in intensity of use is a trend toward greater specialization in type. In floor area, apartments and offices increased from 51 to 75 per cent of aggregate redevelopment between the two periods. Industry and warehousing construction, and low-density residential, on the other hand, declined substantially.

Outside of the commercial core, the intensity of new construction appears unrelated to conditions in the existing inventory and to the traditional decline with distance from the core. The rate of redevelopment exhibits a reverse "J" shape being lowest in the middle zones of the city and rising to peaks in the city center and on the periphery.

In this sense then, redevelopment represents a new pattern superimposed on the old. The new pattern, however, has been highly selective. Detailed analyses indicate a strong tendency toward clustering in small areas. This is particularly true for high-density construction, which appears concentrated at distinct nodes usually within the higher income sectors of the city. Such nodal points or areas offer a combination of location, access, and environmental advantages not present in other areas. Over time these nodes have been shown to shift in importance as the effects of zoning controls and the inherent fluidity of the real estate market mechanism alter the relative ease and costs of redevelopment in different areas.

The fact that all major categories of use are involved, in terms of the redeveloped areas as well as new construction, indicates the multiplicity of processes in redevelopment. In addition to the conversion of residential land, and the filling in of vacant properties, considerable replacement has taken place among other land users in the normal process of structural adaptation. To some extent the changes described above result from simple aging and obsolescence of structures and the necessity to replace what is presently in existence. The expansion of certain uses however, also expresses changes in the demand for land at different locations, resulting in land use succession and the replacement of less by more intensive uses. If aging itself was the dominant process of change then more consistent rates of replacement among land use types might be expected. If economic replacement was dominant on the other hand, redevelopment would follow directly from intensity of use, and would be confined to fewer categories than appear in these statistics. Redevelopment is thus a function of some composite form of these factors.

CHAPTER VII

AREA AND SITE CORRELATES OF STRUCTURAL CHANGE

Introduction

The factors which underlie the spatial patterns and relationships in redevelopment documented in the preceding chapter, are obviously complex. Even in theoretical terms, it is difficult to isolate these factors from other processes generating change in the city. Very generally, the apparent relationships have been discussed but not empirically tested. If spatial variations in redevelopment can be explained, as is commonly asserted, by the factors hypothesized in Chapter V, then it should be possible to account for these patterns of activity statistically given appropriate empirical measures.[1]

This chapter has three analytical objectives. First, to select characteristics for areas which approximate each set of theoretical location factors discussed in Chapter V. Second, to assess the degree of spatial association between these hypothesized determinants and the volume and rate of redevelopment summarized in Chapter VI. The approach is based on the formulation of a model of redevelopment as a process of spatial change that can be tested using multiple regression techniques. The primary purpose is to sort out the relative effects of different location factors and test the initial hypotheses, rather than to devise a strong redevelopment model. These objectives need not be independent, of course, and the latter may follow logically from a systematic treatment of the former. The third section of the chapter deals with the replacement process in individual properties. Each property is examined before and after redevelopment to establish the nature of land use succession that results. This provides the means of relating the analysis of aggregate redevelopment activity between areas to the concise impact of new construction on the spatial structure of the city within areas.

As the mix of location determinants in land use change is quite different for each

---

[1] We cannot expect, of course, to establish new theories or to disprove existing theories on the basis of a single case study, regardless of the detail or exactness of the data. What can be done here is to account for the spatial pattern of change in Toronto, and to make qualified judgments concerning the theoretical implications of the results, in the light of the discussion in the first three chapters.

category of use, and because the market mechanisms for each operate somewhat independently, a model incorporating aggregate redevelopment activity would be both cumbersome and confusing. In this study, time and space limitations necessitated the selection of two categories, office and residential redevelopment, for the detailed regression analysis. Both offer several advantages for purposes of analysis,[1] and as they account for some 70 per cent of all redevelopment activity in Toronto, the limitation is not severe.

The Area Redevelopment Model

The Rationale

The framework and techniques employed in this analysis in part derive from land development studies. In most of these studies, given units of growth are allocated to subareas of the city on the basis of pre-selected location factors. The units of growth or development usually consist of population and employment predictions translated into urban land requirements. However, the problems of allocating this growth to developed areas of central cities, and more importantly, of isolating the processes of change involved, have been generally ignored.[2] Despite the complexity of accounting for redevelopment in comparison to suburban development, an attempt to formulate a systematic approach in this direction would represent a valuable addition to existing theory.

What location factors are used in these development models, and how useful is the analytical framework for predicting the location of private redevelopment? F. Stuart Chapin, who has experimented at considerable length with residential forecasting models, refers to the replacement process in developed areas as follows:

> " . . . the model is adaptable to take into account the succession of one use by another . . . it can be done by introducing into each interative period redevelopment units (by specific use) for distribution among developed cells.[3]

---

[1]In both cases the analysis is simplified by more rigorous land use definitions, greater homogeneity of product throughout the urban area, and generally more meaningful comparisons between land area and building space.

[2]Three of the most common criticisms of land development models are: that they are relatively coarse grain, that they have major operational shortcomings, and that changes in the existing stock of buildings are not included. See, for example, Frederick Hayes, "Operations Research: A Statement of Requirements," Part I, Analytic Techniques in Urban Planning and Renewal, Planning 1964 (Chicago: American Society of Planning Officials, 1965).

[3]F. Stuart Chapin, Jr., and S.F. Weiss, Factors Influencing Land Development (Chapel Hill: University of North Carolina, 1962), p. 41. See also, T.G. Donnelly, F. Stuart Chapin, Jr., and S.F. Weiss, A Probabilistic Model for Residential Growth (Chapel Hill: University of North Carolina, 1964); F. Stuart Chapin, Jr., and S.F. Weiss,

Chapin contends that the allocation of such units could be carried out according to the degree of blight in each cell. But here the suggestions end. The degree of blight is obviously an important consideration, but only as a negative factor excluding redevelopment from selective areas.

For our purposes, Chapin's studies point to the type of variables which might be useful in predicting the pattern of redevelopment activity. In the analysis of land in urban use in Winston-Salem and Greensboro,[1] the most important variables were found to be accessibility to highways, work places, and services, and the availability of sewerage and vacant land. For dwelling density, the main predictors were accessibility, assessed value of land, sewer availability, and vacant land. However, the factors most likely to differentiate the relative attractiveness of central locations for new growth, such as the degree of blight and residential amenities, were dropped. Moreover, with the exclusion of collinear variables the power of both models dropped substantially.[2]

Lakshmanan's treatment of population and employment change is particularly relevant here as an example of this approach because it separates central area and suburban growth. In fact, he found it necessary to formulate distinct models for the two areas precisely because of the different processes at work, as discussed here in the three introductory chapters. For central areas, Lakshmanan found population growth to be a function of available land (AL), the proportion of housing stock constructed in the previous decade (PH), the proportion of population non-white (NW), and the area prestige level (PRG).[3] The coefficient of determination ($R^2 = 0.88$), suggests that the model is successful.

Yet problems arise in the application of this model to the redevelopment case in

---

Some Input Refinements for a Residential Model (Chapel Hill: University of North Carolina, July, 1965); F. Stuart Chapin, Jr., "A Model for Simulating Residential Development," Journal of the American Institute of Planners, XXXI, No. 2 (May, 1965), 120-125. In the latest papers, which broaden the conceptual base by inclusion of more behavioral variables, an attempt is made to integrate the role of housing turnover and changes in the developed areas to those in suburban areas. However, as the results are preliminary, a full assessment of this attempt must wait.

[1]Chapin and Weiss, Factors in Land Development, pp. 12-18.

[2]The coefficients of determination for land in urban use and dwelling density dropped to .449 and .314 in Winston-Salem, and to .605 and .448 in Greensboro.

[3]T.R. Lakshmanan, "An Approach to the Analysis of Intraurban Location Applied to the Baltimore Region," Economic Geography, IV, No. 4 (October, 1964), 348-370. The resulting equation is as follows:

Δ Population (P_C) = 36 AL + 100.6 PH - 108 NW - 5.9 PRG + 12400 (Central city)

partial corr. coeff. (P_C)	AL = 0.89	NW = -0.40	d = .001
	PH = 0.48	PRG = -0.53	$R^2 = 0.88$
			n = 29

general and to the Toronto situation in particular. Neighborhood population change, referring back to Chapter III, may result from residential redevelopment, building conversion, or non-residential succession, which represent three quite different processes not logically incorporated into the regression hypotheses. Limitations are also present in the types of variables selected. In most central cities, vacant land is at a premium, and it exhibits only minor spatial variability between areas. As a factor in redevelopment location we would expect vacant land to appear as a critical variable only at the level of individual sites. In Toronto, the vacant land variable appears insignificant between areas and the proportion non-white factor is irrelevant. This leaves only the prestige variable, which is simply income, and the direction of previous structural growth, and thus a fairly weak model for our purposes.

The Area Model[1]

In theory, each subarea within a city has a potential to attract new building investment dependent on its position and character relative to all other areas. This potential is determined by the interplay of a host of factors, and the resulting pattern of new construction reflects the cumulative effects of varying combinations of these factors.

The regression hypothesis has already been established in Chapter V. The allocation of private redevelopment to individual subareas within the city is hypothesized to be a function of the character and distribution of the existing stock of buildings, the physical and social amenities of the area, the difficulty of land assembly, and relative accessibility to the center of metropolitan population, the city center, and to mass transit facilities.

The Variables

In selecting variables to approximate the above sets of factors, the purpose is not to find concomitant measures that correlate with structural change, such as population change or land value change, but rather to describe and measure the potential for

---

[1]For a description of the characteristics and rationale of models in geography, see the discussion and references in Peter Haggett, Locational Analysis in Human Geography (London: Edward Arnold, Ltd., 1965), pp. 19-23. Also, the review article by Ira S. Lowry, "A Short Course in Model Design," Journal of the American Institute of Planners, XXXI, No. 2 (May, 1965), 158-165; and Brian J.L. Berry, "Mathematical Models in Geography", paper presented at the annual meetings of the American Sociological Association, Chicago, August 29-31, 1965.

change from conditions apparent before the change occurred.[1] Only in this way will the model be truly predictive.

The first set of independent variables describes the character and distribution of the existing structures and land uses in the city in 1951. As no drastic revision in the existing urban structure within a decade is apparent, and because zoning and propinquity among similar uses tend to channel the location of new construction, the spatial pattern of redevelopment should be strongly determined by this structure. Obviously, industrial redevelopment, for example, will largely occur in existing industrial areas. However, simple measures of the existing structure do not assess the relative attractiveness of specific locations within these areas for new investment. To measure this aspect, quality variables relating to the immediate physical environment must be added. These include the relative age and condition of buildings, the presence of local parks, and the degree of conflicting or mixed uses.[2]

In renewal and redevelopment research, however, these quality considerations are usually described as negative factors excluding redevelopment from certain areas, rather than attracting it to others. This is particularly true of office and apartment redevelopment. However, a model designed to predict where growth will not or did not occur is conceptually less meaningful than one based on where growth did occur. In an attempt to gauge the positive attractiveness of an area, income and rent are included as proxies for socio-economic status.

Accessibility measures are central to any explanatory framework for the location of urban land uses, activities, or populations. Accessibility and centrality are evaluated in the regression analysis by two functions: distance from the peak land value intersection and from the center of metropolitan population, in both linear and logarithmic units.[3] A third measure, proximity to the Yonge Street subway, is included as a binary

---

[1]In some land development studies, the variables selected as location determinants are often not based on a hypothesized cause and effect relationship. Rather, the variables are the simplest and most flexible, in the sense of being subject to control, that are available. They are selected because they work, meaning they enable "explanation" of the dependent variable, even without an a priori basis for understanding the relationship.

[2]There are as well a variety of physical attributes which influence the attractiveness of particular sites for redevelopment, such as slope, scenic qualities, and so on. Here the analysis is explicitly concerned with factors which vary over area and which influence the potential of broad areas rather than sites.

[3]Both distances are measured in standard units from 1:25,000 topographic sheets. The former is measured directly from the peak land value intersection at Yonge and Queen Streets to the centroid of each census tract. Alternative measures to linear distance were investigated, but produced essentially the same results.

variable in recognition of the strategic and localized advantages of this facility.

The final set of empirical measures, average lot size, and proportion of vacant land, are included to test the hypothesis that <u>land availability and ease of assembly</u> are principal location factors in redevelopment. Lot size is the critical variable here because it offers greater spatial variability between areas, yet more uniformity within local areas. Vacant land tends to be more localized, often relevant only to a single site. Also, in reflecting the difficulty of land assembly as well as social environment, lot size may isolate former high-income areas which have since lost the positive attraction of social environment but still retain some physical or structural advantages for redevelopment.

The dependent variables: redevelopment totals by census tract

SFLA	=	Single-family lot area, in acres
SFFA	=	Single-family floor area, in 100's square feet
MFLA	=	Multi-family lot area
MFFA	=	Multi-family floor area
ATLA	=	Apartment lot area
ATFA	=	Apartment floor area
TRLA	=	Total residential lot area
TRFA	=	Total residential floor area
RARL	=	Rate of apartment redevelopment, lot area
RTRL	=	Rate of total residential redevelopment, lot area
OFLA	=	Commercial office lot area
OFFA	=	Commercial office floor area

The independent variables:

Existing structure: Transformations

NRA	=	Net residential acreage (1956	–
PRU	=	Per cent land in residential use (1956)	–
APTS	=	Apartment units (1951)	Sq. root
PAPT	=	Per cent apartment units (1951)	–
SFAM	=	Single-family units (1951)	Sq. root

Environment: Physical

AGE	=	Dwellings constructed before 1920	–
PAGE	=	Per cent dwellings constructed before 1920	–
LIA	=	Local industrial areas in acres	Log 10
PIU	=	Per cent of land in industrial use	Log 10
LPA	=	Local parkland in acres	Log 10
PLP	=	Per cent of area in local parkland	Log 10
DNP	=	Dwellings in need of major repair	–
PDNP	=	Per cent dwellings in need of major repair	–

Environment: Socio-economic

MINC	=	Median income (1951)	Log 10
MRT	=	Median rent (1951)	–
DENS	=	Net population density (1956)	–

Accessibility:

DIST	=	Distance from peak land value intersection	–
DCP	=	Distance from center of metropolitan population	–

Accessibility:

SUB   =   Proximity to subway (binary: 1 adjacent,   –

                              0 otherwise)

EMP   =   Employment (1956)   Log 10

ED   =   Employment density (1956)   Log 10

Land availability; Land fragmentation:

VAC   =   Vacant acres (1956   Log 10

PVAC =   Per cent of area vacant (1956)   Log 10

LOTS =   Average lot size in square feet (single

                          family residential)   Sq. root

Correlates of Structural Change

In large part, the independent variables behave as expected. For example, median income in 1951 correlates +.591 with distance from the city center, +.573 with average lot size, -.616 with population density, and -.700 with employment density. In most cases the correlations are likely reduced by the use of data for the city area only rather than the metropolitan area, nevertheless, they are clearly significant.[1]

Most of the hypothesized relationships of preceding chapters are evident in the correlation matrix. The correlations between the predictor variables and the measures of redevelopment are in the appropriate direction, with some exceptions, but are generally low. For apartment lot area all correlations are below .500 and most are below .300 (Table 20). The highest correlates are with existing apartments units in 1951, and net residential acreage. The former simply says that new construction follows existing concentrations of use and directions of growth. The second is purely a size factor for the areal unit. Neither is discretionary in the sense of differentiating the attractiveness of areas for redevelopment. Among the hypothesized location factors, lot size shows a correlation of +.392 with redevelopment, proximity to subway +.331, age of dwellings -.284, and median rent +.256.[2] Despite the coincidence of apartment and office redevelopment with the higher income sectors of the city, the direct correlation

---

[1] Another interesting variation in the results is that it does not seem to make a significant difference whether the central business district is included or not. Rather than complicating the results, inclusion of the CBD in fact generally improved the statistical relationships. Following the initial tests, it was decided to include the four census tracts in the commercial core in most of the following analyses.

[2] The correlation of percentage population change between 1951 and 1961 with apartment lot area (+.392 and floor area (+.407) is revealing in the context of the general problem formulation. Although we do not make use of this measure as a predictor of new construction, it does reveal the extent to which residential redevelopment expresses and incorporates the processes of population change affecting central city areas.

SIMPLE CORRELATIONS BETWEEN INDEPENDENT VARIABLES
AND APARTMENT AND OFFICE REDEVELOPMENT

Independent Variables[a]	Apartments		Offices	
	Lot Area	Floor Area	Lot Area	Floor Area
1 Med Income 51	0.193	0.160	-0.112	-0.162
2 Singl Fam 51	0.219	0.120	-0.023	-0.145
3 Apt Units 51	0.397	0.519	0.205	0.027
4 Net Pop Dens	-0.242	-0.156	0.037	-0.110
5 Net Res Acre	0.424	0.305	-0.054	-0.196
6 Total Acres	0.219	0.130	-0.017	-0.062
7 Vacant Acres	-0.039	-0.042	-0.045	-0.033
8 Med Rent 51	0.256	0.268	0.017	-0.276
9 Du Need Rep	-0.085	-0.066	0.046	0.044
10 Cons Bef 1920	0.027	0.048	-0.175	-0.222
11 Distance CBD	0.061	-0.002	-0.232	-0.310
12 Near Subway	0.330	0.319	0.642	0.564
13 Population 51	0.155	0.148	-0.082	-0.255
14 Population 61	0.283	0.277	-0.137	-0.274
15 Employment 56	-0.086	-0.068	0.378	0.743
16 Ave Lot Size	0.391	0.348	-0.096	-0.240
17 Local Parkld	0.015	-0.041	-0.010	-0.078
18 Local Indust	-0.172	-0.175	0.208	0.442
19 Dist Popu Cen	-0.090	-0.145	-0.216	-0.122
20 Dwellings 51	0.275	0.255	-0.012	-0.210
21 Perc Apts 51	0.227	0.358	0.224	0.042
22 Perc Need Re	-0.094	-0.081	0.105	0.122
23 Perc Bef 1920	-0.283	-0.270	-0.142	-0.203
24 Perc Res Use	0.159	0.135	-0.251	-0.362
25 Perc Vacant	-0.045	-0.039	-0.033	-0.022
26 Perc Palklnd	-0.012	-0.066	-0.054	-0.087
27 Perc Ind Use	-0.173	-0.172	0.189	0.403
28 Perc Pop 51 61	0.392	0.406	-0.263	-0.344
29 Employ Dens	-0.104	-0.081	0.443	0.854

N = 125   Null error 0.090   Data are transformed

[a]See previous list of independent variables for transformations and name designations.

with median income by census tract is only +.194 for apartments. The correlations between apartment lot and floor area and the distribution of vacant land, distance from the city center, proportion of deteriorated structures, local parkland, and employment density, are statistically insignificant.

The importance of previous directions of growth in orienting redevelopment patterns in the study period is difficult to assess. Existing apartment construction is the only measure of this nature employed, and even it is indirect. Lakshmanan found this to be of considerable value as a predictor of population change in central areas. Here, it is only possible to say that the current emphasis in apartment location in the city has a strong basis in growth in preceding decades.

The absence of a strong correlation between vacant land and redevelopment does not mean that redevelopment occurs entirely on developed properties. In the preceding chapter it was shown that over one-third of the area affected was vacant at the beginning of the period. When considered in the aggregate, however, the distribution of vacant land does not seem to influence the distribution of redevelopment activity. Moreover, vacant land shows no strong relationship with distance from the city center or with other accessibility measures.[1] Redevelopment is a very selective process in the sites affected, and the presence of vacant land must act basically to alter the selection within broad areas but not between areas.

The negative correlation between redevelopment and age of structures suggests that redevelopment is not primarily a function of age and deterioration. At least in the aggregate case, the older structural stock of Toronto is not being removed in the private redevelopment process. This does not suggest that few older buildings are being replaced, as in fact they are, but rather that areas with increasingly older stock do not receive larger proportions of new construction. Age of structure in this case serves both as a measure of the cost of replacement, in terms of building acquisition and original investment lost, as well as the physical attractiveness of the area.

For office redevelopment, proximity to subway and existing employment concentrations exhibit the closest degree of association. However, the hypothesized relationships of offices with population density, median income, vacant land, and lot size, do not appear. As expected, the correlation with distance from the city center is higher than that for apartments, and because of the expanding office center at the subway terminus on Eglinton Avenue, there is a weak but significant correlation with distance from the

---

[1] For the City of Toronto as a whole, vacant land is limited outside of the waterfront area, and exhibits a relatively uniform distribution between census tracts. The simple correlation between vacant land and total acreage is +.77 over 125 tracts, and the correlation between proportion of vacant land and distance from the city center is -.197 (all variables are logarithmic transformations).

center of metropolitan population which falls in that area. There is also weak correlation with areas of declining population and mixed industrial use, in large part deriving from the expansion of offices into the fringe area adjacent to the central core.

The neutral effect of many of the variables commonly ascribed importance in suburban land development studies, points to the complexity of central area redevelopment and the locational freedom of expanding urban activities.[1] Even so, the cumulative interaction of these factors may still serve to account for a significant proportion of the spatial variability of redevelopment activity. To test this hypothesis we turn to the multiple regression analyses.

The Regression Equations

In light of the weak correlations, the regression equations proved only moderately successful. The highest coefficients of determination (R^2),[2] are .543 and .495 for single and multi-family residential land area, respectively, representing about 54 and 50 per cent of the aggregate variability between census tracts. For apartment and office redevelopment, the largest categories, the regression models account for 39 and 40 per cent of the spatial variation in land area and 38 and 31 per cent of the variation in floor area respectively. The R^2 for the rate of apartment and residential redevelopment, that is redevelopment lot area as a proportion of net residential acreage, are slightly lower at .344 and .304.

Revealing differences appear in comparing the equations for total volume and the rate of apartment construction. Spatial variations in the volume of apartment redevelopment, both lot (ATLA) and floor (ATFA) area (Equations 5 and 6), appear as a function of existing acreage (NRA), the proportion of apartments in the area before change (PAPT), proximity to the subway (SUB), and distance from the center of population (DPC). For the rate of redevelopment (Equations 7 and 8), however, the environmental quality factors clearly become more important, although there is a drop in the power of the models. The rate of apartment redevelopment (RAR) emerges as a function of the percentage of existing apartment units (PAPT), age of structure (AGE), average lot size (LOTS), and proximity to subway (SUB). By eliminating the size consideration, the really critical location factors appear as hypothesized. Redevelopment is more wide-

---

[1] In part the locational freedom of new construction documented here is the result of the relatively large areas of the City of Toronto which are to some extent attractive for redevelopment (see the general discussion of special considerations in chapter IV).

[2] The coefficient of determination is the square of the multiple correlation coefficient and can be interpreted as a measure of the proportion of the total statistical variance of the dependent variable that is accounted for by the variance of the set of independent variables.

spread in areas of existing apartment units and larger lot sizes, and in areas of more recent construction. Considering all residential activity together (TRLA and TRFA), to reduce the effects on the regression line of a large number of zero values for apartment redevelopment,[1] the power of the model increases somewhat with the measure of pro-portion apartments replaced by the mixed land use variable (PIU).

The Regression equations:

$$\text{Log SFLA} = \underset{(.0297)}{.135 \text{ NRA}} + \underset{(.0034)}{.012 \text{ DIST}} - \underset{(.1639)}{.402 \text{ ED}} + \underset{(.0559)}{.132 \text{ PLU}} - 1.880 \quad (1)$$
$$(R = .737 \quad R^2 = .543)$$

$$\text{Log SFFA} = \underset{(.0673)}{.290 \text{ NRA}} + \underset{(.0087)}{.028 \text{ DIST}} + \underset{(.1268)}{.402 \text{ PIU}} - \underset{(.3715)}{.710 \text{ ED}} - 1.640 \quad (2)$$
$$(R = .704 \quad R^2 = .495)$$

Total residential lot and floor area:

$$\text{Log TRLA} = \underset{(.0354)}{.160 \text{ NRA}} + \underset{(.0634)}{.181 \text{ LIA}} + \underset{(.0062)}{.013 \text{ LOTS}} - \underset{(.0025)}{.005 \text{ AGE}} - 1.773 \quad (3)$$
$$(R = .726 \quad R^2 = .527$$

$$\text{Log TRFA} = \underset{(.2929)}{.911 \text{ APTS}} - \underset{(.0883)}{.254 \text{ AGE}} + \underset{(.2165)}{.484 \text{ LOTS}} + \underset{(3.087)}{6.23 \text{ SUB}} - 6.916 \quad (4)$$
$$(R = .645 \quad R^2 = .416)$$

Apartment lot and floor area:

$$\text{Log ATLA} = \underset{(.0431)}{.196 \text{ NRA}} + \underset{(.0044)}{.015 \text{ PAPT}} + \underset{(.1279)}{.413 \text{ SUB}} + \underset{(.0045)}{.010 \text{ DPC}} - 2.657 \quad (5)$$
$$(R = .623 \quad R^2 = .388)$$

$$\text{Log ATFA} = \underset{(.1006)}{.392 \text{ NRA}} + \underset{(.0102)}{.036 \text{ PAPT}} + \underset{(.2987)}{0.925 \text{ SUB}} + \underset{(.0100)}{.020 \text{ DPC}} - 2.983 \quad (6)$$
$$(R = .598 \quad R^2 = .357$$

Rate of Apartment Redevelopment, lot area:

$$\text{Log RAR} = \underset{(.0015)}{.004 \text{ PAPT}} - \underset{(.0013)}{.003 \text{ AGE}} + \underset{(.0027)}{.006 \text{ LOTS}} + \underset{(.0429)}{.086 \text{ SUB}} - 2.080 \quad (7)$$
$$(R = .552 \quad R^2 = .304)$$

Rate of Total Residential Redevelopment, lot area:

$$\text{Log RTRR} = \underset{(.0012)}{-.004 \text{ AGE}} + \underset{(.0028)}{.008 \text{ LOTS}} + \underset{(.0300)}{.066 \text{ PIU}} - 1.768 \quad (8)$$
$$(R = .636 \quad R^2 = .344)$$

Office lot and floor area:

$$\text{Log OFLA} = \underset{(.1000)}{.538 \text{ SUB}} + \underset{(.1868)}{.754 \text{ EMP}} + \underset{(.0318)}{.074 \text{ NRA}} + \underset{(.4753)}{1.085 \text{ PVAC}} - 3.219 \quad (9)$$
$$(R = .636 \quad R^2 = .404)$$

$$\text{Log OFFA} = \underset{(.2682)}{1.004 \text{ SUB}} + \underset{(.5008)}{1.750 \text{ EMP}} + \underset{(1.2745)}{3.43 \text{ PVAC}} + \underset{(.0853)}{.207 \text{ NRA}} - 4.559 \quad (10)$$
$$(R = .558 \quad R^2 = .311)$$

---

[1] New apartment construction occurred in less than 35 per cent of the census tracts of the city.

Multi-family lot and floor area:

$$\text{Log MFLA} = \quad .018 \text{ DIST} + .151 \text{ PIU} - 2.306 \tag{11}$$
$$\quad\quad\quad\quad (.0053) \quad\quad (.0641)$$
$$\quad\quad\quad\quad (R = .668 \quad R^2 = .448)$$

$$\text{Log MFFA} = \quad .029 \text{ DIST} + .262 \text{ PIU} - 2.404 \tag{12}$$
$$\quad\quad\quad\quad (.0124) \quad\quad (.1503)$$
$$\quad\quad\quad\quad (R = .599 \quad R^2 = .359)$$

As might be expected from the distinct spatial patterns noted in the previous chapter, the equations for single-family and multi-family construction differ markedly from the other residential models. For multi-family construction (MFLA and MFFA, Equations 11 and 12), only two significant independent variables appear, distance from city center (DIST) and mixed land use (PIU), with R^2's of .446 for lot area and .358 for floor area. The distance variable also appears in the single-family equations (SFLA and SFFA, Equations 1 and 2), following the size measure of net residential acreage. In the single-family case, there is a strong inverse relationship with employment concentration and a direct correlation with the degree of mixed use. The latter correlation is in conflict with our initial hypotheses, but can be explained largely in terms of census tract boundaries which encompass quite distinct industrial and residential areas, thus distorting the over-all means.

The fact that distance is not included as a variable in any equations other than for low-density residential is indicative of the decentralization of urban redevelopment.[1] It appears in these equations simply because the extent of single and multi-family construction is very limited and is confined to the outer margins of the city area. For the same reasons, distance from the city center appears as a dominant factor in attempts to predict suburban development patterns.

Despite the coincidence of office construction outside the central core with areas of higher income, variables measuring environmental amenities do not appear as significant predictors in the regression equations. For office redevelopment (OFLA and OFFA) the important location predictors in the hypothesized set are proximity to subway (SUB), employment concentrations (EMP), the size dimension (NRA), and the percentage of vacant land (PVAC). The first three variables essentially measure the importance of existing centers and directions of growth in employment. The latter is one of the few cases in which vacant land appears, and here it is of minor importance. The power of the models, with R^2's of .404 for lot area and .311 for floor area, are relatively low but in the same range as those for apartment redevelopment.

---

[1] In part, the absence of a correlation between redevelopment and distance from the peak land value intersection results from the inadequacies of the land use classifications. Variations in intensity of use, and thus in the range of possible locations, is enormous within each category of use.

This level of statistical power leaves some doubt as to the validity of Ullman's location factors (see Chapter VI) in explaining the office concentration in the Clayton area of St. Louis, at least in Toronto and with the information available here. One problem with Ullman's approach, as well as the analysis in this study, is that although the factors included represent reasonably hypotheses according to the available literature, there are outlying areas with essentially the same advantages that have not witnessed office construction.

The importance of the subway as a variable in the location of redevelopment, particularly of apartments and offices, is clearly evident. The northward expansion of apartment and office construction in the city, documented in the previous chapter, closely follows the route of the Yonge Street subway. In the office regression analysis (Equations 9 and 10), proximity to the subway is by far the most important predictor of redevelopment.[1] However, it is not possible to attribute a specific proportion of this expansion to the accessibility advantages offered by the subway. The northern sector of the city would likely be the most attractive for redevelopment even without the subway because of its environmental character.[2] In fact, extensive redevelopment was underway in this sector before 1953. Thus, the basis for growth existed, and the subway then acted as a major stimulant.

Patterns of Variation

Residuals from the regression analysis exhibit low systematic patterns of variability relating to social and political constraints and to the highly localized distribution of redevelopment. In terms of apartment floor area (Figure 30), four areas of major over-prediction appear, three outlying tracts and the Rosedale area immediately to the north of

---

[1] For an interesting discussion of the effects of mass transit facilities see E. H. Spengler, Land Values in New York in Relation to Transit Facilities (New York: Columbia University Press, 1930), p. 126.

[2] The recently completed (1966) east-west subway along Bloor-Danforth should provide an interesting comparative test of this relationship. This route passes through quite different socio-economic areas of the city and does not follow a clearly defined and pre-existing direction of growth. The implication from the above discussion is that if the hypothesized associations hold, the stimulus provided by this new facility to new investment will be less than in the northern sector, and it will differ in both pattern and composition. As the location of this route cuts across income and land use sectors of the city, we might expect new construction to occur largely in areas where higher income sectors are traversed. Announced development proposals suggest that this hypothesis is being realized. Consideration should also be given to the possible effects of anticipation of the construction of the Bloor Street subway on the level of investment along the Yonge subway. As the basic data source terminates at the end of 1962, four years before completion of the Bloor route, the effect is unlikely to be substantial. After 1965, however, given a finite demand and construction capacity, the influence of this line appears to have been considerable.

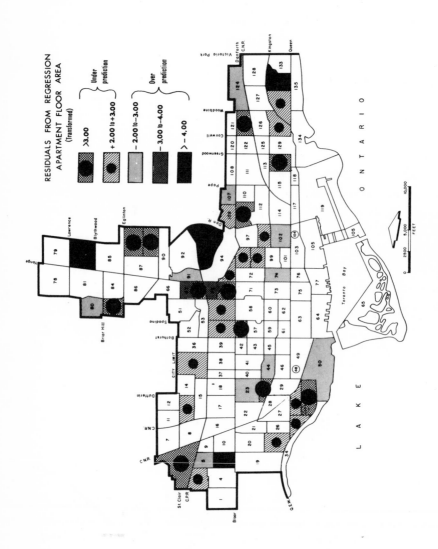

Fig. 30--Patterns of Regression Residuals: Apartment Floor Area Analysis

the downtown core. Not only is the outlying location of these areas revealing, they also share certain common social and environmental characteristics. All four areas are medium to upper income, and offer the social context that is attractive to apartment redevelopment. In part because of such characteristics, and the political power they represent, these areas have been successful in resisting the pressures for high-density construction. Rosedale is a particularly good example, but the Beaches area (Tract 132), Keele Street (Tract 6), and north Yonge (Trace 82), follow similar patterns. Present indications are that all four areas will likely receive new apartment construction in the relatively near future.[1]

At the other end of the scale, considerable under-prediction occurs in widely scattered areas, as the apparent result of two quite different factors. First, the inability of the model to adequately capture the agglomeration effect in new construction is evident in the high positive residuals in areas of extensive redevelopment, such as Parkdale and the area north of Bloor Street. For the same reason, outlying concentrations of apartment construction, particularly in the east and north sectors, appear as high positive residuals. In the northern sector this is partly due to the fact that such areas lie away from the subway line. Second, some tracts in the extreme east and west of the city embrace both industrial and residential uses, although not in the sense of local mixed use, and therefore, despite local residential amenities, they rank low in the ranking of attractiveness for census tracts. This is true for example, of the Junction area (Tract 2) and portions of the C.N.R. Kingston Road area (Tracts 125 and 127).

For the office regression analysis, the spatial pattern of residuals, although not included here, indicates that much the same considerations are applicable, particularly the agglomeration effect. In this case the extreme concentrations in the northern sector of the city along the subway route appear as large residuals throughout. For much of the rest of the city, where office construction has been relatively scarce, extensive over-prediction occurs. The fact that this situation exists despite the inclusion of the subway variable is further indicative of the degree of localization in office redevelopment.

Evaluation of the Model

As means of assessing more fully what factors are associated with the spatial pattern of urban redevelopment, the above research design has been quite useful. Emphasis has been given to factors which measure the relative potential of areas in the city for apartment and office redevelopment. However, the ability to predict the resulting location

---

[1]City of Toronto Planning Board, Planning and Development News, Information Bulletin No. 28, January-February, 1966.

of redevelopment given these factors in an operational regression formulation, was only moderately successful.

Over and above the obvious complexity of factors, it is difficult to adequately incorporate the different levels at which factors influencing the location of redevelopment seem to operate. Existing concepts at least as evidenced in the literature, are not sufficiently pointed to precisely isolate critical variables in the redevelopment process.

A second type of error derives from the spatial behavior of private redevelopment itself. There is sufficient correlation between the hypothesized variables, such as accessibility, lot size, and income, and the distribution of redevelopment, to warrant the conclusion that redevelopment is greater in areas with above average measures on these factors. However, the regression equations are unable to capture the extreme degree of localization and concentration documented in the preceding chapter.[1] The cumulative effects of agglomeration in redevelopment are not replicated in any of the predictor variables. All variables reflect essentially continuous spatial distributions, while redevelopment is markedly discontinuous. The missing value in the equations is the triggering mechanism which initiates redevelopment in some areas and not in others with approximately equal potential.

A third possible source of residual variance includes institutional constraints on redevelopment. To some extent, the importance of the "triggering" mechanism derives from such conditions. In this study, the effects of municipal policy and neighborhood resistance were evaluated in the general discussion in Chapter VI, but were not incorporated in the regression analysis. They were not tested here because of the emphasis on more general patterns of change which are less subject to direct municipal control than single properties or small areas, and because of the difficulty of measuring such effects meaningfully. Most such attempts have been unsuccessful. Czamanski, for example, employed measures of the type of ownership, existing zoning, anticipated zoning, anticipated zoning change, and potential change in use, as predictors of changes in land values for individual lots.[2] The first three at least are critical factors in redevelopment. However, all of the above were determined subjectively, and in the analysis all proved to be statistically insignificant. The example is relevant here because

---

[1] Further errors appear because of the inclusion of floor area statistics. Not only are the equations trying to predict a discrete spatial distribution with continuous variables, but unit variables are used to predict volume. The effect of the latter is apparent in that in each case the power of the regression model is lower for floor area (TRFA: $R^2 = .414$), than for lot area (TRLA: $R^2 = .505$).

[2] Stanislaw Czamanski, "Effects of Public Investments on Urban Land Values," Journal of the American Institute of Planners, XXXII, No. 4 (July, 1966), 204-216. The variables which did prove to be significant were age of structure, lot size, and accessibility, all of which are included in this analysis.

theoretically the potential for an increase in land values in central areas would in fact reflect redevelopment potential.

Also, the results inevitably lead to questioning the suitability of census tracts as appropriate units with which to measure the environmental context. The only way in which this question can be thoroughly treated is by comparing empirical results for different sizes of units, above and below the census tract level. Unfortunately, time and space constraints render this impossible with the available data sources.[1]

Compared to the results of many land development studies, the coefficients of determination for the above equations are not unexpected. In most cases, Chapin's equations for population density and land in urban use produced R^2's of less than .500 despite the greater uniformity of relevant conditions. What may then have been isolated in this analysis is that part of the total variability in the location of redevelopment which can be attributed to general spatial factors. That is, the first two of the three levels of spatial determinants suggested in Chapter V. What remains of the total variance to be accounted for can then be allocated (in addition to error variance) to factors deriving from individual site and property conditions.

In part, the complexity of location factors in redevelopment dictated the selection of large areas (census tracts) as the geographic units of analysis. Attempting to account for the spatial distribution of structural change at this level avoids many of the complexities of redevelopment which enter at the level of the individual site. These include such factors as the ease of securing titles, existing ownership and development rights, willingness to sell, demolition costs, and so on, most of which are not quantifiable and are not subject to systematic analysis. Bury found this to be the case in his use of site variables as predictors of residential location in suburban areas.[2] He was able to allocate only 20 per cent of the spatial variability in single-family residential construction to specific site factors.

If our stated premise is valid, however, that site factors only enter in as important location factors in redevelopment within and not between broadly defined areas, then such factors should have little effect on the prediction for large areas. That is, if these

---

[1] A brief examination of the data with planning districts as spatial units showed similar but slightly stronger relationships. Planning districts divide the city into groups of about six census tracts (see Fig. 10 and Appendix C for district definitions). None of the empirical results are incorporated here because of the lack of comparative information.

[2] Richard L. Bury, "The Efficiency of Selected Site Characteristics as Predictors for Location of Land Use Shifts to Residential Purposes" (unpublished Ph.D. dissertation, Department of Economics, University of Connecticut, 1961).

areas actually do encompass the full range of alternatives. The areal division of the city into census tracts as units of analysis only meets this criterion with partial success. It is desirable, therefore, to tie the analysis of redevelopment patterns at the census tract level to the conversion of land uses in single properties over time.

In the following section a detailed examination is made of individual properties undergoing redevelopment. Combining the analysis of area correlates of redevelopment with an evaluation of site conversion, should facilitate incorporation of the full range of spatial patterns in redevelopment into a model framework.

Land Use Succession and the Replacement Process

This section adds the final dimension to the analysis, that of changes in individual properties and the succession of land uses generated by the redevelopment process. What types of redevelopment occurred, for example, on commercial land or in areas of single-family use? What proportion of properties remained in the same use through the rebuilding process? What is the nature of land use succession and how does this vary between areas of the city? Is there a systematic replacement of one type of use by another as ecological theory suggests? Answers to these questions may provide insight into the dynamic nature of the replacement process in urban structural change.

It is hypothesized that there is consistency in the type and spatial patterning of land use succession resulting from private urban redevelopment. That is, there is only a limited range of functions which redevelop and occupy the area of any other use. The replacement process in the standing stock of structures in a city tends to produce a more intensive use of the land, as economic theory would predict, and this replacement tends to form a distinct hierarchy based on the intensity of use. Furthermore, it is hypothesized that this process exhibits regularities over space in direct relation to distance from the city center.

The Conversion Matrices

To assess the relative frequency and geographic extend of land use succession in the redevelopment process requires a direct comparison of individual properties through time. For each area (census tract) of the City of Toronto, tables were prepared showing the number of properties, and land area in acres, of each type of use in 1951 that underwent redevelopment, according to the type of use after redevelopment.

Preparation of the tables was based initially on the 1951 land use designation.[1]

---

[1] Briefly, the procedures used in preparing the basic work tape prior to compiling the summary tables were as follows. The input data were stored on two tapes, one

Each 1951 property was examined, its use recorded and then compared to the use of the same property (or property equivalent) in 1962. The property acreage was then entered in the appropriate cell in the table for that census tract. This procedure was repeated for nearly 7, 200 pairs of properties, or parts of properties, building up a comprehensive picture of land use conversion in the city.

The results for the entire city are summarized in Tables 21 through 26.[1] Reading across the rows of Table 21 gives the number of each type of 1951 property which were converted through redevelopment to each of the other uses. Similarly, Table 24 records the amount of land area in acres undergoing conversion.[2] Reading down the columns of these tables gives the frequency and scale with which each land use type received redevelopment. For example, column 03 in Table 21 indicates that of 713 properties redeveloped in apartments, 351 were single-family, 28 multi-family, 158 were

---

containing the change or redevelopment properties (1962), and the other containing the same properties before change (1951). These were then edited in the following manner:

(1) All properties in 10 census tracts, including major institutional, recreational, public, and waterfront industrial areas were deleted (see Appendix C).

(2) All multiple records for single properties were deleted, leaving only one record on the tape of the characteristics for the dominant use in that structure.

(3) All properties classified as public and not deleted in step (1) were then deleted (see Appendix B).

(4) The same property was then located on both tapes, deleting all those not classified as private before and after redevelopment.

(5) In cases involving an amalgamation of several 1951 properties into one 1962 property, the latter was subdivided into portions equal in size to the land area of each 1951 property (see Appendix A).

(6) A new master tape was prepared with two records for each of 7, 200 properties or equivalents, one for 1951 and the other for 1962 characteristics. About 1, 000 properties were deleted through the above procedures.

(7) In preparing the final summary tables of land use conversion, the original 50 categories of private use were condensed to 14 to conform to previous aggregating procedures (see Appendix B).

[1] Land Use Classification Code, Tables 21 to 26, 1951 Existing Use:

01 Single- family	05 Offices	09 Hotel-Motel
02 Multi-family	06 General Commercial	10 Warehousing
03 Apartments	07 Auto (Commercial)	11 Industrial
04 Other Residential	08 Parking	12 Trans: Auto, Truck
13 Under Construction	14 Vacant	

[2] The acreage figures are actually more meaningful measures of relative importance of conversion among uses because of obvious differences in the size of property holdings between uses, for example, in single-family and industrial areas, and because of the necessity to split properties to achieve comparability through time.

TABLE 21

LAND USE SUCCESSION

NUMBER OF PROPERTIES CONVERTED IN REDEVELOPMENT: BY LAND USE CATEGORY
BEFORE AND AFTER CHANGE, CITY TOTALS, TORONTO, 1951 and 1962

1951 Existing Use	1962 Redevelopment Use														
	01	02	03	04	05	06	07	08	09	10	11	12	13	14	Totals
01	123	158	351	37	225	89	117	638	5	102	57	2	158	201	2263
02	3	7	28	2	10	4	1	21		1	1		9	10	97
03			10	1	4	3		5		1			5	3	32
04	20	19	158	2	72	44	35	209	1	31	24		67	72	754
05		1	4		49	8	3	37	3	4			12	2	123
06	3	3	7	3	77	155	50	121	6	15	24	2	63	33	562
07					15	16	115	12		2	2			10	172
08	14	8	11	3	29	15	20	81	3	10	2	1	27	29	253
09						1		2	3				4	1	11
10	2	5	4	1	14	17	17	115	1	63	28	1	8	37	313
11		3	1	1	12	13	15	65	1	18	68		8	11	216
12	1		2	3	4	1		7		1	1	1	1		22
13			1		2	1	3	1	1	2	1				12
14	572	310	136	119	102	111	136	507	1	133	84	3	39	93	2346
	738	514	713	172	615	478	512	1821	25	383	292	10	401	502	7176

TABLE 22

LAND USE SUCCESSION

PROPORTIONS OF 1951 PROPERTIES CONVERTED TO EACH TYPE OF REDEVELOPMENT USE:
ROW PERCENTAGES FOR TABLE 21

1951 Existing Use	1962 Redevelopment Use														Totals
	01	02	03	04	05	06	07	08	09	10	11	12	13	14	
01	5.4	7.0	15.5	1.6	9.9	3.9	5.2	28.2	.2	4.5	2.5	.1	7.0	8.9	
02	3.1	7.2	28.9	2.1	10.3	4.1	1.0	21.6		1.0	1.0		9.3	10.3	
03			31.3	3.1	12.5	9.4		15.6		3.1			15.6	9.4	
04	2.7	2.5	21.0	.3	9.5	5.8	4.6	27.7	.1	4.1	3.2		8.9	9.5	
05		.8	3.3		39.8	6.5	2.4	30.1	2.4	3.3			9.8	1.6	
06	.5	.5	1.2	.5	13.7	27.6	8.9	21.5	1.1	2.7	4.3	.4	11.2	5.9	
07					8.7	9.3	66.9	7.0		1.2	1.2			5.8	
08	5.5	3.2	4.3	1.2	11.5	5.9	7.9	32.0	1.2	4.0	.8	.4	10.7	11.5	
09				9.1		9.1		18.2	27.3				36.4		
10	.6	1.6	1.3		4.5	5.4	5.4	36.7	.6	20.1	8.9	.3	2.6	11.8	
11		1.4	.5	.5	5.6	6.0	6.9	30.1	.5	8.3	31.5		3.7	5.1	
12	4.5		9.1		18.2	4.5	13.6	31.8		4.5	4.5	4.5	4.5		
13			8.3	25.0	16.7	8.3		8.3		16.7	8.3			8.3	
14	24.4	13.2	5.8	5.1	4.3	4.7	5.8	21.6		5.7	3.6	.1	1.7	4.0	

TABLE 23

LAND USE SUCCESSION

PROPORTIONS OF EACH TYPE OF REDEVELOPMENT TAKING PLACE ON EACH TYPE OF
1951 PROPERTY: COLUMN PERCENTAGES FOR TABLE 21

1962 Redevelopment Use

1951 Existing Use	01	02	03	04	05	06	07	08	09	10	11	12	13	14	Totals
01	16.7	30.7	49.2	21.5	36.6	18.6	22.9	35.0	20.0	26.6	19.5	20.0	39.4	40.0	
02	.4	1.4	3.9	1.2	1.6	.8	.2	1.2		.3	.3		2.2	2.0	
03			1.4	.6	.7	.6		.3		.3			1.2	.6	
04	2.7	3.7	22.2	1.2	11.7	9.2	6.8	11.5	4.0	8.1	8.2		16.7	14.3	
05		.2	.6		8.0	1.7	.6	2.0	12.0	1.0			3.0	.4	
06	.4	.6	1.0	1.7	12.5	32.4	9.8	6.6	24.0	3.9	8.2	20.0	15.7	6.6	
07					2.4	3.3	22.5	.7		.5	.7			2.0	
08	1.9	1.6	1.5	1.7	4.7	3.1	3.9	4.4	12.0	2.6	.7	10.0	6.7	5.8	
09						.2		.1	12.0				1.0		
10	.3	1.0	.6	.6	2.3	3.6	3.3	6.3	8.0	16.4	9.6	10.0	2.0	7.4	
11		.6	.1		2.0	2.7	2.9	3.6	4.0	4.7	23.3		2.0	2.2	
12	.1		.3		.7	.2	.6	.4		.3	.3	10.0	.2		
13			.1	1.7	.3	.2		.1		.5	.3			.2	
14	77.5	60.3	19.1	69.2	16.6	23.2	26.6	27.8	4.0	34.7	28.8	30.0	9.7	18.5	

TABLE 24

LAND USE SUCCESSION

CONVERSION OF LAND AREA IN REDEVELOPMENT: BY LAND USE CATEGORY BEFORE
AND AFTER CHANGE, CITY TOTALS, TORONTO, 1951 and 1962 (00's acres)

1951 Existing Use	1962 Redevelopment Use														
	01	02	03	04	05	06	07	08	09	10	11	12	13	14	Totals
01	3477	6791	24903	1490	7719	2582	3126	16801	172	2778	1693	100	4886	6981	83499
02	94	425	2015	91	542	84	33	824		21	23		415	274	4841
03			2955	185	357	266		272		18			517	3135	7705
04	697	823	10783	225	3276	2949	1218	6068	38	1012	529		2470	1820	30908
05		31	522		3255	361	68	2113	44	1052			1131	141	8718
06	56	145	251	95	1901	5637	1747	5154	197	932	1692	100	1696	1501	21104
07					1433	881	9151	792		39	77			716	13089
08	567	258	684	90	1769	795	1498	4744	120	494	41	152	2297	1120	14629
09				81		34		174	215				179		683
10	67	272	1934	57	1332	7437	1870	6531	48	23133	12521	520	677	4664	61006
11		122	890		844	1001	1073	3157	32	6897	22776		1241	707	38797
12	14		180		144	41	106	400		25	29	81	70		1090
13			64	116	519	33		29		647	31			106	1545
14	23218	10005	12452	5213	5203	4274	7342	22339	118	33058	20343	145	1880	8699	154289
	28190	18872	57633	7643	28294	25375	27232	69398	984	70106	59755	1098	17459	29864	441903

TABLE 25

LAND USE SUCCESSION

PROPORTIONS OF 1951 LAND AREA CONVERTED TO EACH TYPE OF REDEVELOPMENT
USE: ROW PERCENTAGES FOR TABLE 24

	1962 Redevelopment Use														Totals
	01	02	03	04	05	06	07	08	09	10	11	12	13	14	
01	4.2	4.1	29.8	1.8	9.2	3.1	3.7	20.1	.2	3.3	2.0	.1	5.9	8.4	
02	1.9	8.8	41.6	1.9	11.2	1.7	.7	17.0		.4	.5		8.6	5.7	
03			38.4	2.4	4.6	3.5		3.5		.2			6.7	40.7	
04	2.3	2.7	34.9	.7	10.6	6.3	3.9	19.6	.1	3.3	1.7		8.0	5.9	
05		.4	6.0		37.3	4.1	.8	24.2	.5	12.1			13.0	1.6	
06	.3	.7	1.2	.5	9.0	26.7	8.3	24.4	.9	4.4	8.0	.5	8.0	7.1	
07					10.9	6.7	69.9	6.1		.3	.6			5.5	
08	3.9	1.8	4.7	.6	12.1	5.4	10.2	32.4	.8	3.4	.3	1.0	15.7	7.7	
09				11.9		5.0		25.5	31.5				26.2		
10	.1	.4	3.2		2.2	12.2	3.1	10.7	.1	37.9	20.5	.9	1.1	7.6	
11		.3	2.3	.1	2.2	2.6	2.8	8.1	.1	17.8	58.7		3.2	1.8	
12	1.3		16.5	7.5	13.2	3.8	9.7	36.7		2.3	2.7	7.4	6.4		
13			4.1		33.6	2.1		1.9		41.9	2.0			6.9	
14	15.0	6.5	8.1	3.4	3.4	2.8	4.8	14.5	.1	21.4	13.2	.1	1.2	5.6	

1951 Existing Use

TABLE 26

LAND USE SUCCESSION

PROPORTIONS OF LAND AREA OF EACH TYPE OF REDEVELOPMENT TAKING PLACE ON
EACH TYPE OF 1951 LAND USE: COLUMN PERCENTAGES FOR TABLE 24

1962 Redevelopment Use

1951 Existing Use	01	02	03	04	05	06	07	08	09	10	11	12	13	14	Totals
01	12.3	36.0	43.2	19.5	27.3	10.2	11.5	24.2	17.5	4.0	2.8	9.1	28.0	23.4	
02	.3	2.3	3.5	1.2	1.9	.3	.1	1.2					2.4	.9	
03			5.1	2.4	1.3	1.0		.4					3.0	10.5	
04	2.5	4.4	18.7	2.9	11.6	7.7	4.5	8.7	3.9	1.4	.9		14.1	6.1	
05		.2			11.5	1.4	.2	3.0	4.5	1.5			6.5	.5	
06	.2	.8	.9	1.2	6.7	22.2	6.4	7.4	20.0	1.3	2.8	9.1	9.7	5.0	
07			.4		5.1	3.5	33.6	1.1		.1	.1			2.4	
08	2.0	1.4	1.2	1.2	6.3	3.1	5.5	6.8	12.2	.7	.1	13.8	13.2	3.8	
09				1.1		.1		.3	21.8				1.0		
10	.2	1.4	3.4		4.7	29.3	6.9	9.4	4.9	33.0	21.0	47.4	3.9	15.6	
11		.6	1.5	.7	3.0	3.9	3.9	4.5	3.3	9.8	38.1		7.1	2.4	
12			.3		.5	.2	.4	.6				7.4	.4		
13			.1	1.5	1.8	.1				.9	.1			.4	
14	82.4	53.0	21.6	68.2	18.4	16.8	27.0	32.2	12.0	47.2	34.0	13.2	10.8	29.1	

mixes residential, and so on. Tables 22 and 25 provide row percentages, and Tables 23 and 26 column percentages, for the above summaries. The row percentages can be taken to measure the probability of conversion for any type of property undergoing redevelopment. The column percentages likewise measure the probability that redevelopment will take place on any given type of property. Note that this is not the probability that redevelopment will occur, but rather what the outcome will be in land use change when it occurs.

Land Use Succession in Redevelopment

Theoretically, one might expect to find a large proportion of the changes along the main diagonal of each matrix, indicating no change of use within major categories. Land use patterns tend to persist once established, due in part to "natural" processes and in part to the channelling effects of zoning discussed in Chapter V. Although redevelopment commonly involves a change in zoning, the property usually remains in the same general category of use, but because of the costs of land, witnesses an increase in intensity.

The results indicate that the conversion of land to a different use through redevelopment is considerable, and that wide variations occur between uses. Table 27 ranks each of the major categories in terms of the proportion of 1951 land area and number of properties affected which remained in the same use after redevelopment. This This ranking acts both as a measure of stability within land use types as well as of the degree of containment or isolation between types. Almost 70 per cent of the commercial automobile areas involved in change remained in the same use, compared to 58 per cent for industrial uses, 39 per cent for apartments, and 37 per cent for warehousing.[1] As expected, only a minor proportion of low-density residential uses were redeveloped for that use. Note that except for the lower end of the scale, this ranking bears only a weak relationship to intensity of use and therefore in the aggregate to the economics of land use succession.

Variations in land use stability in redevelopment derive from two quite distinct

---

Splitting of 1951 properties was carried out in the compilation of the basic data source, which splitting of 1962 properties was performed in the preparation of the above tables (see footnote on the preceding page, the section on data in chapter IV, and Appendix A).

[1] The figures for industrial and warehousing uses are somewhat exaggerated, as noted in chapter vi, by the inclusion of properties subjected to only minor structural modification. The nature of the problem in data compilation as previously discussed is such that errors would appear largely in the diagonal of the conversion matrices. Most errors involve the invlusion of properties which did not in fact change and thus would inflate the degree of stability.

TABLE 27

PROPORTIONS OF 1951 LAND AREA AND PROPERTIES THAT REMAINED IN
THE SAME USE THROUGH REDEVELOPMENT, CITY OF TORONTO

Major Category of Use	Land Area Percentages[a]	Properties	Intensity Rank[b]
Automobile Commercial	69.9	66.9	9
Industrial	58.7	31.5	5
Apartments	38.4	31.3	3
Warehousing	37.9	20.1	7
Offices	37.3	39.8	2
Parking	32.4	32.0	12
Hotel	31.5	27.3	1
General Commercial	26.7	27.6	4
Multi-family	8.8	7.2	6
Trans: Auto, Truck	7.4	4.5	11
Vacant	5.6	4.0	13
Single-family	4.2	5.4	10
Other Residential	.7	.3	8
Under Construction	--	--	--

[a] From Tables 22 and 25

[b] The intensity rank is based on the aggregate floor area ratio for the entire structural
inventory in that use in the city in 1962

but interrelated factors. First, occupance of a site by certain types of use in effect
"contaminates" that site for other uses by the unattractive environment created. The
site is essentially removed from the locational choices open to these uses because they
are considered incompatible. The standard example in planning is the conflict between
industrial and residential uses, with the latter seldom invading the territory of the
former. The persistence of land uses also has an obvious economic basis. The occupance of a site by high-intensity uses such as offices, usually renders it economically
infeasible for succession to occur involving less intensive uses. In the above table, the
first argument, the environmental context, would apply primarily to commercial, industrial and warehousing uses, and the economic argument to apartments, offices and hotels.
These two groups tend to be mutually exclusive in land use succession, even without
consideration of differences in intensity and costs of land.

Despite the operation of these different processes in succession, there is a
consistent pattern in the type of land conversion that takes place in redevelopment. This
consistency is apparent both within major categories of use, reflecting the stability of

land uses, and in changes in intensity of use. For example, of all single-family residential properties (use 01) undergoing redevelopment (first row of Table 22), 30 per cent went into new residential use, 28 per cent to parking, and 10 per cent to offices. In total, 42 per cent of all residential properties remained in the same use. In contrast, of the 1951 industrial areas (use 11) subjected to redevelopment, only 2 per cent became residential, while 8 per cent went into parking use, and 17 per cent to warehousing. There was no major shift in the use of industrial land through redevelopment.

The fact that more than half of total residential redevelopment took place on previously non-residential land suggests the scale of land use rearrangement in the city. Chapter VI pointed out that residential acreage remained relatively stable as a proportion in the redeveloped areas. Obviously the areas were not the same. Residential uses expanded at the expense of some uses, and in turn were replaced by others. The unexpected appearance of new single-family construction can be accounted for noting the type of area affected (column 01 in Tables 23 and 26). Over 77 per cent of single-family units were constructed on vacant land, while the rest were constructed on existing single-family land or parking areas. In large part this construction occurred without structural replacement as part of the "filling-in process." In fact more 1951 vacant areas were converted to single-family use than to any other use (row 14, Table 22).

As expected, low-density uses suffered most in the process of rebuilding. Of the 7,200 properties examined fully one-third were in single-family use and one-third were vacant prior to redevelopment. Another 20 per cent were in low-density commercial, mixed residential, and parking uses. The magnitude of this conversion process is given in Table 21 by comparing the row totals, the number of properties of each type at the beginning of the period, with the column totals, the number of properties at the end of the period.

Although low-density uses were most widely subjected to redevelopment, the nature of replacement tends to form a distinct hierarchy based on intensity of use in which all types of properties are involved. To illustrate this point, Table 28 ranks each of the categories of use in the preceding conversion tables according to aggregate intensity in the existing stock. The upper right triangle contains the number of properties which declined in intensity through redevelopment, and the lower left triangle those registering an increase in intensity. All conversions should fall along the main diagonal or in the lower left triangle indicating replacement by increasing higher density uses. As the ranking is by average floor area ratios for the entire city, however, some variation from the hypothetical case should be expected.

To a large extent the hypothesis is validated, as evidenced by the small number of entries in the upper right triangle. Two clear exceptions emerge, however. There

TABLE 28

REDEVELOPMENT CONVERSION MATRIX: NUMBER OF 1951 PROPERTIES IN
EACH LAND USE CATEGORY FOLLOWING REDEVELOPMENT, RANKED BY
INTENSITY OF USE

1951 Existing Use[a]	1962 Redevelopment Use												
	1	2	3	4	5	6	7	8	9	10	11	12	13
1 Hotel	3											2	
2 Office		49					4					37	
3 Apartments			10										3
4 General Commercial		77	155	24					50			121	
5 Industrial				68		18						65	
6 Multi-family		10	28		7					3		21	
7 Warehousing			17	28		63							37
8 Other Residential		18	47	8				2				65	
9 Auto Commercial		15	16						115			12	10
10 Single-family		225	351			158			117	123		638	201
11 Trans: Auto, Truck		4	2						1		1	2	
12 Parking		29		15					20	14		81	29
13 Vacant	1	102	136	111	84	310	133	119	136	572	84	507	93

[a]Ranked by average intensity of use determined from the aggregate standing stock in
that category for the entire city.

Notes: Excluding all categories which accounted for less than 5 per cent of all
conversions by land area, and excluding the under construction category.

has been widespread conversion of certain types of properties, particularly single-
family, industrial and warehousing, into parking, and to a lesser extent to vacant land.
In the case of industrial and warehousing uses much of this change reflects changes
within property holdings rather than replacement of existing structures. On the other
hand, over 630 single-family properties (or equivalents) were demolished and converted
to parking use in the eleven years under study.[1]

---

[1]The demolition of existing structures for parking use to some extent may be
considered as a transition stage in the process of rebuilding for another use. This is
certainly true for the appearance of vacant land in the statistics. At one point in time,
the date at which data compilation was terminated, over 500 properties formerly occupied by other uses were classified as vacant.

Land use succession in redevelopment exhibits the following systematic sequence of conversion. Of all vacant land receiving new construction (Table 22) for example, 6 per cent went into warehousing, 22 per cent into parking, and 24 per cent into single-family residential, all of which are low-density uses. More vacant land was converted into low-density use than to intensive uses such as apartments and offices. The latter uses in turn, expanded at the expense of the former, particularly residential, which dominate in the conversion of vacant land. Only 8 per cent of all vacant land was converted to apartments and only 3 per cent to offices. Reading from Table 26 for column percentages, note that 82 per cent of all single-family construction, 53 per cent of mixed residential and 47 per cent of warehousing construction took place on vacant lands. In contrast, only 21 per cent of apartments, 18 per cent of offices, and 16 per cent of general commercial redevelopment involved vacant land, being considerably more widespread in existing low and mixed intensity areas.[1]

Nevertheless, the results substantiate the initial hypothesis that the replacement process involves a systematic conversion of existing uses by those at the next higher level of the intensity scale. Through time there is a definite trend toward a "higher and better" use in economic terms in response to the demands for space and location.

Moreover, suggesting that a step-like pattern exists in the replacement process, agrees with the cyclical concept of structural change formulated in Chapter III. Although it is not possible to isolate the nature of this cycle for the same property through time, the systematic replacement of similar properties at different intensities indicates that a redevelopment cycle does in fact exist.

Spatial Patterns of Land Use Succession

Ecological theory describes the spatial pattern of land use succession as involving concentric expansion of zones of different use outward from the city center, each zone invading and replacing one of less intensive use. In theory, the central business district expands into the adjacent industrial-warehousing area, which in turn expands into the older residential zone. In most cases, residential uses are incapable of outbidding other uses for central locations and therefore bear the brunt of most such expansions. Succession may result from many different processes, only one of which is generated by redevelopment as examined in this study.

Although this concept of succession as a spatial process is over-simplified, it does provide a general framework for understanding site selection and land use conversion in redevelopment. In the aggregate, there is an apparent relationship between

---

[1]The correlation between per cent vacant land and per cent land in residential use is -.322.

the nature of replacement taking place and distance from the city center, even though redevelopment exhibits a discontinuous pattern in both rate and magnitude. Examining the types of properties affected also indicates the relative changes in the importance of site factors in redevelopment over space. Apartments are selected as the first example because of the greater uniformity of the product across the city.

Figure 31 represents a highly generalized illustration of the proportion of apartment redevelopment occurring on vacant land. The spatial pattern is clearly concentric, with values ranging from zero per cent for most of the central area to 100 per cent in the outlying extremes of the city.[1] This means more than simply that vacant land increases with distance from the center, although this is to some extent true. It suggests that land converted in redevelopment varies in intensity of use directly with distance rather than the type of redevelopment. More importantly, it indicates that as a factor in redevelopment location, vacant land becomes increasingly important away from the central area. The wide locational freedom of apartments throughout most of the city enables developers to seek out vacant areas to reduce the costs of acquisition and site preparation once the immediate advantages of central location have been reduced. As the large part of apartment redevelopment has been shown to occur in the middle and outer reaches of the city, the value of centrality must be outweighted by these costs.

Not only is the pattern of replacement by intensity of use related to distance, but the type and stability of land uses involved also varies outward from the city center. Evidence of this concentric variation in residential succession is provided by Figure 32. The proportion of residential land remaining in that use through redevelopment is lowest in and around the central core and along the main industrial railroad routes. In these areas older residential structures have been removed by the succession of non-residential uses. Outward from the central area and from the industrial belts the proportions increase, reaching 80 to 100 per cent at the outer margins of the city. Note that the Rosedale area (Tract 94) immediately to the north of the commercial core stands out as an area of land use stability much as it did in the previous regression results.

Repetitive mapping of various combinations of the summary tables would show much the same results. However, the spatial patterns are by no means as consistent or widespread as these generalized illustrations suggest. The distribution of new construction, particularly in offices and apartments, is discontinuous over space and highly

---

[1] In part, the declining proportion of apartment redevelopment occurring on vacant land is both a cause and effect of the increase in intensity of apartment building toward the center. The average number of units per building within the inner ring of the city, from 0 to 2 miles, is 41.3, compared to 36.0 in the 2 to 5 mile belt, and 23.2 in the 5 to 8 mile belt. Metropolitan Planning Board, Apartment Survey, 1961 (Toronto: The Metropolitan Planning Board, 1962), p. 32.

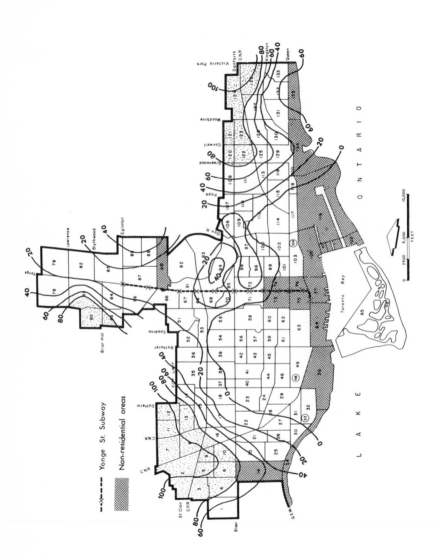

Fig. 31--Generalized Pattern of Land Use Succession in Redevelopment: Proportion of Apartment Construction Taking Place on Vacant Land

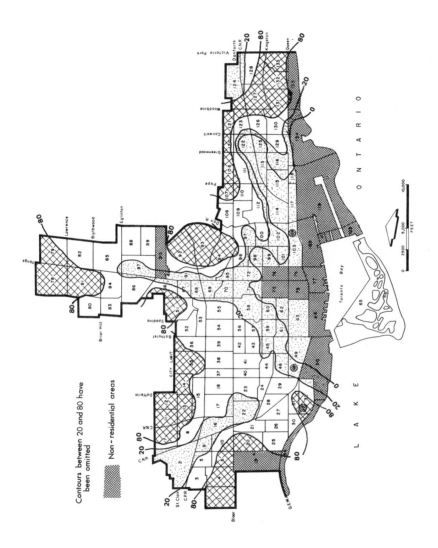

Fig. 32--Land Use Stability: Proportion of Residential Land Remaining in the Same Use Through Redevelopment

localized around certain nodes. Sharp contrasts with the existing stock of the city in terms of intensity and location have been documented. Nevertheless, in the aggregate, redevelopment involves a systematic succession of land use with a step-like increase in intensity related to distance from the city center, and to existing patterns of density of use.

Relating Site and Area Models

At this point we are in a position to bring together the analyses and models of redevelopment at the area and site level, and to suggest an approach to an operational model of structural change. Throughout the study it has been argued that both area and site factors operate to influence the patterns and processes of redevelopment. From an operational viewpoint it is essential to include both aspects of the process if the nature of redevelopment and its impact is to be studied comprehensively.

The regression estimating equations attempted to find means of allocating redevelopment activity to small areas of the city. This was done on the basis of a set of hypothesized location factors, with some success for residential and office construction, and could be extended to include the full range of land use types in the basic data source. However, the resulting estimates reveal nothing about the type of properties affected, or about the nature of replacement in land use that results.

The matrices of land use conversion in redevelopment provide the basis for translating the regression estimates for the aggregate distribution of redevelopment into the precise impact on the land use distribution of the city. When converted to percentages, the matrices offer a measure of the probability that given land use types will be redeveloped and converted to another use. Moreover, as the matrices have been compiled for small areas of the city, they have the distinct advantage of incorporating the existing spatial structure, and therefore the character of the redevelopment process, unique to each area.

Integration of the two approaches, that is, the regression equations and the probability matrices, is conceptually simple, but empirically cumbersome. The suggested statistical procedure to achieve this objective is as follows. The regression equations allocate a given level of investment in redevelopment to each subarea of the city. The resulting regression estimates then appear as the initial inputs at the top of each column in Table 26 for each area (census tract), and can then be assigned or distributed to each existing land use type according to the probabilities of conversion in that column. This would in effect allocate the input over the particular spatial structure of any given area.

The procedure would follow as such:

Let $\hat{X}_{ij}$ represent the regression estimate of the amount of redevelopment of type i in area j. In the Toronto case, i = 1, 14 and j = 1, 125. Therefore, X is a matrix of 14 x 125 elements for the entire city, each row of which is a vector of 14 land use types for each area j.

Let P_{kij} equal the probability of conversion of each 1951 land use type k to redevelopment land use type i in area j, given that redevelopment occurs. Therefore, P is a symmetric matrix of probabilities of the order of k x i, with k = i = 14, for each of j areas.

Then, to distribute the regression estimate for redevelopment type 1 in area 1, that is $\hat{X}_{11}$, across the existing distribution of land uses in that area, the result is the product of:

$\hat{X}_{11}$ x P_{k11} with k = 1, 14, which produces a column vector of 14 elements, measuring the extent of conversion of each of the existing 14 land use types generated by the given level of redevelopment of type 1 employed as input.[1]

To illustrate the procedure:

Let $\hat{X}_i$ = the estimate of new apartment construction for the entire city, in square feet of floor area. This is taken as given from national economic forecasts.

This estimate is then distributed among each of the 125 census tracts of the city on the basis of the relationship established in the regression analysis:

$$\hat{X}_{ij} = .196 \text{ NRA} + .015 \text{ PAPT} + .413 \text{ SUB} + .010 \text{ DPC} - 2.657 \tag{5}$$

where

$\hat{X}_{ij}$ = log. apartment lot area (ATLA) for tract j, with j = 1, 125

and

NRA = log. net residential acreage of the tract
PAPT = log. per cent dwellings in apartments
SUB = proximity to subway: 1 if adjacent, 0 otherwise
DPC = log. distance from the center of metropolitan population.

This given an estimate of the land involved in residential redevelopment for apartment use in each tract.

These estimates are then applied to column 03 (apartments) in Table 27, the proportions of land area of each type of use converted by apartment redevelopment, for each tract in the city. (Note that Table 27 applies to the entire city; similar tables were prepared for each tract.) This then distributes the regression estimates $\hat{X}_{ij}$ over the existing land use distribution of that tract.

As a planning model the procedure can be repeated successively varying either the redevelopment input values or the regression parameters which allocate these inputs,

---

[1] The present data source is insufficient for this procedure to accomplish anything more than a replication of the data for Toronto itself. Both the conversion probabilities and the regression estimates are limited by a single base period and by limited samples in many of the census tracts of the city. To provide a sound basis for calculating the coefficients and probabilities the analysis should be repeated for different time periods and for different areal units or groups of units.

or both. Altering the inputs provides the control mechanism for assessing the impact of different levels, types, and patterns of investment in new construction. Over time, however, regression parameters and conversion probabilities would themselves change. The approach up to this point is essentially static, based on an attempt to replicate change processes in one time period. By altering the parameters the time element can be introduced to account for the dynamics of the redevelopment process.

Synthesis

The purpose of the approach in this chapter was not primarily to develop a redevelopment model. It was initially designed to assess the inter-relationships between sets of hypothesized location factors and the spatial pattern of private redevelopment. The multiple regression analysis provided one means of assessing the composite influences of these factors rather than an attempt to simulate redevelopment patterns through time.

Despite operational limitations, both the approach and the results have useful planning applications. For example, the tables of land use conversion permit a direct assessment of the impact of the private redevelopment process on the spatial structure of the city. Moreover, the analysis provides the concise empirical evidence necessary to answer questions relating to the types of properties undergoing redevelopment to variations in replacement within and between areas of the city, and to changes in the relative composition of land use distributions and patterns of density. By comparing these trends with given policy objectives concerning improvement of the urban structural inventory, the nature, extent, and location of public intervention in controlling and guiding the private market should be more clearly evident. It is clear from the analysis, for instance, that private redevelopment in Toronto, is not affecting the majority of the urban area, and thus of its deteriorating building stock. The composition of redevelopment is narrowly specialized in those categories which do not involve a large proportion of the urban population.

As an aid to research, the models can be employed iteratively over several time periods to assess the future impact of structural change. Although the preceding chapter revealed wide fluctuations in the character and scale of private redevelopment, even within the study period thus making extrapolation of trends difficult, it could be done with more frequent measures and refinements of the parameters of change than time permitted in this study. By repeating the procedure with varying combinations of inputs for each type of redevelopment, alternate spatial patterns of land use and structural change can be evaluated. What would the impact on the city in terms of land conversion be, if the scale of residential redevelopment were to be increased by a substantial amount?

What types of properties would be affected if redevelopment were encouraged in specified areas of the city? Questions such as these, provide scope for further research.

CHAPTER VIII

CONCLUSIONS AND IMPLICATIONS

Redevelopment is a continuous and volatile source of urban growth and structural change. Defined as a replacement process in the building stock of the city, redevelopment becomes one aspect of a series of structural adaptations to accommodate changing demands for space and location. Most such demands are accommodated within the existing stock by a change in the location or amount of space utilized by a given activity. Replacement occurs only when there is strong demand for reuse of the site and when the existing building becomes inadequate. At the same time, redevelopment appears as the final phase in the cyclical change over time in the life of individual buildings and the growth of neighborhoods.

Private Redevelopment: Patterns and Processes

The underlying rationale for redevelopment as a process of change is basically economic. New construction occurs to meet demands that cannot be met within the existing building stock, and when it represents a profitable course of action. Two processes have been shown to operate, both based on the concept of obsolescence. First, obsolescence may derive directly from deterioration and depreciation, the need to replace what is presently in existence over time, and second from economic succession. The latter factor is essentially a competitive growth effect, when an existing use is outbid by another for occupancy of a given site. In reality, these processes occur together in differing degrees for each type of activity and between subareas of the city.

The spatial pattern that mirrors the operation of these forces is complex and variable. Regularity in the pattern becomes apparent only when data for thousands of scattered properties are aggregated over a sufficient area and condensed to manageable classes of land use. The spatial behavior observed is not simply that of concentric or axial patterns, and it contrasts sharply with the existing spatial structure of the city. Redevelopment is too highly localized, specialized in type, and variable through time to mold neatly into these simplified constructs.

The location of redevelopment within the city is a function of the relative potential of each area to attract new investment. A combination of neighborhood amenities,

173

accessibility, and relative location establish the potential for given types of redevelopment within broad areas of the city. Distance associations and proximity among related uses, for example, set bounds on the location alternatives open to most types of activities. Within these areas, neighborhood factors then further differentiate redevelopment potential by measuring relative differences in the quality of the immediate socio-economic and physical environments. Within the range of location alternatives determined both by general access and environmental advantages, site factors, such as property size, the presence of vacant land, and physical attributes, enter to influence the selection of a particular property for redevelopment. As such, these factors generally act to affect the choice of site within but not between broad areas.

The specific factors associated with the spatial distribution of redevelopment, for example apartment construction, include the location of existing concentrations of apartments, proximity to the subway, and distance from the center of metropolitan population. Clearly, accessibility is the primary location factor determining economic feasibility, with no explicit correlation with residential amenities. On the other hand, the rate of redevelopment varies directly with past directions of growth and apartment construction, with proximity to the subway and average size of lot, and inversely with the average age of existing structures. The latter two measure the importance of amenities and environment as location variables, as well as the ease and costs of land assembly. In contrast, when aggregated over large areas, redevelopment bears little relationship to the distribution of vacant land and the degree of mixed and conflicting land uses. The spatial distribution of redevelopment is not a direct function of aging and deterioration.

The operation of these factors in the redevelopment process produces a distinct spatial pattern. Apartment redevelopment, for example, at least within the city limits of Toronto, is concentrated in the higher income sectors. Within these sectors, there is still further clustering centered on about a dozen points of maximum accessibility. Over time, these clusters have shifted as redevelopment migrates from one local area to another, but have remained within the higher income sectors. This clustering effect in spatial patterning stems in part from zoning, but more important, from the external economies that result from proximity among related uses, and similar social groups, and the catalytic reaction of one major redevelopment project in attracting others.

The dynamic nature of this process appears in the following pattern of change. Among several local points which offer similar attractions for redevelopment, the one first selected depends upon the nature of zoning and community resistance to change. In other words, the mechanism which "triggers" redevelopment in one area rather than another is the ease of breakthrough in institutional constraints. Once selected, an area receives the concentrated efforts of redevelopers until its relative potential is exhausted. Activity then shifts to another location, and the process is repeated.

In part because of this locational instability, the distribution of redevelopment in general does not show a consistent decline with distance from the city center. In terms of magnitude it is too discontinuous and localized over space. Excluding the core and fringe area patterns, growth tends to generate from points in the urban spatial structure which offer a combination of attractions for redevelopment from the above factors.

Structural replacement in the redevelopment process exhibits a systematic succession of land uses indicative of the degree of selectivity in site selection as well as the importance of land costs. Less intensive land uses are replaced by more intensive uses in a step-like hierarchy directly related both to intensity of use and to distance from the city center. Offices and apartments expand into areas of low-density residential, mixed commercial and parking uses, while these in turn expand into areas of even lower density, particularly vacant land. The degree of stability in land uses undergoing redevelopment, measured as the proportion of land area remaining in the same general category of use, is likewise related to intensity of use, but also to the degree of conflict in environmental character between uses. For example, in the inner part of the city most land undergoing redevelopment was converted to another use while in the outer areas almost all residential land was redeveloped for residential purposes, except those bordering industrial zones.

In summary, the redevelopment process has produced a significant contribution to the structural inventory and spatial arrangement of land uses in the City of Toronto. Areas equivalent to 11 and 12 per cent of the land and building area of the city respectively, underwent redevelopment during the period 1952 to 1962 inclusive. New construction and major structural modifications added some 46 million square feet of floor space on over 8,300 properties, affecting over 1,400 acres of land. Among the more important features of this activity which substantiate the preceding generalizations are the following:

(1) The rate of redevelopment (within unchanging city boundaries) has been one per cent a year in both land and floor area. Over time, the rate of change in the building stock has been increasing while that in land area has been declining.

(2) Redevelopment is concentrated in those uses at opposite ends of the density scale, with apartments and offices the most intensive, and parking and commercial automobile among the least intensive. Over time, the differential in intensity between the two groups has been increasing.

(3) Redevelopment is highly specialized. Apartment and office construction accounted for nearly 75 per cent of all floor area added to the building stock and the proportion increased sharply within the 1952-1962 period.

(4) At the other end of the scale in terms of land area, commercial automobile and parking uses expanded most rapidly, accounting for nearly 25 per cent of the land area undergoing change.

(5) Redevelopment reflects marked shifts in land area requirements. New industrial and warehousing construction in the city required more land than existing industries, while residential construction, 90 per cent of which is apartments, required considerably less land.

(6) The increasing scale of land area required by new construction is also evident in that there were almost 50 per cent fewer properties in the redeveloped areas in 1962 than at the beginning of the study period.

(7) Redevelopment is highly selective in the types of properties affected. About one-third of all new construction in the city took place on vacant land, and an equal proportion on properties occupied by single-family residential uses.

(8) Yet, within the redeveloped areas, aggregating over 8,300 properties, all land uses expanded except low-density residential, with other low-density uses expanding largely at the expense of vacant land.

(9) Each of the major types of redevelopment exhibits a distinct spatial pattern largely independent of all other patterns. When the change statistics for all types of redevelopment were factor analyzed, five basic patterns emerged, representing the major land use groups, and accounting for almost 62 per cent of the aggregate spatial variability in redevelopment.

(10) Redevelopment is highly localized. The central core and northern sector of the city received about 35 per cent of all floor area added and 76 per cent of all office construction.

(11) Specifically, the spatial pattern of apartment and office redevelopment is clearly sectorial rather than concentric. Apartments appear as clusters in the three higher income sectors of the city and offices are concentrated in the central area and in a northward extension following the subway through the highest income sector.

(12) In the aggregate, the rate of redevelopment, measured as the proportion of total land area, drops sharply from a peak in the commercial core, reaches its lowest point in a concentric zone about 3 to 4 miles from downtown (the traditional "grey" area of stagnant conditions) and from this zone rises outward to the city boundary.

Implications for Theory

Traditional concepts of spatial organization and change in both the structural and functional bases of cities are not capable of incorporating the full degree of complexity in the location of redevelopment. Spatial relationships, as evidenced in redevelopment patterns, are obviously changing, and although a major part of the urban area is not involved in redevelopment, the directions of change and the transformations in small areas are striking. The process by which cities are rebuilt through continuous replacement has been generally ignored by researchers concerned with the city, although there is widespread verification of the results of a lack of rebuilding.

Concepts, such as concentric and sectoral variations in land use patterns, and invasion and succession as descriptions of expansion in socio-economic zones, are far too simplistic a view of a complex process. The spatial pattern of redevelopment does exhibit some association with distance zones and quality distinctions between sectors. However, these patterns are so highly generalized as to be of limited value in under-standing the mechanisms of change involved, since they obscure much of the variability within local areas.

Demands for space and location have changed markedly in recent decades. Expanding urban activities, particularly apartments and offices, are relatively flexible in locational choice, suggesting less consistency in the emerging spatial patterns than has existed before. It is perhaps for this reason, that some theoreticians, such as Webber and Foley,[1] are now emphasizing what are essentially aspatial urban theories. What is needed than is a more comprehensive treatment which incorporates both the spatial dimensions of land use, activity, and structural changes combined, and the aspatial aspects of urban growth.

The concepts presented in this study, although far from providing this compre-hensive framework, do represent a complex addition to existing theories. Redevelopment as a replacement process in the building stock recognizes and incorporates both the effects of aging and deterioration and the changing demands for urban locations.

Implications for Policy

The most critical implication for public policy formulation lies in the selective nature of the redevelopment process, both in terms of the areas and types of activities involved. Many areas of the City of Toronto, containing a large proportion of the older and deteriorating building stock in the city, witnessed no major structural modification during the study period. Moreover, the declining rate of redevelopment, measured in land area, implies that over time progressively less of this stock will be affected by private redevelopment.[2] Not only are the highest rates of redevelopment found among the intensive land uses, but most uses are showing a relative decline in land requirements within the central city. The same amount of new construction in apartments took place in the years 1959-1963 as in the period 1952-1956, but on 40 per cent less land area.

The repercussions of rebuilding at higher densities have been referred to by numerous authors.[3] In strict economic and spatial terms, Miles Colean argues that high-

---

[1] Webber et al., Explorations Into Urban Structure, particularly the Introduction and the first two essays.

[2] Preliminary figures for 1965 and 1966 indicate that the removal of older dwellings, particularly low-cost dwellings, expanded considerably from that recorded during the study period. Although a considerable proportion of this increase has resulted from replacement by apartment and office construction, most seems to be the result of new road and subway construction, and expanding public and institutional building.

[3] For example, W.H. Lundlow, "Urban Densities and Their Costs: An

density redevelopment effectively reduces the possibility of extensive area rebuilding by usurping a portion of a finite demand that might have gone to other sites.[1] Martin Anderson employs similar reasoning in his criticism of the Federal urban renewal program in the United States, to refute arguments of increased taxable assessment in the redevelopment phase of public renewal projects.[2]

The implication of these trends for renewal policy is that accelerated investment in private new construction may not affect an increasing portion of the city area or its aging building stock. The changing parameters of land and building space requirements and the increasing scale of decentralization dictate a different approach to renewal planning than in the past. As the city covers a given geographic area, emphasis must be given to the changing nature of spatial relationships in both land and building and the demand for particular types of location. There is a necessity to bring a larger proportion of urban land into the sphere of private redevelopment activity if the building stock of the city is to be improved, while simultaneously allowing for the economies of scale offered by increased densities and spatial clustering. Public activity may take up part of the slack but clearly the largest source of investment for redevelopment will come from the private sector.

Increased density and localization in private redevelopment have been accompanied by increased locational mobility. Apartment and office construction is not narrowly confined to any particular environment or location. Within the broad areas chosen by these types of redevelopment there have been considerable shifts in emphasis among local areas. Such characteristics make accurate prediction of the resulting spatial pattern difficult, but at the same time they leave wider scope for municipal guidance of the location of new construction.

Public policy decisions themselves have exerted considerable influence on the form of change in urban spatial structure that takes place. The importance of the subway in altering the location of new construction in Toronto is a clear example. Decisions with regard to other municipal investments in structures and facilities also should be made with a view to their impact on the private market mechanism and to achieving desired directions of change. This does not mean that public efforts should follow trends in the private sphere, but rather that conflicts can be reduced while in fact improving the public planning process.

Exploration into the Economics of Population Densities and Urban Patterns," Urban Redevelopment: Problems and Practices, Part II, ed. C. Woodbury (Chicago: University of Chicago Press, 1953), pp. 101-223.

[2] Colean, op. cit.

[3] Anderson, The Federal Bulldozer, p. 82.

Directions for Research

Several different lines of relevant research suggest themselves. There is need for considerably more research into the factors generating change in some areas of the city while others with apparently similar conditions remain untouched. New facilities such as a subway attract extensive redevelopment activity, particularly apartments and offices. Yet, how much of this activity would have occurred anyway, and what are the relative proportions of total redevelopment in the city affected by this facility? The degree of spatial association among factors in redevelopment, and particularly the trade-off between different factors and areas in the process of site selection, is not at all well understood.

From an empirical viewpoint the present analysis could be profitably extended in two directions. First, to include a wider range of structural changes, such as rehabilitation and other modifications to the existing stock, to assess both the relative impact of these in relation to redevelopment and the factors that lead to a shift from one to the other. Second, further research could add the functional component to the analysis by following the types of activities involved in redevelopment. New buildings provide the physical space for urban activities, but what is the relationship between activity movements in this space and changes in the space itself? What movements result from redevelopment, what activities are involved, and from what areas do these movements derive?

In addition to being a part of a series of structural changes, redevelopment in the central city is an integral part of a larger metropolitan economy. Construction activity outside of the city should be examined in detail as an alternative location for private investment. There is evidence that substantial shifts in the relative composition and importance of suburban development and central city redevelopment can take place. What are these shifts, what factors are responsible, and what is the impact on the form of the city?

There is also clearly insufficient knowledge relating to the relationship between social and physical space in the city and the degree to which changes in one are affected by and reflected in the other. What types of social change coincide with the redevelopment process in different areas of the city? To what extent are social changes previews of structural change and particularly of redevelopment? Certainly minor structural modifications act as indicators of future shifts in the pattern of redevelopment activity. The same may be true of social changes. Questions of this nature may serve to bring together some of the rather distinct subdivisions of urban research and to lay the basis for comprehensive social and physical planning.

In terms of analytical procedures, it would be worthwhile to extend the regression allocation and site succession models to provide a broader basis for analysis and prediction. This would involve test cases in which the spatial units and time periods were altered to allow for more rigorous determination of the parameters of change.

To complete the total picture of urban rebuilding involves the addition to the present analysis of the public sector. Public investment as a direct factor in change exert considerable influence on the urban structural inventory. Although there has been considerable research into the location and impact of urban renewal programs little is known about the relationships between public investment in general and structural changes generated in the private market. To what extent are there conflicting or accelerating effects?

There are at least two reasons for continued interest in the redevelopment process in cities. Change within developed areas of the city is one part of a larger context of urban growth and development, and its directions and implications are major components in planning. Redevelopment is the process on which the future growth and form of older areas of the city is largely dependent. Second, most cities are faced with widespread problems of structural decay and obsolescence. Although cities are dynamic, change does not and cannot take place in all areas at the same time or rate. Structural decay and the absence of redevelopment are evidence of maladjustments in the process of urban growth and renewal.

From a policy viewpoint, the real choice for cities is not between public renewal and that generated by the private market, but between scattered, uncoordinated replacement of buildings, and planned, programmed renewal. The formulation of an overall renewal strategy to a significant extent depends on an understanding of the continuous processes of change that are now operating in the city. The treatment of the problem in this study provides one approach to this understanding, and suggests a conceptual context for more extensive research.

APPENDIX A

PROCEDURES FOR OBTAINING INFORMATION ON STRUCTURAL
CHANGE, CITY OF TORONTO, 1952-1962[1]

Objective: To list all properties that underwent <u>structural change</u> or <u>expansion</u> in the decade 1952 to 1962, and to provide comparable land use and assessment statistics for the years 1951 and 1962. The information for 1951 is designed to provide a complete property inventory prior to the period of change analysis.

Assumptions: It is assumed that all buildings appearing on the affected properties in 1951 were removed in the process of change, either they were replaced by new construction or were demolished and the land left vacant.

Definitions: Structural change refers to all new building construction, demolition of existing buildings, and major structural expansions. No information is included of changes in use within existing buildings not subjected to modification.

Procedures:

    I. A. <u>Extract</u> from 1962 land use (assessment) listings the following ledger numbers[2] and list them by city block.

        1) <u>all new construction</u>, as determined by age designations B, C, and D, representing the years 1952-1962.

        2) all areas that are now <u>vacant</u>,[3] (1962). If the property was vacant before 1952 as well, it was ignored.

      B. <u>Record</u> the following 1962 information for each ledger number listed above.

              i) location[4]
             ii) street number
           iii) lot width (in feet)

---

[1] Adapted from City of Toronto Planning Board, Outline of Procedures, 1964. As this source of information is unusual, it was thought useful to include the precise procedure followed during the compilation to facilitate possible replication. During two summer field periods the City Planning staff checked the validity of this information in the field.

[2] Ledger numbers are the basic designations attached to each property in the assessment records and tax accounts. These act as a critical link in seeking out corresponding properties between 1951 and 1962.

[3] The examination of vacant land includes land use codes 47, 51, 57, 95, 96, in reference to major use, and 57G, 96G, 51G, for secondary uses. See Appendix B. These may include properties with a small building assessment, such as parking lots or storage areas, in which structures are present but of minor importance.

[4] The location measures include planning district, census tract, block number, and location within block.

     iv) lot area (in hundreds of square feet)

      v) 1962 land use code

     vi) age

II. Mapping the properties involved.

   The location and boundaries of each property were determined and plotted on large scale (100 ft = 1 inch) land use maps. From these maps the ledger number(s) for properties in 1949[1] that corresponded to the areas involved in change in 1962 were listed.

III. The Metropolitan Assessment Departmen then took these 1949 ledger numbers of changed properties, located the corresponding number in the 1949 assessment work books, and listed the following information:

     1) land assessment

     2) building assessment

     3) total floor area

     4) total lot area

     5) age of building

     6) dominant land use

IV. The total information for both 1951 (that is, 1949) and 1962 change properties from the Planning Board and the Assessment Department was then transferred to punch cards for preliminary processing.

Changes in Property Subdivisions

   A problem arose in the case of a split or amalgamation of 1949 properties in 1962. Other than the straight change, where one 1949 property of equal dimensions existed for one property in 1962, 3 major classes of irregularities appeared.

     1) 1949 property split

     2) 1949 amalgamation

     3) Lanes and streets amalgamated with 1962 properties

   Only the first two need concern us here. The critical controlling factors in the procedure, in that they provide the basis for direct comparison of the condition of a property before and after change, are the 1962 property dimensions (area) and ledger number. Without the tedious and painstaking task of establishing uniformity in these changes, systematic comparison would be impossible.

   In the case of a split of a 1949 property, each part is treated as a percentage of the whole as it existed in 1949. Each sub-divided part has a different 1962 but common 1949 ledger number. Each part has the same dimensions as the 1962 properties and the assessments are divided proportionately. If no building demolition was involved, the split piece of land was classified as vacant.

   Where two or more 1945 properties were amalgamated in whole or in part into a 1962 property, each has a similar 1962, but different 1949 ledger number, in the

---

[1]The 1949 assessment maps and work books were used because this was the date of the latest major reassessment of the City of Toronto. The Planning Board made every attempt to ensure that the properties in 1949 were similar to those which existed just prior to 1952. The choice of 1952 as the beginning of the change analysis period was predetermined by the age breakdown in the original listings.

preliminary listings. In the final summaries the 1949 ledger numbers were disregarded and the properties were assigned the corresponding 1962 ledger numbers. The land areas involved in "change" are thus equal for the same ledger numbers regardless of the number of properties involved in either year.

Data Presentation: Summary

The resulting information can be thought of as consisting of three data arrays, stored on IBM tapes.

1) a complete inventory of all properties in the City in 1962
2) a summary of all properties that underwent change between 1952 and 1962.
3) a summary of the change properties (land area equivalents) prior to 1952.

APPENDIX B

LAND USE CLASSIFICATION: MINOR USES

*Denotes public, institutional, and other uses excluded from analysis

RESIDENTIAL

01.   Residential single-family, lot size one acre one acre or more
02.   Detached single family, including shacks--lot size less than one acre
03.   Semi-detached single-family
04.   Row house
05.   Duplex, triplex, double-duplex, quadruplex, fiveples, and double-triplex
06.   Apartment designed as such, including a sixplex or larger
07.   Any residence which would be coded 01-04 inclusive containing office or studio
08.   Converted detached or semi-detached
09.   Residence contained in commercial property
10.   Rooming or boarding house
11.   Private old people's or nursing home, non-institutional
12.   Residential or apartment hotel
13.   Residential club, fraternity or sorority, university residence or dormitory
14.   Summer cottage used for permanent residence
15.   Summer cottage used as such
16.   Residence in partially-completed building
17.   Trailer on private lot
18.   Permanent trailer camp
19.   Unclassified residential
*20.-34.   SCHOOLS, INSTITUTIONS, PLACES OF ASSEMBLY

OFFICES

35.   Commercial office, including bank, medical centre and clinic not being hospital, also government offices not in public buildings but in rented space; wholesale showroom
*36.-38.   Federal, Provincial, Local government offices in public buildings
39.   Unclassified office establishment

COMMERCIAL

40.   General retail, including sub post office not in public building
41.   Restaurant, tavern
42.   Personal service
43.   Commercial service with ancilliary industry
44.   Commercial school and commercial trade school
45.   Commercial service in the open
46.   Auto sales showroom
47.   Used car lot
48.   Auto gas station or service station
49.   Auto repair and service shop
50.   Auto parking garage
51.   Parking lot
52.   Commercial hotel

COMMERCIAL --continued

    53.   Motel or tourist cabin, tourist home or lodge, trailer court
    54.   Unclassified commercial

WAREHOUSES

    55.   Warehouse, not including storage building in industrial plant
    56.   Truck depot and wholesale market
    57.   Storage yard
    58.   Grain elevator, tank farm and other storage of liquid or gaseous fuel or bulk commodity
    59.   Unclassified warehousing

INDUSTRY

    60.   Manufacturing industry in enclosed buildings
    61.   Manufacturing industry chiefly in the open
    62.   Extractive industry in the open
    63.   Spare
    64.   Unclassified industry

UTILITIES AND SERVICES

    *65.-69.   Public and commercial utilities and services

TRANSPORTATION

    70.   Buildings and depots of railway, rapid transit, street car and bus lines
    71.   Lines and yards on private rights-of-way of railways, street cars, rapid transit
    72.   Airport and terminal building
    73.   Auto transportions, taxi, car and trailer rentals
    74.   Truck transportation, truck rental and delivery service
    75.   Public dock and wharf, boat rental, scheduled shipping line terminal
  76-78.   Spare
    79.   Unclassified transportation

  *80.-89.   PUBLIC AND PRIVATE OPEN SPACE

  *90.-94.   AGRICULTURE AND FORESTRY

MISCELLANEOUS

    95.   Land being developed, building being demolished, building under construction
    96.   Vacant land not in use but immediately capable of some use for urban or farm purposes
  *97.-99.   Waste and other lands

Classification of Major Land Uses

Major Use	Description	Minor Land Use (99 categories)
	Residential	
1	Single-family	01-04
2	Multiple-family less than 6 units	05

Major Use	Description	Minor Land Use
3	Multiple-family more than 6 units	06
4	Converted single-family	08
5	Other residential	07, 09-19
	Schools, Institutions, Places of Assembly	
6	*Schools and universities	20-26
7	*Places of Amusement and Assembly	28, 29
8	*Places of Worship, Hospitals and *Special buildings	27, 30-34
	Offices	
9	Commercial and miscellaneous offices	35, 39
10	*Government offices	36-38
	Commercial	
11	General commercial	40-45, 54
12	Commercial connected with Automobile	46-49
13	Parking Garages and Lots	50, 51
14	Hotel, Motel etc.	52, 53
	Warehouses	
15	All warehousing uses	55-59
	Industry	
16	All industry uses	60-64
	Utilities	
17	*All utilities etc.	65-69
	Transportation	
18	Auto and truck transportation	73, 74
19	Other transportation	70-72, 75-79
	Open Space	
20	*Commercial open space, Parks, *Playgrounds, etc.	80-82
21	*Miscellaneous open space	83-89
	Agriculture and Forestry	
22	*All agriculture and forestry[1]	90-94
	Miscellaneous	
23	Under construction	95
24	Vacant	96
25	*All other miscellaneous uses	97-99

[1] An asterisk denotes public, institutional, and other uses excluded from the analysis. The category Other Transportation consists largely of public facilities and is excluded from most statistical summaries.

APPENDIX C

ZONES OF ANALYSIS

Planning Districts--Census Tracts[1]

No.	Planning District	No. of Tracts	Census Tract No.								
1	Harbour West	(5)	48	49	50	63	64				
2	Downtown	(4)	73	74	75	76					
3	Spadina	(7)	56	57	57	59	60	61	62		
4	Don	(7)	96	97	98	99	100	101	102		
5	Yorkville	(5)	69	70	70	72	95				
6	Annex	(2)	54	55							
7	Christie	(3)	37	38	39						
8	East Junction	(3)	16	17	18						
9	Dufferin	(5)	22	23	24	28	28				
10	Trinity	(8)	40	41	42	43	44	45	46	47	
11	Humberside	(3)	1	3	4						
12	South Junction	(4)	5	6	9	10					
13	Parkdale	(11)	19	20	21	25	26	27	30	31	32
			33	34							
14	North Junction	(3)	2	7	8						
15	Oakwood	(7)	11	12	13	14	15	35	36		
16	Deer Park	(6)	51	52	53	66	67	68			
17	Rosedale	(4)	91	92	93	94					
18	Eglinton	(8)	83	84	85	86	87	88	89	90	
19	Lawrence Park	(5)	78	79	80	81	82				
20	Danforth West	(7)	106	107	108	109	110	111	112		
21	Danforth East	(5)	120	121	122	123	124				
22	Beaches	(8)	126	127	128	130	131	132	133	135	
23	Greenwood	(8)	113	114	115	116	117	118	125	129	
24	Harbour East	(6)	77	103	105	105	119	134			
25	Island	(1)	65								
	Totals	135									

[1] See Figure 10 in text (chapter III) for map.

Census Tracts Deleted from the Analysis

Tract No.	Description
19	High Park
33	Chy Hospital
34	Lakeshore Drive
48	Ontario Hospital
65	Toronto Island
90	Mt. Pleasant Cemetery
102	Regent Park North and South Public Housing
104	
105	Waterfront Industrial Area (from residential analysis)
119	" " " " " "

Special Tracts

58	University of Toronto
73	
74	
75	Downtown Area
76	
134	Sewage Disposal Plant

SELECTED BIBLIOGRAPHY

General

Alonso, William. Location and Land Use Toward a General Theory of Land Rent. Cambridge: Harvard University Press, 1964.

Chapin, F.S., Jr. Urban Land Use Planning. 2nd ed. Urbana: University of Illinois Press, 1965.

Colean, Miles. Renewing our Cities. New York: Twentieth Century Fund, 1953

Firey, Walter. Land Use in Central Boston. Cambridge: Harvard University Press, 1947.

Fisher, Robert M. (ed.). The Metropolis in Modern Life. New York: Doubleday & Co. 1955.

Fiser, Webb S. Mastery of the Metropolis. Englewood Cliffs, N.J.: Prentice Hall, 1962.

Gruen, Victor. The Heart of Our Cities The Urban Crisis: Diagnosis and Cure. New York: Simon & Schuster, 1964.

Hoover, E.M., and Vernon, R. Anatomy of a Metropolis. New York Metropolitan Region Study. Garden City, N.Y.: Doubleday & Co., 1962.

Jacobs, Jane. The Death and Life of Great American Cities. New York: Random House, 1961

Mayer, H.M., and Kohn, C.F. (eds.). Readings in Urban Geography. Chicago: University of Chicago Press, 1959.

Murphy, Raymond E. The American City: An Urban Geography. New York: McGraw-Hill Co., 1966.

Park, R.E., Burgess, E.W., and McKenzie, R.D. (eds.). The City. Chicago: University of Chicago Press, 1925.

Ratcliff, Richard U. Urban Land Economics. New York: McGraw-Hill Co., 1949.

Webber, Melvin M., et al. Explorations into Urban Structure. Philadelphia: University of Pennsylvania Press, 1964.

Wingo, Lowdon, Jr. Cities and Space The Future Use of Urban Land. Baltimore: Johns Hopkins Press, 1963.

Dynamics of Urban Spatial Structure

Alonso, William. "A Theory of the Urban Land Market," Papers and Proceedings of the Regional Science Association, VI (1960, 149-156.

Berry, Brian J.L. "Internal Structure of the City," Law and Contemporary Problems, XXX, No. 1 (Winter, 1965), 111-119.

_____. Commercial Structure and Commercial Blight. Department of Geography Research Paper No. 85. Chicago: University of Chicago Press, 1963.

Blumenfeld, Hans. "Are Land Uses Predictable?" Journal of the American Institute of Planners, XXV, No. 2 (May, 1959), 61-66.

_____. "The Tidal Wave of Metropolitan Expansion," Journal of the American Institute of Planners, XX, No. 1 (February, 1954), 3-14.

Boyce, Ronald R. "Changing Patterns of Urban Land Consumption," Professional Geographer, XV, No. 2 (March, 1963), 19-24.

Bury, Richard L. "The Efficiency of Selected Site Characteristics as Predictors for Location of Land Use Shifts to Residential Purposes." Unpublished Ph.D. dissertation, Department of Economics, University of Connecticut, 1961.

Chapin, F.S., Jr., and Weiss, S.F. Factors Influencing Land Development. Chapel Hill: Institute for Research in Social Science, University of North Carolina, 1962.

Duncan, B., and Duncan, O.D. "Variables in Urban Morphology," in Research Contributions to Urban Sociology. Chicago: University of Chicago Press, 1963.

Foley, Donald L. The Suburbanization of Administrative Offices in the San Francisco Bay Area. Research Report No. 10 Berkeley: Bureau of Business and Economic Research, 1957.

Griffin, D.W., and Preston, R.E. "A Restatement of the Transition Zone Concept," Annals of the Association of American Geographers, LVI, No. 2 (June, 1966), 339-350.

Hansen, Walter G. "How Accessibility Shapes Land Use," Journal of the American Institute of Planners, XXV, No. 2 (May, 1959), 73-76.

Harris, Britton. Some Problems in the Theory of Intra-Urban Location. Penn-Jersey Paper No. 3. Philadelphia: Penn-Jersey Transportation Study, 1961.

Hill, Donald M. "A Growth Allocation Model for the Boston Region," Journal of the American Institute of Planners, XXXI, No. 2 (May, 1965), 111-119.

Horwood, E.M., and MacNair, M.P. "The Core of the City: Emerging Concepts," Plan Canada, II, No. 3 (December, 1961), 108.

Hoyt, Homer. The Structure and Growth of Residential Neighborhoods in American Cities. Washington: U.S. Government Printing Office, 1939.

_____. "Recent Distortions of the Classical Models of Urban Structure," Land Economics, XL, No. 2 (May, 1964), 199-212.

Hurd, Richard M. Principles of City Land Values. New York: The Record and Guide, 1924.

Lakshmanan, T.R. "An Approach to the Analysis of Intra-urban Location Applied to the Baltimore Region," Economic Geography, XL, No. 4 (October, 1964), 348-370.

Lowry, Ira S. Model of Metropolis. Memorandum RM-4035-RC. Santa Monica: Rand Corporation, 1964.

Mitchell, R.B., and Rapkin, C. Urban Traffic A Function of Land Use. New York: Columbia University Press, 1961.

Muth, Richard F. "Economic Change and Urban vs. Rural Land Conversions," Econometrica, XXIX, No. 1 (January, 1961), 1-23.

Niedercorn, J.H., and Hearle, E.F.R. Recent Land Use Trends in 48 Large American Cities. Memorandum RM-3664-FF. Santa Monica: Rand Corporation, June, 1963.

Rannells, John. The Core of the City. A Pilot Study of Changing Land Uses in Central Business Districts. New York: Columbia University Press, 1956.

Rodwin, Lloyd. "The Theory of Residential Growth and Structure," Appraisal Journal, XVIII, No. 3 (July, 1950), 295-317.

Row and Jurkat, "The Economic Forces Shaping Land Use Patterns," Journal of the American Institute of Planners, SSV, No. 2 (May, 1959), 77-81.

Simmons, James. The Changing Pattern of Retail Location. Department of Geography Research Paper No. 92. Chicago: University of Chicago Press, 1964.

Stefaniak, N.J. "A Refinement of Haig's Theory," Land Economics, XXXIX, November 4 (November, 1963), 429-433.

Ullman, Edward L. "The Nature of Cities Reconsidered" Papers and Proceedings of the Regional Science Association, IX (1962), 7-24.

Vernon, Raymond. The Changing Economic Function of the Central City. New York: Committee for Economic Development, 1959.

Voorhees, Alan M. "Urban Growth Characteristics," Urban Land, XX, No. 11 (December, 1961), 3-6.

Wabe, J.S. "Office Decentralization: An Empirical Study," Urban Studies, III, No. 1 (February, 1966), 35-55.

Wendt, Paul F. The Dynamics of Central City Land Values San Francisco and Oakland, 1950-1960. Research Report No. 18. Berkeley: Institute of Business and Economic Research, University of California, 1961.

_____. "City Growth and Urban Land Values," Appraisal Journal, XXVI, No. 2 (April, 1958), 254-269; and XXVI, No. 3 (July, 1958), 427-443.

Wheaton, L.C. "Public and Private Agents of Change in Urban Expansion," in Explorations into Urban Structure. Edited by M.M. Webber et al. Philadelphia: University of Pennsylvania Press, 1964.

Willhelm, S.M. Urban Zoning and Land-Use Theory. New York: The Free Press of Glencoe, 1962.

Willhelm, S.M., and Sjoberg, G. "Economic vs. Protective Values in Urban Land Use Change," American Journal of Economics and Sociology, XIX (January, 1960), 151-160.

Wingo, Lowdon, Jr., Transportation and Urban Land. Washington: Resources for the Future, Inc., 1961.

_____. "An Economic Model of the Utilization of Urban Land for Residential Purposes," Papers and Proceedings of the Regional Science Association, VII (1961), 191-205.

Winsborough, H.H. "City Growth and City Structure," Journal of Regional Science, IV, No. 2 (Winter, 1962), 35-50.

Yeates, Maurice. "Some Factors Affecting the Spatial Distribution of Chicago Land Values," Economic Geography, XLI, No. 1 (January, 1965), 57-70.

Urban Renewal and Redevelopment

Abrams, Charles. The City is the Frontier. New York: Harper & Row, 1965.

Alonso, William. "The Historic and the Structural Theories of Urban Form: Their Implications for Urban Renewal," Land Economics, XL, No. 2 (May, 1964), 227-231.

American Institute of Real Estate Appraisers. Urban Renewal and Redevelopment. Chicago: American Institute of Real Estate Appraisers, 1964.

Anderson, Martin. The Federal Bulldozer   A Critical Analysis of Urban Renewal 1949-1962. Cambridge: M.I.T. Press, 1964.

Bailey, Martin. "Notes on the Economics of Residential Zoning and Urban Renewal," Land Economics, XXXV, No. 2 (August, 1959), 288-292.

Bloom, Max R. "Fiscal Productivity and the Pure Theory of Urban Renewal," Land Economics, XXXVIII, No. 2 (May, 1962), 134-144.

Borchert, J.R., Stewart, E.E., Hasbrouck, S.S. Urban Renewal: Needs and Opportunities in the Upper Midwest. Urban Report No. 5 Minneapolis: Upper Midwest Economic Study, 1963.

Breger, G.E. "The Economics of Urban Blight and Economic Guidelines for Urban Renewal." Unpublished Ph.D. dissertation, Department of Economics, University of Arkansas, 1964.

Claire, W.H. "Urban Renewal and Transportation" Traffic Quarterly, XIII, No. 3 (July, 1959), 414-422.

Colborn, F.M. The Neighborhood and Urban Renewal. New York: National Federation of Settlements and Neighborhood Centers, 1961.

Colean, Miles L., and Davis, A.P. Cost Measurement in Urban Redevelopment. New York: National Committee on Housing Inc., 1945.

Davis, Otto, and Whinston, A.B. "The Economics of Urban Renewal," Law and Contemporary Problems, XXVI, No. 5 (Winter, 1961), 105-117.

Duke University, School of Law. "Urban Renewal Part II," Law and Contemporary Problems, Vol. XXVI (Winter, 1961).

Dyckman, J.W., and Isaacs, R.R. Capital Requirements for Urban Redevelopment and Renewal. Action Series in Housing and Community Development. New York: McGraw Hill Co., 1961.

Frieden, Bernard J. The Future of Old Neighborhoods Rebuilding for a Changing Population. Cambridge: M.I.T. Press, 1964.

Gans, Herbert J. "The Failure of Urban Renewal: A Critique and Some Proposals," Commentary, XXXIX, No. 4 (April, 1965), 29-37.

Grebler, Leo. Urban Renewal in European Countries: Its Emergence and Potentials. Philadelphia: University of Pennsylvania Press, 1964.

Greer, Scott. Urban Renewal and American Cities. The Dilemma of Democratic Intervention. New York: Bobbs-Merrill Co., 1965.

Hearle, E.F.R., and Niedercorn, J.H. The Impact of Urban Renewal on Land Use. Memorandum RM 4186 RC. Santa Monica: Rand Corporation, June, 1964.

Hemdahl, Reuel. Urban Renewal. New York: Scarecrow Press, Inc., 1959.

Hunter, David L. The Slums Challenge and Response. New York: The Free Press of Glencoe, 1964.

Justement, Louis. New Cities for Old. City Building in Terms of Space, Time, and Money. New York: McGraw-Hill Co., 1946.

Lichfield, Nathaniel. Cost-Benefit Analysis in Urban Redevelopment. Research Report No. 20 Berkely: Real Estate Research Program, University of California, 1962.

Marris, Peter. "The Social Implications of Urban Redevelopment," Journal of the American Institute of Planners, XXVIII, No. 3 (August, 1962), 180-186.

Nash, William W. Residential Rehabilitation: Private Profits and Public Purposes. New York: McGraw-Hill Co., 1959.

Nourse, Hugh O. "The Economics of Urban Renewal," Land Economics, XLII, No. 1 (February, 1966), 65-74.

_____. "The Effect of Public Housing on Property Values in St. Louis," Land Economics, XXXIX, No. 4 (November, 1963), 433-441.

Rapkin, C., and Grigsby, W.C. Residential Renewal in the Urban Core. Philadelphia: University of Pennsylvania Press, 1960.

Ratcliff, Richard U. Private Investment in Urban Redevelopment. A Study of the Disposal Phase in Urban Renewal Research Report No. 17. Berkeley: Real Estate Research Program, University of California, 1961.

Robinson, I.M., Wolfe, H.B., and Barringer, R.L. "A Simulation Model for Renewal Programming," Journal of the American Institute of Planners, XXXI, No. 2 (May, 1965), 126-133.

Ross, Thurston H. "Market Significance of Declining Neighborhoods," Appraisal Journal, XXIII, No. 2 (April, 1955), 203-211.

Schaaf, A.H. Economic Aspects of Urban Renewal: Theory, Policy and Area Analysis. Research Report No. 14. Berkeley: Institute of Business and Economic Research, 1960.

Schussheim, M.J. "Urban Renewal and Local Economic Development," Journal of the American Institute of Planners, XXVII, No. 2 (May, 1961), 118-120.

Slayton, William L. "Urban Renewal Philosophy," Planning 1963. Chicago: American Society of Planning Officials, 1963. Pp. 154-159.

Smith, Wilbin S. "Traffic and Rebuilding Cities," Traffic Quarterly, XIII, No. 1 (January, 1959), 156-168.

Steger, W.A. "The Pittsburgh Urban Renewal Simulation Model," Journal of the American Institute of Planners, XXXI, No. 2 (May, 1965), 144-149.

Stokes, C.J., Minitz, P., and Van Golder, H. "Economic Criteria for Urban Redevelopment," The American Journal of Economics and Sociology, XXIV, No. 3 (July, 1965), 249-256.

Vereker, C., and Mays, J.B. Urban Redevelopment and Social Change. Liverpool: Liverpool University Press, 1961.

Vernon, Raymond. The Myth and Reality of Our Urban Problems. Cambridge: Harvard University Press, 1962.

Willbern, York. The Withering Away of the City. Birmingham: University of Alabama Press, 1964.

Wilson, James Q. (ed.). Urban Renewal The Record and the Controversy. Cambridge: M.I.T. Press, 1966.

Wingo, Lowdon, Jr. "Urban Renewal: A Strategy for Information and Analysis," Journal of the American Institute of Planners, XXXII, No. 3 (May, 1966), 143-154.

Winnick, Louis. "Economic Questions in Urban Redevelopment," American Economic Review, LI, No. 2 (May, 1961), 290-298.

Woodbury, Coleman (ed.). The Future of Cities and Urban Redevelopment. Chicago: University of Chicago Press, 1953.

_____. Urban Redevelopment: Problems and Practices. Chicago: University of Chicago Press, 1953.

Real Estate and Building

Backman, Jules. "The Real Estate Market and the General Economy," Appraisal Journal, XXXII, No. 1 (January, 1964), 21-28.

Barlowe, Raleigh. Land Resource Economics. The Political Economy of Rural and Urban Land Resource Use. Englewood Cliffs, N.J.: Prentice Hall, 1958.

Colean, M.L., and Newcomb, R. Stabilizing Construction: The Record and Potential. New York: McGraw-Hill Co., 1952.

Fisher, E.M., and Fisher, R.M. Urban Real Estate. New York: Henry Holt & Co. 1954.

Fisher, E.M. Urban Real Estate Markets: Characteristics and Financing. New York: National Bureau of Economic Research, 1951.

Grebler, Leo. Experience in Urban Real Estate Investment. New York: Columbia University Press, 1955.

Haskett, Jack. "A Real Estate Investment Plan," Canadian Business, XXXVIII, No. 8 (August, 1965), 94-99.

Isard, Walter. "A Neglected Cycle: The Transport-Building Cycle," Review of Economics and Statistics, XXIV, No. 4 (November, 1942), 149-158.

Jennings, C.R. "Predicting Demand for Office Space," Appraisal Journal, XXXIII, No. 3 (July, 1965), 377-382.

Maisel, Sherman J. A Theory of Fluctuations in Residential Construction Starts. Reprint No. 34. Berkeley: Center for Research in Real Estate and Urban Economics, University of California, 1963.

Nelson, R.L., and Aschman, F.T. Real Estate and City Planning. Englewood Cliffs, N.J.: Prentice Hall, 1957.

North, N.L., and Ring, A.A. Real Estate Principles and Practices. 5th ed. Englewood Cliffs, N.J.: Prentice Hall, 1960.

Rapkin, Chester. The Real Estate Market in an Urban Renewal Area. New York: City Planning Commission, 1959.

Ratcliff, Richard U. Real Estate Analysis. New York: McGraw-Hill Co., 1961.

Rowlands, D.T. Urban Real Estate Research. Research Monograph No. 1 Washington: Urban Land Institute, 1959.

Shenkel, W.M. "Opportunities in Downtown Real Estate," Journal of Property Management, XXVII, No. 4 (Summer, 1962), 196-204.

Turvey, Ralph. The Economics of Real Property An Analysis of Property Values and Patterns of Use. London: Allen & Unwin, 1957.

Wehrly, M.S., and McKeever, I.R. Urban Land Use and Property Taxation. Technical Bulletin No. 18. Washington: Urban Land Institute, 1952.

Weimer, A.M., and Hoyt, H. Principles of Real Estate. 4th ed. New York: Ronald Press, 1960.

Housing Markets

Angles, Charles K. "Housing and Urban Redevelopment," chapter iv in An Approach to Urban Planning. Edited by G. Breese and D.E. Whiteman. Princeton: Princeton University Press, 1953.

Clark, W.A.V. "The Dynamics of Rental Housing Areas in U.S. Central Cities." Unpublished Ph.D. dissertation, Department of Geography, University of Illinois, 1964.

Davis, J. Tait. "Middle Class Housing in the Central City," Economic Geography, XLI, No. 3 (July, 1965), 238-251.

Derrickson, G.F. "Recent Homebuilding Trends in Major Metropolitan Areas," Construction Review, VI (September, 1960), 5-10.

Foote, N.N., et al. Housing Choices and Housing Constraints. New York: McGraw-Hill Co., 1960.

Gordon, R.A. "Population Growth, Housing, and the Capital Coefficient," American Economic Review, XLVI, No. 3 (June, 1956), 307-322.

Grebler, Leo. Housing Market Behavior in a Declining Area. New York: Columbia University Press, 1952.

_____. "The Housing Inventory: Analytical Concept and Quantitative Change," American Economic Review, XLI, No. 2 (May, 1951), 555-568.

Grigsby, William C. Housing Markets and Public Policy. Philadelphia: University of Pennsylvania Press, 1963.

Kristof, Frank S. "Housing Policy Goals and the Turnover of Housing," Journal of the American Institute of Planners, XXXI, No. 3 (August, 1965), 232-245.

Lowry, Ira S. "Filtering and Housing Standards," Land Economics, XXXVI, No. 4 (November, 1960), 362-370.

Maisel, Sherman J. "Policy Problems in Expanding the Private Housing Market," American Economic Review, XLI, No. 2 (May, 1951), 599-611.

Meyerson, Martin. Housing, People and Cities. New York: McGraw-Hill Co., 1962.

Rapkin, C., Winnick, L., and Blank, D.M. Housing Market Analysis: A Study of Theory and Methods. Washington: Housing and Home Finance Agency, 1953.

Smith, Wallace F. The Low Rise Speculative Apartment. Research Report No. 25. Berkeley: Center for Real Estate and Urban Economics, University of California, 1964.

_____. Filtering and Neighborhood Change. Research Report No. 24. Berkeley: Center for Real Estate and Urban Economics, University of California, 1964.

Winnick, Louis P. Rental Housing: Opportunities for Private Investment. New York: McGraw Hill Co., 1958.

Toronto and Canadian Sources

Berry, B.J.L., and Murdie, R.A. Socio-Economic Correlates of Housing Condition. A Study Prepared for the Urban Renewal Study, Metropolitan Toronto Planning Board. Toronto: The Metropolitan Planning Board, 1965.

Bureau of Municipal Research. "Redevelopment in Downtown," Civic Affairs. Toronto, April, 1964.

_____ . "The Impact of Property Taxes in Metro," Civic Affairs, Toronto, February, 1964.

Carver, Humphrey. "CRP: The Canadian Experience," Planning 1965. Chicago: American Society of Planning Officials, 1965. Pp. 200-226.

Canada, Central Mortgage and Housing Corporation, Canadian Housing Statistics 1965. Ottawa: The Central Mortgage and Housing Corporation, 1966.

Corelli, Rae. The Toronto That Used To Be. Toronto, 1964.

Firestone, O.J. Residential Real Estate in Canada. Toronto: University of Toronto Press, 1951.

Hooper, N.A. "Toronto, A Study in Urban Geography." Unpublished Master's dissertation, Department of Geography, University of Toronto, 1947.

Illing, Wolfgana M. Housing Demand to 1970. Staff Study No. 4, Economic Council of Canada. Ottawa: The Queen's Printer, 1964.

Kerr, D., and Spelt, J. Industry and Warehousing in the City of Toronto. Toronto: City Planning Board, 1961.

_____ . The Changing Face of Toronto - A Study in Urban Geography. Memoir 11, Geographical Branch, Department of Mines and Technical Surveys. Ottawa: The Queen's Printer, 1965.

Masters, D.C. The Rise of Toronto 1850-1890. Toronto: University of Toronto Press, 1947.

Pickett, Stanley H. "Canadian Experience in Urban Renewal," Planning 1965. Chicago: American Society of Planning Officials, 1965. Pp. 139-147.

Rose, Albert. Regent Park. A Study in Slum Clearance. Toronto: University of Toronto Press, 1958.

_____ . Rehabilitation of Housing in Central Toronto. A Study Prepared for the City of Toronto Planning Board and Central Mortgage and Housing Corporation. Toronto: The City Planning Board, September, 1966.

Simmons, James. Toronto's Changing Retail Complex: A Study in Growth and Blight. Department of Geography Research Paper No. 104. Chicago: University of Chicago Press, 1966.

Smallwood, Frank. Metro Toronto: A Decade Later. Toronto: Bureau of Municipal Research, 1963.

Spelt, Jacob. "The Development of the Toronto Conurbation," Buffalo Law Review, XIII, No. 3 (Spring, 1964), 557-573.

Toronto, Advisory Committee on the Urban Renewal Study. Urban Renewal: A Study of of the City of Toronto, 1956. Toronto: Advisory Committee on the Urban Renewal Study, 1956.

Toronto, City Planning Board. Downtown Toronto. Background Studies for the Plan, Technical Series No. 1. Toronto: City Planning Board, 1963.

_____. Improvement Programme for Residential Areas. Toronto: City Planning Board, 1965.

Toronto, Metropolitan Planning Board. Apartment Survey 1961. Toronto: Metropolitan Planning Board, 1962.

Toronto, Metropolitan Urban Renewal Study. The Role of Private Enterprise in Urban Renewal. A Study Prepared by M.V. Jones and Associates. Toronto: The Metropolitan Planning Board, 1966.

Wilson, G.W., Gordon, S., and Judek, S. Canada: An Appraisal of its Needs and Resources. A Report Prepared for the Twentieth Century Fund. Toronto: University of Toronto Press, 1965.

THE UNIVERSITY OF CHICAGO
DEPARTMENT OF GEOGRAPHY
RESEARCH PAPERS (Lithographed, 6 × 9 Inches)

* Out of print.

91. HILL, A. DAVID. *The Changing Landscape of a Mexican Municipio, Villa Las Rosas, Chiapas*
NAS-NRC Foreign Field Research Program Report No. 26. 1964. 121 pp.
92. SIMMONS, JAMES W. *The Changing Pattern of Retail Location*   1964. 212 pp.
93. WHITE, GILBERT F. *Choice of Adjustment to Floods*   1964. 164 pp.
94. MC MANIS, DOUGLAS R. *The Initial Evaluation and Utilization of the Illinois Prairies, 1815–1840*
1964. 109 pp.
95. PERLE, EUGENE D. *The Demand for Transportation: Regional and Commodity Studies in the United States*   1964. 130 pp.
96. HARRIS, CHAUNCY D. *Annotated World List of Selected Current Geographical Serials in English*   1964. 32 pp. $1.00
97. BOWDEN, LEONARD W. *Diffusion of the Decision To Irrigate: Simulation of the Spread of a New Resource Management Practice in the Colorado Northern High Plains*   1965. 146 pp.
98. KATES, ROBERT W. *Industrial Flood Losses: Damage Estimation in the Lehigh Valley*
1965. 76 pp.
99. RODER, WOLF. *The Sabi Valley Irrigation Projects*   1965. 213 pp.
100. SEWELL, W. R. DERRICK. *Water Management and Floods in the Fraser River Basin*   1965. 163 pp.
101. RAY, D. MICHAEL. *Market Potential and Economic Shadow: A Quantitative Analysis of Industrial Location in Southern Ontario*   1965. 164 pp.
102. AHMAD, QAZI. *Indian Cities: Characteristics and Correlates*   1965. 184 pp.
103. BARNUM, H. GARDINER. *Market Centers and Hinterlands in Baden-Württemberg*   1966. 172 pp.
104. SIMMONS, JAMES W. *Toronto's Changing Retail Complex*   1966. 126 pp.
105. SEWELL, W. R. DERRICK, *et al. Human Dimensions of Weather Modification*   1966. 423 pp.
106. SAARINEN, THOMAS FREDERICK. *Perception of the Drought Hazard on the Great Plains.* 1966. 198 pp.
107. SOLZMAN, DAVID M. *Waterway Industrial Sites: A Chicago Case Study.*   1967. 138 pp.
108. KASPERSON, ROGER E. *The Dodecanese: Diversity and Unity in Island Politics.*   1967
109. LOWENTHAL, DAVID, editor, *Environmental Perception and Behavior.*   1967
111. BERRY, BRIAN J. L. *Essays on Commodity Flows and the Spatial Structure of the Indian Economy.*
1966. 350 pp.
112. BOURNE, LARRY S. *Private Redevelopment in the Central City (Toronto).*   1967